Acknowledgements

Our gratitude to the following people:

Niall Fitzpatrick for sending us the diary.

Jeremy Lowe for his eye for detail and advice.

Milena Vitorovic for her creativity and immense patience.

Alex Wade for his expertise and guidance.

Georgina Aldridge at Clays for all her help.

About The Author

Born in Dublin (The Liberties) in 1927, Vera had a strict Catholic upbringing. Her father died when she was just 10 years old and her mother was left to bring up three young children on her own. The Liberties is one of the oldest parts of Dublin, home to the Guinness factory, a place rich in community and history. Though the actual district was torn down in the 19th century, the name 'Liberties' has retained its unique character and culture. It would have led to her sense of community, family and faith. Though she calls it a 'curse to be poor', and dreams of winning the Pools (a form of betting based on predicting the scores of football matches), it is clear that Vera is proud of her working-class roots.

One aspect of Irish life at that time was the absolute centrality of the Catholic Church. You will see in the diary that Vera goes to Mass most days. Prayers to God and the saints trip from her lips as extensions of her belief-system and thought patterns – her world view is anchored by family and faith and she works tirelessly for both. This is not what most people would understand as 'going to Church', a weekly obligation; it is a natural and inextricable part of her life, built into her daily routine.

She moved to London in 1965, married Bernie (a neighbour whom she had grown up with in Dublin) in Tottenham in 1966, and they had their first child in 1967. Married life proved rather difficult; money was always short and the relationship was very strained at times. Vera was missing home and jobs were hard to come by. In her diary you see not just her own struggles but, through glimpses, Bernie's own difficulties in adjusting, cut off from a community he had known, and stranded in a life that had lost some meaning. It's easy to see Bernie as a villain – he comes across as lazy and selfish – but there is here also the sadness of someone severed from what he knew, and where he once had purpose and identity.

Tottenham is and was known for its multicultural population, and this diversity comes up in Vera's diary, with Afro-Caribbeans, Irish, Indians, Pakistanis and other races and cultures, all part of a thriving area of London. But you can also sense the tensions that led to the 1985 Broadwater Farm riot in the area, in attacks on shops, the emergence of skinheads and punks whose fashion Vera's son, Ciarán, innocently adopts, the rise of football violence, and the struggles of police to cope.

It is easy to forget that the early 1980s was a rather bleak time. The country was still in recession, and unemployment at a record high of three million. There was a loss of manufacturing and industry, with widespread discontent. Vera alludes to the Thatcher government's attempts to take on and destroy the trades unions. Bernie is often on strike. There was little to no state support, social support or workers' rights. Home comforts didn't match the luxuries we take for granted: no internet, no mobile phones, only four TV channels. Appliances were unreliable and expensive, and much of the diary is spent detailing Vera's daily efforts to deal with things breaking down and not working properly. Police take hours to arrive and do little to help. For Vera, money is always tight.

Big superstores like Tesco and Wickes are coming in and starting to drive the smaller traders out. All of this Vera observes as the days go by.

Unlike Bernie, whose job at a factory is precarious, Vera worked for a private firm as a sample machinist. Vera's love of dressmaking started at a very young age. She would make dresses for her dolls and later when she left school it became her full-time occupation. She was kept busy making clothes for friends and neighbours too. Her life was always hectic and eventful but she never lost her love of dressmaking.

The diary covers a single year when Vera launches into an ambitious and unbelievably difficult attempt to remodel the house. Looking back, we, as her now grown children, can't actually believe how she didn't have a nervous breakdown, given the chaos of that time, as she juggled work with an endless shopping list of activities and problems: a house like a builder's yard, daily DIY, an unreliable car, an unhelpful husband, an inconsistent workman, frequent trips to hardware stores, constant interruptions, and bouts of ill-health. And she always found time to make clothes for us in her lunch hour, hear the complaints and sufferings of her neighbours and friends, give support for the church and perform a litany of other daily tasks that she records faithfully – in a diary she wrote every day! Irish women from the Liberties were built tough.

Things gradually improved as time went on and the children got older. When Bernie died in 1990 she continued as she had always done, dedicating the rest of her life to her children, and then her five grandchildren.

Vera passed away in 2014 in Surrey.

Foreword

I first read this diary in February 2015, some 32 years after it had been written. Although I knew of the diary's existence, and remember watching my mother write in that day's entry very faithfully of an evening, as a child it never held any interest for me, or for my sister or brother. It was just something Mum had decided to do for her close friend and neighbour, Ann Fitzpatrick, as a way of keeping Ann informed about what was going on in her day-to-day life.

Ann and Vera lived a few roads away from each other in Tottenham in the 70s, and they would see each other nearly every day, either on the school run, up at the church, or in each other's houses. Ann and her family moved back to Ireland in 1979, and I am sure this must have been upsetting for my mother as they were such good friends. They shared many interests and were both very creative, Ann with her flower arranging and Mum with her dressmaking.

I have very fond memories of Ann and her family. I always remember the walks back from school, Ann with her four children and Mum and the three of us. It was always a slow meander home. The route meant that we always arrived at Ann's road first, and it was never a quick goodbye. Ann and Mum would stand on the corner, chatting for ages about everything and anything while the seven children tried to entertain themselves to pass the time, soon getting bored and irritated that they were taking so long – we wanted to get home.

Ann and Vera kept in touch by post and phone for the next 30-odd years, only meeting on a few occasions. Both were busy raising their families. Ann opened a beautiful florist shop in Ireland, which is still there today.

The diary was given to Ann in 1984. After that, I never heard or really thought about it at all.

It was a few days after my mother died in November 2014 that I telephoned Ann to tell her the news. She was very upset, and we reminisced about Mum and the time when Ann had lived in Tottenham and the fond memories we shared. It was then that Ann reminded me about the diary. She said how much she had enjoyed reading it and how funny it was, and how from time to time she and her family would take the diary down from the shelf and read extracts from it. I told her that none of us had ever read it, and she promised she would send it to me. About three weeks later, I got the shocking news that Ann had suddenly and unexpectedly died – only 26 days after Mum.

I later learned that on the morning of the day Ann died, she had been to her local church to ask the parish priest there to sign a Mass card for my mother. It must have been found in Ann's handbag when she died, and a few weeks later I received the card by post from her son Niall. I was amazed when I looked at it and saw that it was dated the day Ann died. It was a very poignant moment for me, knowing Ann had been thinking about my mother on the day she passed away.

Niall posted the diary to me in February 2015, for which I was extremely grateful. It was in pristine condition, and it was the best memento of my mother I could have. I was very excited; finally I was going to be able to sit down and read the diary for the first time.

I remember feeling slightly apprehensive, thinking, what on earth could my mother have written?

It was like stepping back in time. I was hearing my mother's voice in my head again, with her classic phrases and sayings. I went through a range of emotions reading it: tears of laughter and tears of sadness; surprise and amazement at some of the things that had happened. All the memories came flooding back, except now I was experiencing that time again through an adult's eye.

I doubled over laughing at some of the things she had said, and was struck by her observations and the way she thought deeply about life. Nothing seemed to run smoothly for her, but she managed to retain her great sense of humour. She always seemed to be so busy, and everywhere around her was perpetually in a state of chaos, and I was amazed at her stamina and determination to get things done. I still question why she embarked on such a huge project to remodel the house, which is the catastrophic core of this diary, at such a busy time in our lives – I think it must have been very important to her at the time. I am now at an age near to when my mother wrote the diary, and, as a mother myself of grown-up children, I can really understand all the efforts she made for us, although I did not see it or appreciate them at the time.

My sister and brother then read the diary, which brought back many memories for them too. It was such a lovely way to remember my mother, and, instead of feeling the great sadness at her passing, which we would otherwise have felt at that time, our grief was transformed by the presence of the diary; we spent the next few months laughing and talking about the those days it records and all those memories she had left us with, now never to be forgotten.

The decision to publish the diary was not taken lightly, but after mulling over the idea for the past two-and-a-half years we eventually thought that it would be lovely to share it with others. I remember speaking to my mother a few years before she died, and detected a sadness that maybe she felt she had not achieved as much as she could have done in her life. She was very talented, but I think she felt she was limited by her circumstances. She wrote the diary with such dedication, knowing that it was for Ann; and this in itself, I believe, was a great achievement. The fact that Ann looked after and cherished the diary is also a testament to her feelings for my mother.

To see the diary in print is something I believe both my mother and Ann, two remarkable ladies, would have approved of, and it is because of this belief that the diary has finally been printed.

Fiona Byrne, 2018

Contents

Editor's Note

Vera wrote very much as she spoke, and this made some editing decisions necessary.

The first is that she used only two basic forms of punctuation, the comma and the full-stop. This means that all of her sentences are basically 'run-on' sentences, i.e. largely a sort of train of thought style. This can often lead to difficulties of understanding, particularly in longer sentences. To remedy this, I have added, where necessary, dashes and semi-colons. Dashes I have used just to show where she wants to qualify a thought – to explain it in further detail, or to indicate a character, place, idea and so on. I have chosen a dash over a colon because colons are more like 'formal' writing that don't sit well with her informal style.

Semi-colons I have used only sparingly, for the same reason. I have only added them where I want to keep the length of the sentence, but need to break it up just to indicate a slight change of emphasis or direction. Vera prefers long sentences to short, so generally I haven't added full-stops because these produce a staccato character that spoil her easy, conversational flow. In any case, whenever you see a dash or a semi-colon, you will know these have been added!

I have retained as much of her original phrasing, punctuation and grammar as possible. No diary is really meant to be corrected for grammar and spelling, except to make it easier to read where absolutely necessary. It almost certainly wouldn't have been checked over by Vera for any of these things, so readers should be aware of this and to expect grammatical 'errors'. To correct them would have knocked the life out of the diary and removed her characteristic voice, charm and wit.

The second issue is that Vera uses some phrases and words that come from Irish-English. These are generally speaking a product of spoken Irish and on occasion might be difficult to understand in written English. Wherever this happens I have added a note in square brackets to explain the meaning of the word or phrase. We mulled over how to handle these words and phrases, considering footnotes or a glossary, but deciding that in-text explanations were the best way. Obscure historical references have also been handled this way.

Jeremy Lowe, 2018

Who's Who

(Some names have been changed to protect privacy)

BERNIE: Vera's husband

TERRI (15), FIONA (14) & CIARÁN (13): Vera's children

MARY: Vera's sister, worked as housekeeper for Father Hegarty

ANN, JIM & NIALL: friends and neighbours

PETER, SHEILA, PATRICIA & HELEN: friends and next-door neighbours

LEENA & TINA: neighbours who owned the corner shop

DAN, COLETTE, JAMES & SALLY: neighbours

BOB & PATTIE: neighbours

MARY MAC & JACK: old friends

JOHNJOE & MARY: friends and neighbours

JUDY, MICHAEL & ADAM KELLY: friends and neighbours

ANNA: Vera's first cousin.

KEVIN & COLM: Anna's husband and son

NAN KAVANAGH: Vera's first cousin

MICK: Vera's first cousin

DORRIE: Mick's wife

SONNY: Vera's brother

DECLAN: Sonny's son

FATHER HEGARTY: parish priest

FATHER RODERICK: priest

DICK JOHNSON: assistant to priests

JUNE: Mary's friend and landlady

BEN & LAURA: Vera's employers at first firm

HARRY, MR ABRAHAMS & MR JACOBS: Vera's employers at second firm

LIZZIE, JO, DORIS, PENNY & CATHY: work colleagues at second firm

January 1983

BACK TO THE SAME OLD ROUTINE

Saturday 1st January

Dear Ann

Here I am with my new diary and my Replay pen and have nothing exciting to relate for the first day of 1983.

Stayed in bed until 12.30, which is very unusual for me – haven't had a lie-in for years, didn't get to bed until four o'clock this morning ringing in the New Year. Had some people in from across the road, a very nice couple from Dublin with two young children. They bought the second house on the opposite side of our road – you know, the one the old couple lived in. Jim used to talk to the man there, can't think of their name. I suppose you heard they both died. You'd want to see that house now. This couple (Dan and Colette) have it really lovely. Dan is a carpenter, he can do anything. Have my cousin, Nan Kavanagh, over for Christmas; her mother (my aunt Sara) died last February and she is very lonely. I also had Mary staying with me over the Christmas, I suppose you heard she left here last year, but that's another story.

Sunday 2nd January

Went to eight o'clock Mass, which Ciarán still serves and I still sell the bingo tickets at. After Mass, went over to my friend, Mary Mac, with Nan and the girls. Had a cup of coffee there and then home to get the Sunday dinner ready. After dinner, went to bed for my usual Sunday afternoon nap, which sets me up for the week. Had my tea brought up to me by Terri, who is her usual kind and considerate self; wish I could say the same about Fiona, they are two very different people. Terri still wants to be a nurse, but whether she gets the O-levels she needs remains to be seen. You know she's not very bright, but she does try. She got an award in school last year for effort and willingness to help during the year, I was very pleased for her. Fiona is aggressive, head strong and very sure of herself, and with little or no effort seems to sail through exams. She is five foot four inches now, very slim and nice looking, doesn't eat sweets, cakes or drink minerals [fizzy drinks] in case they spoil her teeth or skin. It's a pity she doesn't have the manner to go with her looks, but I suppose it takes all sorts to make a world and please God she'll change.

Monday 3rd January

Took Nan to Euston Station, she'll be back in the summer, please God. Didn't stop raining all day, I suppose the fine weather was too good to last. Felt like doing a bit of knitting today so I started an Aran sweater. I was going to make it for Fiona, but she was so cheeky I told Ciarán he could have it when it's finished – when that will be God only knows,

2

don't get much time for knitting. Adam Kelly was here today and himself and Ciarán fell out over something or other. They had a few words and Adam finished up telling Ciarán that they are better people than us, at least they own their own house and their father is self-employed, and that makes them middle-class people, and his jumper costs £35.00 and Ciarán's was just a cheap one out of Marks. Ciarán was quite upset. You should have heard me telling him how unimportant money is (God forgive me for lying) and that 'clothes don't make the man', it's what you are that counts and how you behave. I'm hoping he's got the message. Watched that film, 'Papillon', on telly tonight. Remember? Yourself and Jim went to see it and Bernie took me the week after and nearly had a fit when he got to the box office and heard the price it was in. He is still living in the past regarding prices.

Tuesday 4th January

Started back to work today, hated every minute of it, kept wishing I could win the Pools. I'm still working for Ben and Laura. They have a two-and-a-half-year-old daughter now called Katie. She is really beautiful and so intelligent. They have got on very well in business, which is great considering how bad things are here. We are moving to new premises in Primrose Hill at the end of the month, I believe it's a very posh area. Ben said we will mix with a better class of people there. I told him I had nothing in common with better class people. After work, the mad rush home to get the dinner ready by five o'clock, then after dinner cut out some curtains and quilts for my bedroom. Slipping back into the old routine of work and more work as if I'd never had a holiday. Had very bad storms here today. Our television aerial bent over, hope it doesn't come through the roof. We bought a new colour telly a few months ago (a Phillips) – a neighbour got it from some bloke he knows, it was only £150.00, I think it must have fallen off the back of a lorry.

Wednesday 5ᵗʰ January

Had to take Terri to Dr. Watson tonight, she has a very bad rash on one finger of each hand and she has quite a lot of spots on her face. After he had prescribed some cream and tablets for her and made his usual cheeky comments to me, he turned to Terri and said, "I suppose the next time you come to see me you'll be wanting me to put you on the pill". Well, after I picked myself up off the floor, he said, "You needn't look so shocked, you'd be amazed at the number of 15 year olds on the pill, and don't think your daughter will be any different to all the rest". And how, "It was better to be on the pill than have unwanted pregnancies". After he had finished talking, I pulled myself up to all of my five foot one and a half inches and I said, "We are Catholics and I think my daughters will have enough respect for their religion and themselves not to be like all the rest". He just laughed at me. Please God I don't have to eat my words, now I've got another worry to add to my list. When we got home, Bernie was having one of his turns – you know, the one where he gets down on his knees and swears vengeance on everybody, and me in particular. The telly wouldn't work because of the aerial and he was going berserk over it. What a life.

Thursday 6ᵗʰ January

Still quite stormy today, could feel it coming right through the car. Sold 'old LEG' for £150.00 two years ago this month and bought a Marina for £600 at an auction, haven't had much joy with it. When it rains you need your wellies and umbrella in it, it leaks. Bernie keeps saying when he's made redundant (God forbid) we can buy a good new car with the money he'll get. Talk about getting your priorities right. I can just see Bernie amongst the unemployed and me lording it in a posh new car – doesn't matter if we don't eat. He's talking about this redundancy for the past twelve months, he loves spreading doom. I really think he'd love to be made redundant and just sit all day watching telly. I can see myself doing a moonlight flit. Started stripping the paint off the doors and staircase. I'm just fed up with white paint work. Going to dye them all dark oak and varnish them. After trying all the paint strippers that were ever made and found none of them any good, finally bought an electric paint stripper which is great. It's like a new toy to Bernie, I'm hoping he won't get tired of it before the work is done. The girls bought me an electric sander for Christmas, they are nothing if not practical – never had such a useful present.

Friday 7th January

The weather is a bit better today – at least the storm is over. Went to work as usual and discovered my car, for some reason best known to itself, is only doing 20 miles to the gallon. I'd be as well off petrol-wise with that Rolls Laura is giving me when they make their first million; I suppose by then I will be too old to drive. An Indian couple with a six-year-old girl have opened the shop next door to us – God help them, they are not doing much business. I am praying every day they will make a go of it, they are so nice, we couldn't have better neighbours. It cost them a couple of thousand to do it up. It was closed for three years, and what with most of the factories closed up down our road there's not much business for a small shop. Terri spends all of her free time in there. They like her to go in – they feel if people see a white person there they might feel more inclined to shop there. They wanted to pay for her going in, but I wouldn't let them. Terri's been working all day Saturdays in Geary's [cake shop] off Fore Street for the past twelve months or more; she gets £8.49 for that, she gives me half and puts the rest in the Leeds [Building society], she's very good natured.

Saturday 8th January

Went to Walthamstow market at nine o'clock this morning, bought some curtain lining, 50p a yard, then went on to work to do my quilts. I don't do any machining at home now. I do all my cutting out during the week, then take it into work on Saturdays – it saves me messing up the place at home. Worked until 3.30 then home to prepare the dinner. Collected Terri and my seven loaves of bread from Geary's. Had our dinner and then went over to Dan's and Colette's for a drink. Kitty Shanahan and her husband John were there – I think you know them, they live on Maple Road. She talks nineteen to the dozen, nobody can get a word in edgeways when she's around, but she's an interesting person, so I quite enjoyed myself. Colette's two children had gone over to our house. According to Fiona they had a great time playing hide-and-seek in and out of our wardrobes – that was after they had gotten tired of playing cards – even Colette's six-year-old is an expert at playing cards. Left Colette's at 12.45, and when all here had gone to bed, I sat watching a film on the telly until 1.45.

Sunday 9th January

Got up very tired this morning at seven o'clock. We all went to eight o'clock Mass as usual. Then I took my three children, Colette's son

6

James and Adam Kelly (who has patched up his differences with Ciarán) to Petticoat Lane. The moment we got there it started to rain, and by the time we got round the Lane we were just like drowned rats. When we got home they all wanted to go swimming, so into the car again and took them off to Edmonton swimming pool. Home again, just to get back into the car and take Bernie to the off-licence for his usual Sunday beers, which he has while I'm preparing dinner. After dinner, went to bed for my usual Sunday afternoon nap, which is my treat of the week. Terri brought my tea up at six o'clock. Then I had a bath and went down stairs to watch a load of rubbish on the telly. Had a couple of fresh-cream trifles – Terri's working in Geary's is ruining my figure. Keep telling myself I'll never eat cakes again but I just can't resist fresh cream. Went to bed at 12.30 after making a solemn vow never to go to Petticoat Lane again.

Monday 10th January

I hate Monday mornings and work – wouldn't go at all only I need the money. There's so much I want to do at home and haven't the time to do it, but once I'm on the road I keep telling myself how lucky I am to have the health and strength to be able to work. It's just that I wish my work was at home and not somewhere else. Ben and Laura were late getting in today. Their little girl, Katie, is not well – she has a very bad cold. They haven't slept all night with her, they both looked exhausted. Ben's mother looks after Katie while they are at work, she is very good to them. They stay at Ben's parents' home all the week, and just go home to their house in Essex at the weekends. We have a new pattern-cutter, she is 21 years old and very nice. She comes from Kent every day, her mother is from Northern Ireland. Got home after work to find Fiona was helping in the shop next door and Terri was in Geary's; the manageress had rung to know would she go in as one of the staff is off sick. Did some more work on my quilts and curtains before going to bed at 11.30.

Tuesday 11th January

Pandemonium broke loose this morning with them all getting ready for the first day back to school after the Christmas holidays. I really do need another toilet and bathroom. Tempers were really frayed, with Fiona contemplating suicide as a means of avoiding going to school and Ciarán threatening to run away and join the army; I forgot to ask him if he meant the Salvation Army, and Terri didn't say much but she had her tragedy queen face on. I could have screamed when I saw the bathroom – wet towels everywhere, some even thrown back on the shelves with the dry ones, soap left in the water, toothpaste oozing out of the tube, you'd think the demolition squad had been in. I really can't understand how it takes so many towels to dry three people, especially as Ciarán doesn't consider his neck, ears or hands part of his body. A similar scene in the kitchen – dirty cups, saucers and cereal bowls, buttery knives and jammy ones, breadcrumbs all over the cooker and floor. It's at times like this I wish they would all run away and join the army. Tidied up and went to work exhausted. 4.30, return of the demolition squad in better humour than when they left. Sat down to dinner at five o'clock when, all of a sudden, total darkness – we had a power cut, a mad rush to get candles. Helen came in from next door and said how romantic it looked eating by candle light. Prefer the electric myself.

Wednesday 12th January

The demolition squad were at it again this morning, this time on a slightly lesser scale, but still the wet towels, this time thrown in the bath, the soap put back in the dish but in a pool of water, the toilet seat soaking wet (Ciarán must have missed his shot). In the kitchen, dirty dishes and cutlery thrown into the sink. The floor looked as if we kept pigs in the kitchen. Washed and tidied up, swearing to kill the three of them when I got them home. Had breakfast and went to work, didn't do very much there as we are waiting on sample lengths to come in. Made one skirt with two big bands either side, I'm sure if the person wearing it turned round suddenly they'd injure everybody within reach. 4.30, return of the home wreckers. I soon wiped the smiles off their faces when I got going on them, I am sure I could be heard on Worcester Avenue. Finished off telling them of the need to keep Britain clean, and especially a certain house in Tottenham, and if they didn't, I would get into my car tomorrow and drive away into the sunset never to return again. Dinner was eaten in silence, but I think they got the message because later on everywhere was spick and span. Bernie was to do some paint-stripping tonight but he couldn't find the scraper so he sat watching telly instead. I did some more work on my quilts and curtains and went to bed at midnight.

Thursday 13th January

My shouting yesterday seems to have paid off. Was really surprised to see the bathroom this morning not looking as if a bomb had hit it. In the kitchen, dishes washed, floor swept, altogether looking nice and tidy. Felt really pleased, that is until the post arrived. Nan (my cousin) took some snaps here at Christmas, she had them developed in Ireland – got them today, wish I hadn't. I looked dreadful in them. Gave me quite a turn to see myself as others see me. Have to stop eating cakes. Five foot one and a half inches and 11 stone with it, is not a pretty sight. A helmet with horns and I could be mistaken for a shortened version of a Viking. Wish I could have a face transplant. Thought the snaps were bad but there was worse to come. My landlord called this morning to tell me my rent is going up by £10.00 a week, which means I will now be paying nearly £25.00 a week; on the other hand, we could buy it for £15,000.00. Short of winning the Pools, there is no way we can buy this house at our age – no hope of getting a mortgage. Mary came to go shopping with Terri and myself. Fiona went to her Confirmation class, Mrs. McClusker is instructing her. She makes it in May, please God. Ciarán went over to James's (Colette's son). Bernie was going to do some paint-stripping but he couldn't find the key to the shed, so he sat watching telly.

Friday 14th January

Woke very tired this morning. Terri brought me my usual cup of tea, which did little to revive me. Hated going to work. If ever I get to Heaven (please God) I'm going to really give that Adam and Eve a piece of my mind, they have a lot to answer for. Pouring rain, and has turned very cold, but really can't complain, the weather has been lovely for this time of year, almost like spring. Had to fill up my petrol tank today. Mentioned to the garage owner that my car was only doing 20 miles to the gallon, told him I had just had it tuned. He said it wasn't done right so I'll have to complain to the people who did the job. I'm robbed buying petrol. Was a bit busier in work today – the sample lengths came yesterday. We are now getting our summer range together. Fiona and Ciarán went to the swimming baths tonight. Terri stayed home and washed her hair. I cut it for her last night; she cried when she saw it, but after she washed it and styled it, it looked really nice, so smiles all round. Only Bernie is not smiling. He told a bloke in work about getting a cheap telly, the bloke said he'd like one. Bernie contacted the neighbour's friend and got the telly. The bloke rings tonight to say it's not a new telly and he wants his money back. Bernie too sick with worry to do any paint-stripping so he sat watching telly instead.

Saturday 15th January

The usual busy Saturday. Up at eight o'clock. Took Fiona to Brent Cross to change two jumpers Nan had bought herself and Terri for Christmas (they were too small for them). Then into work to finish my quilts and curtains; there is so much work on them I'm almost sorry I started – still, they do look nice. Sent Fiona out to get something for our lunch. She came back with a fresh-cream cake and a bottle of milk. As she doesn't eat cakes I had to eat it all – so much for my good intentions. Left work at 2.30. Prepared dinner for the evening, then out again to look at some gas fires I want to buy for the sitting room and dining room. Saw some which look exactly like a real coal fire, you can even lift the coal out with a tongs and it remains lit – the only snag is, the fireplaces would have to be opened up to fit them in. Dan is doing some brick surrounds for me so I'll ask him to open them up. Collected Terri at 5.45 with her usual bag of cakes from Geary's, it's all a conspiracy to ruin my figure. Adam Kelly and James stayed to dinner. Ciarán went out this morning at six o'clock to try and get a job doing a milk round – he had no luck. Bernie phoned the neighbour's friend (the telly man) to tell him his work mate wanted his money back. He said he would give it back, so Bernie is happy again, too happy to do any paint-stripping so he sat watching telly all day.

Sunday 16th January

The weather is beautiful, just like summer, the sun is so warm. We all went to eight o'clock Mass, which Adam Kelly and Ciarán served. After Mass, drove the two of them to Queensway market. Adam wanted to buy a flick knife for when he goes camping with the Scouts. Bernie, the girls and myself went to see a new warehouse which has just opened beside Bernie's work – as a matter of fact Bernie's firm sold the land it's built on. We looked at all the things we are going to buy when we win the Pools. Bernie's favourite was a sun house. He said he could sit in it all day, so, Pools or no Pools, I am going to save up and buy it for him for when he retires so that I don't have to watch him sitting indoors all day watching telly – I'll even put a telly in it. At 10.30, drove all the kids to the swimming pool. Dan went up after and took them all on video. After dinner, Terri went in to help in the shop next door, and Fiona and Ciarán went over to Dan's to watch themselves on video tape. Fiona said it was hilarious, they didn't know they were being taken. In one part of it Ciarán went up the ladder to the top diving board and bounced up and down; he'd done all the limbering up motions, and just when it looked as if he was about to dive off, he turned round and calmly walked off down the ladder, which proves he is not as silly as he looks, thank God. The telly man came and gave back the £150.00. Bernie was so happy he opened a bottle of Advocate [Vera's original spelling] and watched telly all night.

Monday 17th January

Another lovely day today weather-wise but not otherwise. That horrible Monday morning, it seems to come round so quickly after the weekend. Had to have the home-tune man call to do a job on my car. While waiting for him, decided to look for some curtains I had lost, couldn't find them in any of the places they should have been. Thought I'd look in Ciarán's wardrobe. Got a very strong smell of paraffin. Was horrified to find between the bottom of his bed and wardrobe one of those yellow warning lamps usually seen beside skips. I was so upset I nearly rang the school to send Ciarán home so that I could kill him. Went into the sitting room and discovered one of the windows had been left open all night – you think you are safe in your home, with Ciarán around you're not. After my car was fixed, went to work, where I spent all day planning what I would do with Ciarán when I got hold of him. By the time I got home from work I had cooled down a bit. When Bernie heard about the lamp he nearly had a stroke. When Ciarán came home gave him a few whacks, told him he was a thief and he'd have to tell it in confession. He's confined to his room for the rest of the week when he comes home from school. Later on, asked him why he did such a stupid thing. He said he thought the lamp would come in very handy if we had another power cut. Now I'm wondering how I'm going to put it back… with my luck somebody is sure to see me and ring the police. No happy faces today.

Tuesday 18th January

Ciarán was told off in school for being late, so he left home at 7.15 this morning, hope he is in time. Did the usual mopping up operations after the horrible three before going off to work myself. Katie was in today, she is so lovely. She has a new game with plastic fish, so we both sat fishing for a while, then Ben came in and took her to Brighton for the day so that Laura and I could get some work done. We are very busy now, it's all go. After work, went to make some more enquiries about the fires I'm buying. Met a very nice receptionist there who told me her life story. She is 25 years old, got married to a man three years ago who told her she'd never have to work again. She had a great time for one month then without any notice her husband was told they were making him redundant – they were both shattered. He was idle for 18 months before he got another job, and in that time they had to sell their house and go and live with her father. Whatever sort of a job he has now, she said they were better off financially when he was on the dole, such is the system here. Dan called over tonight to take measurements for the brickwork, he is going to do round the fires and into the recesses. He didn't go until midnight so there was no paint-stripping done, Bernie fell asleep.

Wednesday 19ᵗʰ January

Felt anything but well this morning. Really didn't feel like going to work, but we are so busy thought I'd better make the effort. Haven't had a day out of work through illness since I went to work for Laura and Ben. I wish they had another sample machinist then I might have the odd day off. Managed to struggle through the day, and on the way home from work promised myself I'd go to bed early with a hot drink, but the best-laid schemes of mice and men etc. After dinner, felt a bit better and did some housework and washing. Then went over to Colette's for an hour. Came home, got the supper ready. Was just going up to bed, after helping Terri with the washing up, when there was a terrible commotion outside on the road. The Spurs crowd were coming from the match. They had lost to Burnley (a second division), and, bad losers that they are, they were bent on trouble. Two Burnley supporters, a young boy and a man, were walking back to their coach when about 25 Spurs fans attacked the boy. The man tried to defend the boy and was stabbed in the back and side. A few people ran out of their houses and the crowd scattered leaving the man lying on the ground. Colette phoned the police and ambulance who took him off to Middlesex Hospital. This is a usual occurrence here. In the end, didn't get to bed until 12.30.

Thursday 20th January

Very, very cold this morning, everywhere covered in frost, winter has come at last. Did the usual chores before going off to work. Shivered all the way, drafts came in from all directions in that rotten car of mine. When I got in, Ben cheerfully informed me he had left the coffee percolator in the new place we are going to. He took it with him when he went to do some work there last night and forgot to bring it back, I could have killed him. Finished up getting a sore throat for the want of a hot drink. Didn't get one until 2.45 just before I set off for home. Bernie was on strike today. They put in for a raise and the firm offered them one-and-a-half per cent; when they refused to accept, the management told them they were getting nothing at all now. This is the attitude of all the firms towards their workers. The Thatcher government is really bringing the people to their knees and the unions have no say at all now. Went shopping with Mary and Terri. Afterwards, took Mary to the presbytery with the shopping for the priests, then on to where she lives (in Hornsey) with a person she used to work with. On the way home bought some chips. Terri and myself ate them in the car, I'm never going to get slim, too fond of eating. Went to bed at midnight. Bernie went early as usual, he needs his beauty sleep.

Friday 21st January

A really lovely morning, brilliant sunshine. Had to fill up with petrol on the way to work. It's costing me £9.35 per week to run that horrible car, still I'd be lost without it, so would the children and Bernie, they don't believe in walking anywhere. Had all my bills in today: gas, electric, phone and road tax, all came to a grand total of £274.00. I'll have to pay my road tax first, the rest will have to wait their turn, it's a curse to be poor. I'm hoping it's my turn to win the Pools this week, still we have a lot to be thankful for, we are all in good health, thank God. Made six samples today. Did a bit of shopping on the way home from work. Had my friend Mary Mac to dinner tonight, she comes about once a month. She usually finds some work to do here, she's a great help. Herself and I were going to do some sanding down on the doors but I felt too tired to do anything so we sat down and relaxed, something I haven't done for a long time. Terri spent her night in the shop next door with the Indian couple, and when they closed they had a tea party with all the cakes they hadn't sold. God help them, their business doesn't seem to be picking up. Jack (Mary's husband) called at 9.30 to collect her, got some advice from him about my plants. They left at 11.15. I didn't get to bed until two o'clock.

Saturday 22nd January

Didn't get up until 8.30, very tired after my late night. Had breakfast. Brought some sheets back to the chapel house – I do some washing for the priests every week. They have no washing machine, and it would mean Mary would have to do them by hand, so it's a help to her. Went to work and made some trousers for Ciarán, black ones, which is his favourite colour (apart from jeans). Left work at two o'clock and went right into the thick of the traffic all heading for Tottenham – Spurs were playing, didn't get home till near three o'clock. Bernie was going bananas as Ciarán had brought three lads home to lunch. I don't know why he was so annoyed, I was the one who had to clean up after them, he was too busy watching racing on telly. Very disappointed I didn't win the Pools today, only got four draws, now I'll have to wait another week. Prepared the dinner for evening, then went with Fiona to buy a swimsuit; she bought a size 34" bust but when she tried it on at home it was too small – she'll have to change it for a 36". Collected Terri from work at 5.30 with her bag of cakes. Then home to get the dinner, which was shared with one of Ciarán's friends. After dinner, washed my hair and watched telly. Ciarán went to Dan's house with Adam and James, was back at 8.45. Had supper at nine o'clock and was in bed by ten.

Sunday 23rd January

The usual rush to get to eight o'clock Mass, at which Ciarán didn't serve due to the fact that a policeman held us up on the High Road and made us late. There were some road works going on and I should have stopped a hundred yards from the traffic lights. There was a sign there to this effect which I hadn't noticed, nor had the motorist in front of me. He wasn't your usual friendly copper. He asked me (very sarcastically) could I not read. Only we were rushing to Mass I would have given him a piece of my mind. After Mass, had breakfast and drove all the kids to the swimming pool. Then, on Jack's advice, I re-potted some of my plants, which took up my time until 12.30. Drove Bernie to the off-licence for the usual drinks then home to get dinner ready. Sunday dinner is always at two o'clock, but today only Bernie and myself had it at that time. The children didn't come in until three o'clock. Had my usual nap, then up at 6.30 after Terri had brought in my tea, and then did some sanding down on the doors. Six kids in tonight with Ciarán. Bernie swearing what he is not going to do with him when they go. It's really open house here. Had supper at 8.30, then a bath. Everyone had baths tonight because of the water strike. Filled up anything which would hold water: bottles, teapots, kettles, jugs, even the bath. Hope the strike won't last long. Ciarán and Adam washed my car – haven't seen it yet, but hear it looks worse than before they did it.

Monday 24ᵗʰ January

Always lock the bedroom doors when I get up in the mornings so that Minnie (the cat) can't get onto any of the beds, and never leave her in the house while I'm at work, but this morning couldn't lock any doors as Bernie had removed them to burn the paint off the mouldings – talk about open plan. Looked for her everywhere, she was nowhere to be found. Thought Terri had probably put her out before going to school. Was really furious when I came from work and she runs to greet me as I turned the key in the door. Could have killed her – can't stand that cat, she's so devious, would have got rid of her long ago only the kids would go mad, also Bernie. They'd all sooner I'd go than that bloody cat. Wouldn't mind only she's not worth feeding, she can't kill a mouse. Had one come in from the garden, she played with it for a while in the kitchen while I was having hysterics then when she got tired she let it go. Had to wait until Father Byrne (as the kids call Bernie) came in and killed it. Ciarán was there when the execution took place and cried his eyes out and pleaded with Bernie not to kill it, he said it was such a lovely little mouse. I think he had visions of himself, Minnie and the mouse living happy ever after, didn't matter that I'd have to leave home. Did some sanding down tonight. Bernie's heart is really not in it, he'd much rather be watching telly.

Tuesday 25th January

Did exactly what I do every working day of the week, the same dull, boring, predicable routine. Really fed up working. Thinking of just working four days a week so that I can have at least one day to myself. They say things always get worse before they get better, well that's just how it is with our house, every day it looks a little bit worse. Fiona said I must be mad to have started it. There's no carpet on the stairs, landing or hall, and after tomorrow there'll be none on the sitting room or dining room. Bought carpet for both rooms last year, never liked it, so having it put on two of the bedrooms and getting plain carpet all over the rest of the house. That will be in about four months' time, that's how long (or longer) I think it will take to get this house done. Don't mind the hard work, it's the aggro I get with it that gets on my nerves. Bernie is always in bad humour when there is work to be done, he'd much rather be watching telly. One of the armchairs is so moulded to his shape from sitting in it so much that nobody else can sit in it comfortably. I don't know if he's got it right and it's myself that's the fool. Dan came over to tell us that he's bought a shop in Phillip Lane (it is beside the bus garage). It has three rooms above it which he will let out to students from Tottenham College, and the shop will sell DIY stuff. Hope things work out alright for him, another one to add to my list of prayers.

Wednesday 26th January

Bernie took the day off work because of the man coming to put the carpets on the bedrooms. Tried to get as much furniture as possible out of the rooms, shoved it all into Ciarán's room. Bernie, his usual miserable self when there is any work to be done, never stopped nagging. Was really glad to get into work for a bit of peace, where Laura and myself had a long discussion on the selfishness of men. Had a fairly easy time in work, just made three samples. We move to our new premises this weekend, please God. Not looking forward to the longer journey every day. Got home from work at 3.30, was quite surprised and pleased to see everywhere nice and tidy – take back all I said about Bernie. The bedrooms look lovely; even downstairs doesn't look too bad. Bernie and the carpet man put the old carpets from the bedrooms on the dining room and sitting room, at least it's better than looking at bare floorboards. Had dinner and went upstairs to do some more work on the doors. Bernie said he'd put the doors back on the bedrooms, told him they'd need a piece off the bottom because the carpet was thicker than the old one, but he couldn't be told anything. Put one of the doors back only to find it wouldn't open properly. Went into one of his little acts where he's having a nervous breakdown. Took the door off, swore he was never doing any more work here, went downstairs and sat watching telly.

Thursday 27th January

Why is life so hard, nothing seemed to go right today. Fiona is not talking to me because last night I accused her of moving a wire brush from where I left it and couldn't find it. Turned out it wasn't she who had moved it but Bernie. She didn't say goodbye when she went to school this morning, nor did she say a word when she came in this evening, but kept giving me looks which spoke volumes – had to restrain myself from hitting her with the frying pan. Mary came to go shopping; Terri didn't come, she was in the shop next door helping Leena – could do with some help myself. Took Mary home with her shopping, went in to see June (the lady she stays with). Got home at 9.15 to be met by Terri, who was going mad because BBC 1 had broken down (she wanted to see 'The Citadel') and I should have been here to fix it. Then had to listen to Bernie going berserk because there were four kids in tonight jumping up and down in the bedrooms and on the beds, I should have been here to stop them. Didn't see Ciarán at all – was in his bedroom, not talking to me because I wouldn't let him go swimming. Had to listen to Bernie for the rest of night telling me what a fool I was to have given Dan £120.00 for material for the fireplaces. He was to have started on them last Friday… didn't come, then he said Monday… didn't come; last night he got Bernie's keys and said he'd start on them today while we were at work… didn't come, didn't even bother to ring to ask why. No happy faces today.

Friday 28th January

A very busy day in work, getting everything packed for moving. When I left at three o'clock, Laura and Jenny were still hard at it. Ben and Sam were away at the new premises putting the finishing touches to it. Said a few words to Ben this morning for not taking myself and Jenny to see where we are going to work. It will be like a mystery tour for both of us on Monday. Jenny knows very little of London, she lives in Kent and commutes every day, and when I pass Bruce Grove I'm lost.

Maybe it wouldn't be such a bad idea if I did get lost – not having such a happy time at home thanks to Dan. Saw a handful of bricks in the front garden when I came home – thought, thank God Dan has started on the fireplaces, but when I looked in the sitting room he had just taken out about ten bricks and nothing at all done in the dining room. Got a terrible, strong smell of gas, discovered Dan hadn't relit the fridge, the water-heater or the heater in the hall when he turned the gas back on at the mains. Very gingerly relit them, praying I wouldn't blow up. Bernie came in then (he's off at 3.30 every Friday), went into one of his little tantrums when he saw how little Dan had done. Felt almost sorry I hadn't left all the pilot lights on without lighting them and put my head in the gas oven. After dinner, discovered more trouble – the water-heater is not working, and not only that it's leaking in three places. Bernie on the verge of one of his heart attacks, swearing what he'll say to Dan when he sees him.

Saturday 29th January

Dear God, you're never bad but you can be worse. Went down to the Gas Board this morning to buy a new multi-point to replace the broken one, only to be told it would have to go on a wall 12 inches away from an open window. Can't go in the laundry room where the old one is because of the new extension, can't go in the kitchen, so the only other place it can go is in the bathroom, which sounds straightforward enough, only it's not, due to the fact we haven't got a wall wide enough to hold the multi-point and have it 12 inches from an open window. So, what we have to do is open up the part of the window which is a fixture and make the open window a fixture; things get more complicated in this house. Fiona said she wishes some kind person would do us a favour and blow it up. Spurs got through to the next round of the Cup, they beat West Bromwich 2-1 – picked them to draw in the Pools, I got four draws again today. Went to the Leeds this morning to draw out £300.00 to pay my bills. Was told the computer was showing £200.00 less than I had in my book. Told the bloke behind the counter to take no notice of the computer, that they are always making mistakes, he didn't think that funny. Too lazy to check it, said he'll post my book to me during the week. Never did like computers. Dan came over today. Bernie greeted him like a long-lost brother, so much for all he was going to say to him. Was to come back tonight to put the doors back on the bedrooms… didn't come, so Bernie is thinking up more things he's going to say to him when he sees him.

Sunday 30th January

A dreadful morning, pouring rain and very breezy. After Mass, Bernie invited Ann Gilmore home to breakfast – could have killed him, the house is in such a state, she's a very nice person. Her husband and Charlie Dougan were trying to sell off (at half price) all the souvenirs left over from the Pope's visit. Took her back to the church at midday so that herself and her husband could go home together. Took the usual crowd of children to the swimming pool. Fiona and Ciarán washed their hair in the showers there. Really miss having no hot water; still, we are lucky: some people here have no water at all owing to the water strike, no sign of it ending. Dan came and put the bedroom doors on, only God and himself knows when the brickwork will get done. Leena came in from the shop, business is getting no better, God help her. She's on her own in that shop from 6.30 in the morning until 6.30 at night when her husband comes from work and takes over while she gets the dinner ready, she has no life. Her husband is very nice but very hard on her. Indian women are certainly not liberated. Washed 26 tea-towels; I'm sure the neighbours must think I take in washing, but that's just a week's supply for ourselves. Three cheers for the man who invented washing machines. I don't know how we managed years ago when we had only two tea-towels and they were washed every night ready for the next day. Had a phone call from Ben to say he'll meet me at North Road to take me to our new premises, so I won't be going on a mystery tour after all. Just had a phone call from Wexford to say my cousin had died as a result of a car crash last Sunday, Lord rest his soul. Very upset.

Monday 31st January

Very upset this morning over the death of my cousin, R.I.P. It seems he was going along in his car when another motorist, speeding behind, crashed into his car, pushing it into a van in front. He had very bad internal injuries. Eilish phoned me last night to tell me the news. She said his wife is in a dreadful state, they were years married and have no family. She is very delicate, and they are afraid the shock will kill her. They were a lovely couple. Mary, Johnjoe and the children stayed with them overnight the year they went to Ireland – they were catching the boat at Rosslare the next day. They have a beautiful bungalow in Wexford at the foot of a hill. Met Ben this morning as arranged, followed him in my car to our new premises. It's in a place called Gloucester Mews off Regent's Park Road. It's a great improvement on the old place – we've got a reception room, an office, a showroom and a very big design room, so things are really looking up. The only thing I don't like about it is the journey, it's quite a bit further than North Road. We are surrounded by very expensive houses, all around the £175,000.00 mark. A lot of actors and actresses live there; you never know, I might get spotted one day. Dan didn't come over to knock the bricks out of the fireplaces, so Bernie did the one in the sitting room. Surprised me, he made such a good job of it; even surprised himself, said he'll do the dining room one tomorrow night, please God. The weather has really changed, snowing today but still not all that cold.

February 1983

A DIY NIGHTMARE

Tuesday 1st February

Mapped out a route last night for getting to work without the aid of Ben. Everything went great until I came to a one-way system which wasn't marked on the A to Z. Stopped to ask a man the way only to discover he was a mute, God help him. He could hear perfectly (he was very nice looking), and with a few hand signs I finally got the message that I was on the right road. Got into work by ten o'clock. Didn't do very much. Laura wasn't in. She looks after Katie on Tuesdays while Ben's mother goes to dressmaking classes. Came unstuck again on the way home from work. Couldn't go back the way I came because of all these one-way systems. Got lost. After driving round all strange places for about half an hour, I finally finished up at Euston Station, which was lucky for me as the car knows the way home from there on its own because of the various relations and friends I've picked up when they come from Ireland to stay with me. Didn't get home until four o'clock.

A mad rush to get the dinner ready on time, but everybody was getting home late today for some reason or another. Ciarán had detention, Fiona was at Popmobility – whatever that is [an exercise craze, with the various routines set to Top 10 hits]. Had to wear my seat belt from yesterday [the legal requirement to wear a seat belt came into force this year], can't get used to it. They are not meant for fat people, feel I'm being strangled – still, it's that or a £50.00 fine. Bernie didn't do the dining room fireplace, he couldn't get anybody to disconnect the gas fire. He wanted to do it himself but I wouldn't let him, afraid he might blow us all up.

Wednesday 2nd February

Another dreadful journey to work this morning. Could only do five miles per hour down Camden Road, which must be at least two miles long, so didn't get to work until after ten o'clock. Ben phoned to say himself and Laura would be late getting in, so, as we had no work to do, Jenny and myself went out to explore our new surroundings. The houses are really very imposing, with steps leading up to the front doors and big pillars on either side, most of them six storeys high, including the basement and the attic. There is a park very near where our premises are, and right beside that is Regent's Park (the zoo end). Left work at 2.50, didn't get home until four o'clock. Got lost again, this time around Archway. Bernie did some more paint-stripping tonight. He's still furious with Dan, we haven't seen him since last week. I hope we'll have the fireplaces done before next Christmas, please God, or I may leave home. Ciarán got two exam results today, he came second out of the class in Geography and fourth in English, so he's quite pleased with himself. He was to play rugby yesterday, but as he had a cold I wrote a note to the teacher asking that he be excused. Because he didn't play he had to write out the Lord's Prayer 40 times; he'd have rather played and got pneumonia.

Thursday 3rd February

Woke up with sore eyes this morning due to the fact I had stayed up so late last night mapping out yet another way of getting to work, all to no avail. I got lost again; it's becoming a habit. Talk about Rome being built on seven hills, London must be built on 107 hills, and I went up and down them all this morning. My journey took in Muswell Hill, Southgate, Highgate, Gospel Oak, The Great North Road, Haverstock Hill, Swiss Cottage and Hampstead, where I finally stopped and asked a policeman the way. I had left home at 8.45, didn't get to work until 10.35. Saw more of London this morning than I've seen in the 18 years I've been here. Clocked up 24 miles, costing me a bomb in petrol. Thinking of packing a suitcase in case I have to stay overnight somewhere, but at least I did manage to get home from work without getting lost – more good luck than judgement, or maybe I'm developing a homing instinct. Mary, Terri and myself were on our way out tonight to go shopping when Leena knocked to know would Terri go into the shop and stay with her until her husband came in, she was a bit frightened. A young lad had been into the shop and stolen 40 cigarettes. She rang the police, and Terri was telling me later on, this lady come into the shop dressed in a padded jacket and jeans, she introduced herself as Mrs. Foley, a police officer – anything less like a policewoman you couldn't imagine, appearances are very deceptive.

Friday 4th February

Quite pleased with myself this morning, just took one wrong turning on my way to work. Went up this road in Kentish Town which turned out to be a street market, was tempted to get out of the car and do some shopping but decided against it. After weaving my way in and out of the stalls, discovered I couldn't get out the other end so had to turn round and go back. Got to work by 9.45. Didn't do a lot of machining as we are still getting ourselves sorted out. Jenny was very happy today – she went for her driving test yesterday and passed (first time); now all she needs is a car, which she said she can't afford at the moment. Bernie and myself arrived home together (he's off at 3.30 on Fridays). There were five gas men outside our door digging a hole in the ground. He asked one of them to disconnect the gas fire in the dining room so that he could open up the fireplace, which he did after dinner. What a job that was, I never saw so much dirt. There was a back-boiler behind the bricks which we didn't know was there, and by the time that was taken out, we could have done with the dirt squad to clean up. I'm beginning to think Fiona is right in saying I must be mad to have started on this house. Dan hasn't put in an appearance yet, hope we won't be left with two empty fireplaces. Bernie had a letter from management today asking him if he would like to take early retirement, but that didn't worry him half as much as the fact that Sean O'Leary tried to have him sacked today. He reported Bernie to a manager for doing something which he thought he shouldn't be doing. Thank God Bernie was in the right or it could have been serious.

Saturday 5th February

Bernie had a letter from management asking him if he'd like to take early retirement; they were sent to all the over sixties – Bernie will be 61 in April, please God. He doesn't know whether to take it or not. Things are very unsettled in his job. If he stays on there may be redundancies in a few months' time and he'd get less money than they are offering him now. If he were sure of getting some sort of a job, even part-time, he'd be better off to retire now. It's hard to know what to do, we'll have to weigh up the pros and cons. This might turn out to be our chance to buy our house, who knows. Felt very depressed all day. Can't stop thinking about what Sean did on Bernie, especially as Bernie got him that job – thought he was our friend, but with friends like him who needs enemies. I'm trying not to feel too bitter towards him, keep telling myself he is more to be pitied. Took a letter over to Mary in the presbytery. Father Hegarty was there, he asked me how I liked his confession box. He was taking the partition away, and has a small table and two chairs in it with a reading lamp in the centre of the table. Told him all he needed was a crystal ball and one would think he was a fortune teller. He roared laughing, he said that's how the children like it. Told him I was glad I saw it, I know now who not to go to confession to – like things a little more discreet myself. For the rest of the day did all the usual Saturday chores.

Sunday 6th February

After Mass, took Fiona to see our new premises in Primrose Hill, only got lost twice. She was very impressed, thought it was a great improvement on the old place. Came home through Highgate. Fiona was amazed at all the beautiful houses there, she said we'll have to buy a house there when we win the Pools; chance would be a fine thing. I was born a worker and think I'll be one till I die, no hope of early retirement for me; thank God I'm able to work. The children didn't go swimming today. Ciarán and James washed some cars yesterday, and with the money they got they bought some models which they assembled and painted. Nearly killed the pair of them when I discovered they had cleaned the cars with four of my best tea-towels. Terri went into the shop to help out. Leena and her daughter were away visiting her sister and mother. Fiona cleaned out some cupboards in the bedrooms. She said I hoard too much junk. Had to rescue a load of stuff which was being left out for the bin men tomorrow, there is no sentiment in her at all. Dan came over tonight, said he'd definitely start our work tomorrow week, please God. I am now thinking of getting central heating [by 1983 not having central heating would have been unusual, but still, many homes were without it] with what it would cost for the two fires I was going to get. Dan said the price of them would go halfway towards central heating. Knew Bernie was giving me bulls' looks [Irish for angry and reproachful glances – I can't find a derivation for this common phrase] while Dan was talking about it, so didn't dare look at him. Then Leena and her husband came in, had some tea, didn't go until 12.15; by then Bernie too tired to give out – hoping by tomorrow he'll have got over the shock.

Monday 7th February

Very cold this morning. Nearly didn't go to work I had such pains in my stomach, eased off after a while so decided to go. Got in just five minutes before Ben and Laura. Jenny's mother phoned to say she wouldn't be in as she wasn't well. Only made one skirt. Snowing very heavily when I left work at 2.50, not a very pleasant journey home. Going to kill Ciarán when I get him. Himself and James cleaned my car yesterday and twisted both windscreen wipers. Had to get out and try and straighten them, but still wouldn't clear the windscreen properly. Prayed all the way home that I wouldn't have the misfortune to run into a copper, however arrived home safe and sound. The girls and Ciarán came in half frozen. Gave out yards [a common Irish expression – to mean 'complained at length', but with the emphasis on blame] to Ciarán over my car. He had the cheek to ask me did that mean I wouldn't be paying for having the car cleaned. Told him in no uncertain terms that I wasn't paying nor was I allowing him to continue in his car-cleaning business – that I wasn't going to be billed for damage he might do to other peoples' cars. So, needless to say we are not on the best of terms. Gave James a bit of my mind too when he came over – told him they would both have to pay for new windscreen wipers out of their pocket money, he went home really worried. Bernie and myself worked very hard on the house tonight, it's very hard and slow work, but I think we are winning.

Tuesday 8th February

A bitterly cold morning, felt it the moment I woke, the bedroom is like a fridge. Jenny was in today. She had a bad pain in her stomach yesterday, thinks it may be due to the water. The Water Board men are still on strike. We are very lucky here in London, we haven't begun to feel the effects of it yet, but it's pretty grim in some parts of England and Wales and there is no sign of the strike ending. The men seem determined not to go back to work until they have got a better deal. At least we are not wasting water – we can't have a bath here because of our hot water-heater going on strike too. Laura had Katie in today. She had two dolls with her, she calls them Fiona and Jean. She said they were both ill so she had to take them to the doctor (I was the doctor). I prescribed some tablets for them and told her to keep them warm. She brought them back so often for treatment that I had to order them into hospital so that I could get on with my work. Later on, herself, Laura and a friend went off to a fashion show at Olympia. Snowing again today on my way home from work. Getting home a bit earlier now that I'm beginning to know the way. After dinner, two of Ciarán's friends called for him to go swimming, think their parents must be mad. Didn't let him go, which did not improve our relationship. He thinks he is very hard done by, but I think himself and his friends are a bit too young yet to be out at night on their own.

Wednesday 9th February

Another very cold day, had to scrape the frost off my car. Got lost again going to work, still can't get it right. Didn't do one bit of work today. Spent the time talking to Laura about some of my problems and some of hers. Jenny went out to look at the shops in the West End to get some ideas for new designs. Laura is thinking of going into dresses and jackets. Deliberately got home late from work, fed up being taken so much for granted by everyone here, so just for once thought I won't be there when they get home and that will give them something to think about. Terri ran to greet me when I came in, but the others were watching telly while waiting for their dinner. I had cooked a casserole last night which just had to be heated up. Terri had put that in the oven but hadn't done any potatoes to go with it. There was a stony silence all during dinner. They all ate like horses, which proved they weren't worried by my absence, maybe I didn't stay away long enough. Bernie has finally decided not to take early retirement. After himself and the other men concerned had discussed it, they came to the conclusion that the firm was giving them very little money. What they were offering was money from a pension scheme they had paid into, plus their holiday pay and twelve weeks' wages in lieu of notice. It wouldn't add up to eight months' wages and, as he has more than four years to go, he would lose quite a lot of money, so there goes our chance of buying our house.

Thursday 10th February

Had a phone call from one of South's (landlord) workmen to say they'd like to come and do our new multi-point; told him I didn't want it as we were thinking of getting central heating. He said he'd come and fix the chimney stack which was damaged in the storm, and which was the cause of the television aerial bending over. Told him I'll leave the keys in Leena's so that they could do it while I was at work. Didn't do much in work. Laura and Jenny went to the fashion show again today; asked me to go but I didn't feel like it. Got home early from work to discover the workmen had fixed the kitchen ceiling too. For the past twelve months I've been telling South it would fall down on top of us. They hadn't made a lot of mess but there was dust everywhere. While waiting for the dinner to cook, had a quick dust round. Started snowing at four o'clock. Went shopping with Mary after dinner, pouring snow. When I left her home, she said we must be mad going shopping on a night like this – I thought, now she tells me. Snowed worse than ever on the way back home. Traffic was just crawling along. Everybody was being very cautious, thank God. Went over to see Dan about the central heating, could do with it now. He's coming over tomorrow night to measure up for it. Think it's going to cost a bomb – however, hear it pays for itself in the long run. Got home to find Bernie having one of his turns. Our kids and all the neighbouring kids had been having a snowball fight and our hall was full of snow. So all kids are barred from our house. Bernie would even bar our own kids, but who could put up with them only ourselves.

Friday 11th February

Driving along in the pouring snow this morning when I suddenly realised I had forgotten to put my bottom teeth in – had taken them out because my gums were hurting. Thought of going back for them, but decided against it as I was more than halfway to work. Had to keep reminding myself not to smile at passing motorists in case the shock caused an accident. Ben roared laughing when he heard about my teeth. Told him I wouldn't be able to talk much without them, he said, thank God for that. Never did care much for that Ben, hate him now. Laura was much kinder, she said, you look alright without them. Had to have chips for my lunch, thought they'd be easier to eat than slimming biscuits which I usually have. Nightmare journey home from work, snow pelting down, hasn't stopped all day. Had to keep rolling the window down in order to see out, might as well have walked home I was so covered in snow. Had to keep my coat on while I cooked dinner, the kitchen was so cold. Wish we had that central heating. Bernie going mad again tonight. Like Piccadilly Circus here with kids walking in and out. He's thinking of leaving home to get away from them all – can't say that I blame him, it's really getting a bit much. They are treating our house as if it were a club. Bernie did some sanding down dressed in his boiler suit, his filter mask, hood, glasses and rubber gloves, he looked like something from outer space. The kids laughed when they saw him. If he had a ray gun I am sure he'd have exterminated them all.

Saturday 12th February

Terri brought me up a cup of tea just before she went to work. Felt very tired, so went back to sleep. Woke at 9.30 to the sound of voices, Adam Kelly in Ciarán's bedroom. Got up and had breakfast and made some soup for lunch; thought it would be better than a fry this cold weather. Still snowing on and off. After lunch, went to enquire whether I could have the fires I ordered with a back-boiler behind one of them for the central heating. Was very disappointed to hear I couldn't, so now I'll have to have another think about it. These fires look so real, but I have since heard they don't give off enough heat to warm a room, they are merely a frontage for where there is central heating. Went into Sheila's next door. Her house is really lovely, everything is just perfect in it, not a thing out of place. I wish my family were as tidy as hers. Drove two of Geary's shop assistants home in the pouring snow. One of them is Irish, she lives in one of those semi-detached houses in Northumberland Park. After dinner, Ciarán in trouble again. He wanted to go over to James's in soaking-wet shoes. He has a new pair of shoes but he won't wear them. He calls them beetle crushers, and because he wouldn't wear them he wasn't allowed to go to James's, so he threw a tantrum. Finished up saying he might even leave home, so he was sent up to bed. James and another kid called for him and walked straight upstairs to his room – we were furious. After a while, Bernie went up and told them they'd have to go – that Ciarán was being punished.

Sunday 13th February

Pouring snow this morning. On the way to Mass Ciarán threw another tantrum over wearing the new shoes, so he's not to be allowed out for a month in the evenings or at weekends or have any of his friends in. Feeling very sorry for himself all day, and hard done by. He spent most of the time in his room making and painting a model. Gave Mrs. Dunn a lift home from Mass, felt sorry for her walking home in the snow. Beautiful afternoon, brilliant sunshine but very cold. Went for my usual afternoon nap. Woke up feeling terrible. I have a dreadful cold, runny nose and eyes, feel awful. The girls and Helen (next door) were going to a disco in St. Paul's, Wood Green, so, cold or no cold, I had to drive them there and call back for them when it was over. Freezing cold, sure I'll get pneumonia. The girls said the disco was very good, only one boy got beaten up outside. Dan was supposed to come over tonight to measure up for the central heating; he was to start on it tomorrow, no hope of that now. When he will start on it is anyone's guess. Leena came over with beef curry and chapattis, which is an Indian bread somewhat like pancakes except it is very dry. The beef looked lovely except it was greasy – it seems when she was making it her hand slipped and she put in more oil than she intended. I didn't dare eat any of it in case I'd be sick. The girls ate it between them, they said it was lovely. I'd like to try it with less oil.

Monday 14th February

Didn't sleep very well last night. Woke feeling dreadful, aching all over. Didn't think I'd be able to go to work, but after I had breakfast and a couple of tablets, didn't feel too bad, so went off to work; wish I hadn't, it was freezing in our room. The heating had been off all over the weekend. I couldn't stop shivering, couldn't take my coat off, and after a couple of hours and feeling much worse, I said to Laura I'd better go home while I can still drive. The funny thing was I was dying with hunger. Had to stop and get some chips, which I ate on the way home as if I hadn't eaten for a month. After that, really felt as if my number was up. Went to bed for an hour, then got up, prepared dinner, put it in the oven and left it to Fiona to dish up when she came home from school. Couldn't eat a thing, still suffering from the effects of the chips. Lay on the couch for the rest of the evening, silently making my peace with God in case I didn't see morning, and if I didn't, hoping everybody would feel guilty for being so horrible to me lately. Wish I'd made a nice dress to be laid out in; if I recover, must make one. Just when I was thinking of dragging my aching body off to bed, Dan came. If I hadn't felt so bad would have hung out the flags; instead, just lay there listening to all the plans for the central heating which he said he'll start on Wednesday – please God, not going to hold my breath, wondering if I'll live till then.

Tuesday 15th February

Felt a bit better this morning, thank God. Bitterly cold, wish we had that central heating. Had a letter from my cousin Nan telling me that a friend of ours in Ireland had died, Lord have mercy on him.

First met him when I was six years old, lived in fear of himself and his brother for the rest of my childhood. They were really wild and got up to all sorts of devilment, but when they grew up and got sense, they turned out to be two of the nicest people one could wish to meet. It's hard to believe that two such horrible children could turn into such nice adults, so maybe there is hope for my kids. Rang Mary to tell her, and to get some Masses said [requests for specific prayers to be said at Mass for people who have died or who are suffering illness or bereavement can be made] – she was very upset to hear the news. Laura brought Katie to work today; she didn't have her dolls, they are still in hospital, thank God. Didn't feel up to doctoring them – need somebody to doctor myself. We sat looking through books while Laura and Ben were talking to a customer. Had Helen and Leena's youngster, Tina, in tonight. Can't think what attraction this house has for kids, it's in an awful state. When I look round this place, I thank God I didn't die last night – I'd hate to go leaving the house like this, what would people think of me? Dan came over to tell us he is definitely starting the central heating on Thursday, hope we have it in time for next winter. I have a horrible feeling I'm going to wish we'd never decided to have it at all, and just know I'll never hear the end of it from Bernie.

Wednesday 16th February

Fiona wanted to stay off school today to finish a project, she's been doing it since the 1st January – at least, that's what she tells me she's doing any time I ask her to help me, how she hasn't got writer's cramp is a mystery. Told her in no uncertain terms to get off to school, so now she is not talking. We both seem to spend most of our time not talking to each other. Didn't do much in work – waiting on sample lengths to come. Ben brought in some beautiful, big plants, a glass-top table and a couch for the showroom. I told him, Laura, Jenny and myself could use it for a rest room; he said (being sarcastic), I thought the design room was the rest room. Wish it wasn't so far away or I might often escape to it when the going gets too rough at home. Was cooking dinner when Dan rang to know could I give him some money to buy some stuff for the central heating. Had to drop everything and go up to the Leeds. They had taken my book a fortnight ago to correct a mistake in it and hadn't returned it. I explained to the bloke behind the counter about the book and he said he had posted it to me last week. However, he gave me the money and got me to sign a form stating that my book has been mislaid; I forgot to ask him who is supposed to have mislaid it, him or me. Life doesn't seem to run smoothly for me. Bernie did some paint-stripping and I did some sanding down tonight, never saw such a mess. Really want my head tested for putting all this work on myself. Dan come over for the money, wished he'd come over and do the work as quick.

Thursday 17th February

Spoke to the postman this morning about my Leeds' book, said he knew nothing about it and it wasn't in the sorting office or it would have been given to him to post. Phoned the bloke in the Leeds, told him what the postman said. Asked me would I go down to the sorting office and try and sort it out with them; I said alright, but later on, when I had time to think about it, I thought, he's the one who should be sorting it out, not me. Had to fill up with petrol on my way to work, my car doesn't seem to realise it should be doing

35 to 40 miles to the gallon, not 20 to 25 miles as it's doing at the moment. It's a true saying, things are never bad but they could be worse, as was proved today when I came home from work. Yesterday, I thought this house can't look any worse than it is now, how very wrong I was. Today, I had to pick my way through various radiators, a cylinder, two gas fires, a back-boiler and bundles of copper piping, not to mention an assortment of plastic bags containing nuts, bolts, T-joints, U-joints, elbow bends and God knows what other sort of bends, it all added up to complete chaos. Dan had been out shopping for the central heating, and then he tells me that's only half of it. Upstairs not much better. In the bathroom, the bath panel ripped out – never knew baths had legs – in the girls' room clothes everywhere, taken out of one of the cupboards because that's where the cylinder is going, and Ciarán's room as usual looking like a tip. Didn't know whether to leave home or cook dinner, but in the end common sense prevailed.

Friday 18th February

Everywhere covered in frost this morning, took me about ten minutes to get it off my car. Made some nice tops and skirts in work, fashions seem to be getting prettier. Collected some old clothes from a lady on my way home from work, they are for Mrs. Dunn, she is having a jumble sale tomorrow, please God. The proceeds are to go towards the new church hall, they are finally starting work on it at the end of the month. My friend Mary Mac came to dinner today; as a matter of fact she was at home when I got there, Dan had let her in. She laughed when she saw me and said, you never told me you were having a party tonight – Dan had hired some rods and brushes to

41

sweep the chimneys, and while I was getting the dinner ready himself and Bernie started on the dining room one. Had I known the mess it was going to cause I wouldn't have let them do it. I never saw a room in such a state, soot everywhere. Dan and Bernie looked like two comedians from 'The Black & White Minstrel Show' [a popular variety show at the time where performers sang and danced in 'black face'] – the only part of them visible was the whites of their eyes. Bernie's hair was jet black and so was the white boiler suit he had on. Then Dan had to get up on the roof to put this great, big coil down the chimney, what a job that was. It got stuck and wouldn't come down. After much pushing and pulling (Bernie doing the pulling) they finally got it into place. After dinner, they did the sitting room chimney, that one was very clean. The kids went over to Colette's to have showers. Dan and Bernie went for a drink and it was left to Mary and myself to clean up the mess; by the time that was finished we both looked like The Minstrels.

Saturday 19th February

Went to the Leeds first thing this morning to get some money and sign yet another form in connection with the book lost in the post, then down to the Hire Shop to return the rods and brushes used for sweeping the chimneys, then up to Godfrey's to get some new mixer taps for the bath (we are having a shower over the bath) – they cost £50.00. Home to get some lunch ready for Bernie. Terri wasn't in work today, she went to the BBC with the school choir to make a record. After lunch, went back to Godfrey's to get some piping and a few bits and pieces Dan needed, then over to help at Mrs. Dunn's jumble sale. Went into the presbytery with the washing; while I was there repaired the lining in a coat for Father Hegarty. Back to the jumble sale to help pack away all the stuff that wasn't sold. Bought a lovely briefcase for 10p, thought it would do Ciarán for school. When I got home, Terri was back from the BBC, said she had a lovely dinner there for 50p. Leena took the two girls off to an Indian festival, so only Bernie, Ciarán and myself for dinner. Dan warned me not to go up to the bathroom it was in such a state. Thought he was joking, but after dinner just couldn't hold out any longer, just had to go to the loo. What a sight. All the floorboards up, the bath and wash hand basin out. This old house is never going to be the same again. Dan suggested putting a wash hand basin in the girls' room, which I think is a great idea, it could be the answer to someone else getting into the bathroom besides the two girls.

Sunday 20th February

What a day, nothing seemed to go right. Bernie was taking the old taps off the wash hand basin and broke it, had to take it down to the dump, have to buy a new one tomorrow, please God. Ciarán and Adam went to Queensway market to buy a Benny hat, comes from watching too much 'Crossroads' [a soap opera – Benny was a popular character known for his woollen hat], so now I've got the job of knitting one. The two of them with James washed a few cars today. They got a standing order from one lady to wash her car once a fortnight, so they are really going into business. Thought I'd miss my afternoon nap with all the work going on, but I had a lovely sleep on the couch in the dining room – all the work was being done in the bathroom and back bedroom. While I was asleep, Dan turned off the water; nobody here had the good sense to fill the kettle with water, so when it came to getting the tea ready had to send in to Leena's for water. Everything seemed to be going alright until it came to turning the water back on, then Dan discovered the stopcock was broken and the water couldn't be turned on; by now it was ten o'clock and pitch dark. So, himself and Bernie had to get spades and dig up the front garden by torch light. What a performance, but at least they did succeed in getting it fixed temporarily. We now have a huge, big hole in our front garden, and I have a list of things to get in Godfrey's tomorrow. In the meantime, doing a quick Novena [a prayer of petition] that nothing happens to the bath and toilet. Started Ciarán's Benny hat, wish Queensway hadn't sold out of them.

Monday 21st February

Went to pay the rent on my way to work. Told my landlord about the central heating we are having installed, so he gave me a cheque for £260.00 – that is what it would have cost him to put in a new multi-point; I was very pleased, he is a good landlord. It wasn't till I got into work that I realised he hadn't given me my change out of the rent money – phoned him, said he'd give it to me whenever I called in again. Went to buy the new wash hand basin on my way home from work, which cost £40.00, and £4.50 for a ballcock for the water main. The children are on half-term; was quite pleased to see the house a bit tidier than of late, Fiona had been busy. Went up to the toilet and discovered that it wouldn't flush, Dan hadn't put enough water in the tank. He hadn't been here all day – he then came over at 8.30, filled up the tank and said he'd call it a day. At this rate he just might get it done before Christmas. Asked me for another £300.00; this will be £1,170.00 I've given him so far, so I'll have to go to the Leeds before I go to work in the morning. Then he told me he won't be able to put the wash hand basin in the bathroom for another three weeks as he has to do some work on the shop he is going to open, and in the meantime he told me to get a wash hand basin for the girls, and that will have a cupboard underneath. Have a funny feeling there's going to be an awful lot of things left unfinished in this house.

Tuesday 22nd February

Took Fiona to work with me this morning. Terri is working in Geary's in the afternoons – one of the other ladies who works there is having a week's holiday. The only problem is Terri brings home cakes every evening so I'll be putting on a few extra inches. Katie was in today with Laura; Fiona kept her fully occupied, so Laura , Jenny and myself were able to get on with our work. We all had chips for our lunch. Was pleasantly surprised when I came home from work to see Dan had changed his mind about the wash hand basin – he had it all fitted up, cupboard and all built under it. It looked really nice, except when the cold tap was turned on the water ran away into the hot pipe instead of the waste pipe – he said there is air in the pipe. He went up to the loft to try and sort it out, didn't succeed, said he'll do it tomorrow. Gave him the £300.00 which I had got from the Leeds this morning. He was gone when we discovered the toilet wouldn't flush. Bernie had one of his little turns, swearing what he's going to say to Dan tomorrow, but I'm so used to his ranting and raving I take no notice, but I must say I wasn't feeling too friendly towards Dan myself, especially when I had to carry a bucket of water up the stairs to thrown down the toilet when I went to the loo.

Wednesday 23rd February

Said prayers for Dan this morning when I was bringing buckets of water up the stairs for the loo. He came over before I went to work; he didn't even know we had no water in the toilet, so he has a couple of problems to solve today. Got to work late, but worked hard getting samples ready for Littlewoods of Liverpool. Went to Wiseparts on the way home to look at some small wash hand basins for the girls' room. Saw a lovely little one, just 12 inches x 10 inches; it would fit nicely in the space between their wardrobes on the chimney breast, only £16.50, but couldn't get it today as I had no money. Got some money from Bernie tonight, will get it tomorrow. Hope this one will go up without any mishap. Didn't say anything to the girls about it, want to surprise them. Bought some moulding on the way home to go on top of the skirting boards in the dining room, there are big gaps between the skirting boards and the wall. Bernie and myself tackled it tonight but couldn't fix it. I think the boards are warped, have to have another go at it tomorrow night.

Thursday 24th February

Dan was over bright and early, James was with him. Himself and Ciarán were going to Nicky Bowler's for the day, then remembered he had a dental appointment in the Royal Northern about his brace which he hasn't been wearing, groans all round. Drove the two of them down to the Bowlers on my way to work. Made arrangements with Fiona to take Ciarán to the hospital, told them I would pick them up at three o'clock outside the hospital. Didn't have a very happy day in work. Had a few words over a sample I was making and which wouldn't go together right. When I told Laura about it, she thought I was criticising her pattern cutting, which is the last thing I'd do because she is a marvellous pattern-cutter; she started shouting at me. I thought to hell with it, I have enough pressure at home without having it at work as well, so I told her I was going and she got all upset and kept saying how sorry she was. I couldn't stop crying, we've worked together for four and a half years with never a cross word between us, I felt so hurt. However, I didn't leave, but I'll be very careful of what I say to Laura in the future. Collected Fiona and Ciarán on my way home from work. Ciarán not very happy – he has to have some fillings and just wear his brace at night. Mary came over as usual to go shopping, Terri came with us. Went in to see June (Mary's landlady) who's not very well, she has a dreadful cough. When we came home, Bernie told me Dan had run out of copper piping, and is getting another bloke in to help him as he wants to start working on his shop. No happy faces today.

Friday 25th February

Had a letter from the council to say they are calling on Tuesday to inspect the house because of the rent increase, not looking forward to that. Had a phone call from the Leeds to say they had my new book, went to collect it. They had made yet another mistake in it which had to be corrected. Wondering if my money is safe there, but by the time I'm finished paying out for this central heating won't have much to worry about. Finished Ciarán's Benny hat, he looks like the village eegit [Irish for idiot, though with softer, more affectionate connotations] in it, but he thinks it's 'murder', which means 'great' in today's language. These kids speak a language which I really do not know – 'rare bad' also means 'great'. You really risk life and limb just coming into this house. In the hall there is a five-foot-long box full of rubbish, a pile of bricks, a huge sack, various black bags full of I don't know what. The sitting room is completely out of bounds – that is full of what was already in it, plus everything from the dining room, plus a load of copper piping, plus a load of Dan's tools. The dining room is also out of bounds because all the floorboards are up. The kitchen has everything in it from the laundry room (Dan is working on a radiator there), and the cooker is balancing on two floorboards. The girls' room is like a shambles, with a cylinder standing in the middle of the room. Ciarán's room as usual looking like a tip, and Bernie's and my room is full of all sorts of things from the girls' room. Think the only place in this house that is right must be the attic.

Saturday 26ᵗʰ February

Bernie wasn't working this morning, his firm has decided to have overtime only every other Saturday. Terri brought us both up a cup of tea before going off to work. We were supposed to take some rubbish down to the dump, but Bernie decided he had to go to the doctor, his ear was playing him up – just his excuse for going round to the betting shop. So I went instead to collect a radiator Dan had forgotten to order. Had to go to a place on the North Circular Road near Southgate. Had to park my car quite a distance from the shop. A very nice lad who works Saturdays in the shop carried the radiator for me to the car. Told me he goes to the same school as Ciarán; was giving him 50p, but he said he wouldn't dream of taking it – thought, if that was Ciarán he'd probably have his two hands out. Came home and got lunch ready, rasher sandwiches all round, then off with Fiona to buy a shower rail in Godfrey's. She wanted a screen to go round the bath, but realised with the position of the window in the bathroom it wouldn't be possible; was trying to think of a way round the window when the man who was serving us told me they cost £150.00 – immediately stopped thinking and decided on the rail which was £6.00, more my price. Looked at some shower curtains, the cheapest were £6.50. Eileen Buckley gave me some at the bazaar before Christmas, brand new, and told me to get at least £1.50 for them, finished up selling them for £1.00, wish I had bought them all. Collected Terri with her usual bag of what makes me fat, cakes.

Sunday 27th February

After Mass was going to ask Dick Johnson if Eileen Buckley was at the 9.30 Mass, could he ask her to get me some shower curtains, but when I saw him he said Eileen's waiting to go into hospital. He didn't know what was wrong with her – hope it's nothing serious. Tried ringing her a few times today, but every time got an engaged tone – think she must have left the phone off the hook. When taking Bernie to the off-licence saw Red Kitty and her husband on Grange Road, gave them a lift to the church. She told me Nancy O'Connor has bought a house somewhere in Tottenham (can't remember where). She didn't sell her house on Napier Road, but takes in mental patients at £50.00 a week. Two of them went berserk and threw everything out through the windows, I think it's Nancy who needs mental treatment. Took Ciarán and James to Queensway market, then Terri and myself went to Wickes, bought some rings for the shower rail. Just before we left the house to go out again, James and Ciarán came in, when he got to the market Ciarán realised he had forgotten his money, he's a terrible eegit. Dan has all the radiators in now, but Bernie thinks the boiler has him baffled, hope he's wrong. Really worked hard today to try and put this house into some sort of shape, but with all that, there is not one room we could bring anybody into. Bernie said it's like a builder's yard, he has a way with words. Nevertheless, I'm praying nobody takes sick in this house or that we have unexpected visitors. This house is in a worst state now than when we got it.

Monday 28th February

On the verge of a nervous breakdown today, Bernie was right about Dan being baffled by the back-boiler. He spent most of yesterday reading the directions on how to fit it, and it distinctly said to stand the boiler on a four-inch base, but when I came from work he had it all fixed up, but on a level with the floor, which meant the fire in front of it would also have to stand on the floor, which doesn't comply with Gas Board regulations. Then he asked me would I mind if he left off doing the central heating for me and come back in a month's time to finish it – that he wanted to go into his shop and do some work on it. I was really stunned. I told him I'd much rather he'd finish here first. I couldn't talk to him anymore, I felt really sick. How any fair-minded person could leave a house in such a state, I don't know. How I got the dinner ready, I don't know, I was so upset. Couldn't stay in the house after dinner so Ciarán and myself went to the library. When I came back, Bernie said Dan is in Peter's. I gave out yards to Bernie about him. Fiona came in and said Dan is upstairs and can hear you (Bernie hadn't heard him come back). He came downstairs after a while and said, I heard all you said about me, by this time I was so past caring.

He kept insisting the boiler didn't have to go on a four-inch base. He went home, said he'd be over tomorrow, but he was back in half an hour and said he'd put it on the base tomorrow. I think he was cutting corners so that he could get away to his shop. Bernie is having a day off tomorrow.

March 1983

ON THE VERGE OF A NERVOUS BREAKDOWN

Tuesday 1ˢᵗ March

Bernie didn't go to work today – the man was coming from the rent tribunal, so he stayed home to see him. Said he was a very nice man. Apologised to him about the state of the house, made him a cup of tea and told him we had the chance of buying this house for £15,000.00. He told Bernie we should beg, borrow or steal the money, that it was the bargain of the century. Dan rang somebody this morning about the boiler and was told it must go on a four-inch base, so the best part of the day was spent altering that. When I came in from work he said he'd like to talk to me. I said I had to get the dinner ready but I would listen to him while doing so. He said he'd rather I'd sit down and talk, which I did, and to my amazement he started off by telling me he thought I was a very unreasonable person for not agreeing to his leaving the work for a month so that he could go and do up his shop. After I had recovered from the shock, I told him if I hadn't already given him £1,170.00 to date, I'd be perfectly willing to let him go and get somebody else to finish the job, but as it was, it would cost me as much again to get somebody to finish what he had started. After a few more words, he said he was getting a mate of his to come and help him after dinner tonight, which he did. They didn't stop working until 12.30; nobody could go to bed, as they were in and out of the bedrooms all the time. All the family sat in the kitchen, the only place that's warm, thanks to the oven.

Wednesday 2nd March

Everybody exhausted this morning after their late night. Bernie too tired to go to work so he had another day off, that's two days off his summer holidays. Terri brought Bernie and myself a cup of tea in bed, and then told us the bad news that her wardrobe wouldn't open because Dan and his mate had put the cylinder too far out in the other wardrobe and her sliding door wouldn't clear it. While I lay there trying to decide the least painless form of suicide, Bernie got up and had a look at the cylinder. Came back with a look of martyrdom, confirmed what Terri had said, decided we couldn't take any more and that Dan would have to go. Got ready for work while listening to Bernie telling me all he was going to say to Dan. Was so upset, gave two wrong signals on my way to work. Couldn't talk all day had such a dreadful headache. Got home from work to find Dan and Bernie the best of friends, couldn't believe my eyes. When I asked him for an explanation, Bernie said, it's alright, Dan had spent the day fixing the cylinder. Too sick to argue. Got the dinner ready, Dan went home for his, and when at 8.30 Dan hadn't come over Bernie remarked he didn't think he was coming back – offered up a prayer of thanks. But at 8.45 a ring at the door – Dan back, all dressed up, he wanted to have another talk with me. The outcome of which was, another mate is coming again tomorrow night to give him a hand. Pity he hasn't a few more mates, we might be a bit nearer to having central heating.

Thursday 3rd March

Went to work feeling a bit better about things. Getting a bit fed up doing that journey every day, costing me a bomb in petrol, thinking of looking for a job nearer home. Fiona was off school at 1.30, so gave her instructions to cook the dinner. I went to Hendon on my way home from work to get a wash hand basin for the girls' bedroom, but when I got to the shop, there the basin was £46.00 plus £12.50 for the taps plus I don't know what else for the rest of the fittings. Decided there and then they would have to do without it. Didn't get home until near five o'clock due to the fact there was only one lane open on the North Circular Road. Mary had arrived to go shopping and Fiona had let the dinner burn, so we all sat down to burnt pork casserole. Mary said this house is getting worse instead of better, I couldn't agree more. There's so much stuff crammed into the kitchen we had to sit nearly on top of each other at the table and be very careful we didn't jog the person next to us and knock the food off their fork before it reached their mouth, at least we had a laugh about it. I feel like the broken-hearted clown, laughing on the outside and crying on the inside at the state of this house. Went shopping with Mary and Terri. When we came home, Dan's mate had arrived – he wasn't any bigger than Ciarán. 13 years ago he came over here from Dublin – you wouldn't think he'd ever left it, his accent is so flat. He was just like a little leprechaun, hopping up and down the stairs, a great worker and talker and can do both together, a laugh a minute. Himself and Dan didn't leave until two o'clock in the morning.

Friday 4th March

When Terri brought up my cup of tea this morning, couldn't get my eyes to open. Fell asleep without drinking it and didn't wake until the children came up to say goodbye before going off to school. Forced myself to get out of bed, cursing Dan and his mate for staying so late last night; hate to think how Bernie felt getting up at 5.30. Drove to work in a trance. Ben and Laura went out for the day. Jenny left with me at three o'clock, I drove her to the station. Both of us a bit annoyed because we hadn't got paid our wages. Went to Wiseparts on the way home, got a lovely little wash hand basin for the girls' room, a lovely shade of green, 10 inches x 14 inches, just £19.50. Left it in my car so they wouldn't see it. After dinner, we had hot water at last, so everybody, including myself, washed their hair. Rang Eileen Buckley to know could she get us some shower curtains – told me she'd ring her friend and ask her to get them. Also told me she is going into hospital on Monday morning for tests, she has an obstruction – please God it is nothing serious, she is so good; she was made redundant just before Christmas. Was really looking forward to having a rest, and now this made me think, why am I worrying about a house? Fiona is helping Dan since she came from school, he said she is very good. She only has to be shown a thing once and she can do it, she's a real Mrs. Know-All. Dan had the central heating working tonight, but said not to leave it on as the system needs balancing. Bernie said he'll never feel happy with it, but then he's a real defeatist.

Saturday 5th March

Got up at nine o'clock, had breakfast, and then Dan was over with a list of things for me to get. First of all went to Godfrey's, got a load of bits and pieces there, then on to a place on Angel Road for electric cable for the thermostat. When I got home, discovered Godfrey's hadn't given me all I had paid for so had to go back to them again. Got back to be told by Dan that I had got the wrong cable, so into the car again and back for more cable. Home again to get the lunch ready. After lunch, went off to Edmonton to get some timber for cupboards under the girls' wash hand basin. Dan was hoping Fiona would go out while he was doing it because it was supposed to be a surprise. Got to Edmonton to discover the timber shop had closed down, like so many other shops here, so had to go to Wood Green. Got what I wanted there except for the top for the cupboards, which would have cost £22.50. Rang Dan to tell him, he told me to go to a friend of his who has a shop in Stamford Hill, got it there for £11.00. By this time it was 4.30, so had to go to Marks to get some chicken portions for the dinner as I had forgotten to leave something out of the freezer last night. Then I went on to Geary's to collect Terri, who asked me to give a lady a lift home to the Cambridge Roundabout, which I did, then back again to take her home. Then got dinner ready and only after all that did I sit down and have a rest. Finished up falling asleep on the couch.

Sunday 6th March

Before going to Mass this morning, a stand up fight with Ciarán to wear his new shoes, which he calls beetle crushers. He's a dirty little devil, doesn't believe in washing. Himself, Adam Kelly and two other lads served Mass. Couldn't believe it when Dick Johnson told me after Mass that Father Hegarty said they were very good boys and so clean – he couldn't have noticed Ciarán. Were all sitting down to breakfast after Mass when there was a sound on the roof as if there was a deluge, water pouring down all over the roof into the garden. Sent Ciarán over for Dan, who was in bed. When he eventually came over, he said the ballcock had got stuck in the tank and we'd have to get a new one. Went to Wickes, the new place on Angel Road, to get a new one, and some more bits and pieces which Dan had forgotten to tell me about yesterday, it's never ending. Came back, got dinner ready, then after it went to bed. Didn't care if the house fell down, I was so tired. Terri brought me up a cup of tea at six o'clock. When I got up, Dan had nearly finished doing the wash hand basin and cupboards in the girls' room, they are really delighted with it. Asked Ciarán would he like one in his room – thought it might encourage him to wash – but he said he'd rather have a Crombie coat like the skinheads wear. Came downstairs to discover Bernie dying of heat from the central heating, had to explain to him that it could be turned down. Everybody knows how to regulate it except him, he's too busy watching telly.

Monday 7th March

A beautiful morning, just like summer, but it didn't make the journey to work any easier. Vowed when I got to work I'd tell Laura I was going to look for another job nearer home, but when I got in, herself and Ben were in such good humour hadn't the heart to spoil their day. We are very busy, loads of orders coming in. They are taking on another designer and rep at the end of the month. Went to the Leeds on my way home to draw out some money. Couldn't believe my ears when I was told there was an error in my new book. I have £300.00 less than is written in my book, this is the new book that has been corrected at Head Office, I'm really furious over it. Now the new book has to go back to Head Office again. I certainly won't trust them with my money when I win the Pools, have to keep it in my mattress. Mary came this evening with the shower curtains from Eileen Buckley; her husband left them in the presbytery. I'm really pleased with them, they are only £1.25 each, the cheapest of them are over £6.00 in the shops. Dan did a few patching up jobs today. I bought a jacket for the hot water cylinder and when it was put on, Terri's wardrobe door wouldn't open again, I'm really annoyed over it. Dan wants to build the wardrobe out a bit more but I wouldn't have it, would be out of line, so now he has to alter the pipe work all over again. I'm thinking strongly of getting another bed because I think we are going to have Dan here for ever.

Tuesday 8th March

Another beautiful morning, daffodils up in the front and back garden – poor things, I don't know how they managed to grow amongst all the weeds and rubble. The gardens are like the house, in a terrible state. Asked Ben today if I could have next week off, need the time to get things sorted out here, he didn't give me a direct answer. I suppose he's waiting to see will I get enough samples done. Went home a different way from work and finished up in Golders Green – lovely houses there, wish I could afford one of them. Dan for the third time has redone the cylinder. He actually put in another one, which is already lagged – it doesn't look as well as the copper one, but at least now Terri's wardrobe door is opening and closing alright. He also finished the wash hand basin in the girls' room, two nice cupboards each side, which really pleased the girls – hope that will now ease the pressure in the bathroom. The shower is also fixed up. Couldn't believe my ears when Ciarán said he would try it out first. Haven't seen him looking so clean since he started to wash himself, hope the novelty doesn't wear off too soon. He annoyed me to bleach his jeans tonight, he wants them white, can't see them staying very white for long, he's such a dirty little devil. Turned on the gas fire in front of the boiler just now and the room filled up with fumes, have to have Dan back again to see what's wrong with it.

Wednesday 9th March

Very tired this morning, all the late nights are catching up with me. Asked Laura today about having next week off, she said ok, so at least it will give me some time to get things sorted out. Bernie wanted to take next week off also, but I told him I'd rather he didn't, I don't want any aggro – can work much better on my own. On my way home from work went to Godfrey's to get a pipe joint for Dan, bought the wrong one and had to take it back. Thinking of asking him for a job as a messenger – don't know how he'll manage on his next job. Told him about the fire and the fumes. He turned it on and it worked perfectly, said it must have been because it was the first time it was lit that caused the fumes. Bernie and myself got to work after dinner and made a hot-press [airing cupboard] over the cylinder, that wasn't as easy as it sounds. First of all, couldn't find the key for the drill, which had a sanding drum on it. Bernie had one of his little turns, gave out yards about people not putting things away safe after using them; he shut up very quickly when I reminded him he was the last person to use it. Said he'd get one tomorrow – but, not to put off till tomorrow what you can do today, I got the hammer, gave the chuck a sharp blow and off popped the sanding drum, got a bit and tightened the chuck by putting a long screw in one of the holes, and set Bernie to work drilling holes. If looks could kill, I was dead on the spot, he would much rather have sat watching telly.

Thursday 10ᵗʰ March

Got to work late again this morning – ten miles in heavy traffic doesn't make for fast driving. However, when I got in Laura said she'd like to have a talk with me. I knew what she was going to say because Jenny had told me she had said a few words to her last week about being late. It was funny really – only two weeks ago I was moaning to Ben about how long it took me to get to work and he said, well, don't worry, just get here whenever you can. Now here was Laura, in a very nice way, telling me she'd like me to get here earlier, so I told her, also in a very nice way, that I was going to look for a job nearer home, that the effort of getting to work was proving too much for me. What she hadn't taken into account is the fact that Jenny and myself don't have even half an hour to our lunch, some days it's just a quick cup of coffee taken while working. She could employ a pattern-cutter and sample machinist who could come in very early in the morning, but they wouldn't produce half the amount of work Jenny and myself do, we are both faster than average; I didn't say this to her, I'll leave her to find this out for herself. After our talk, she said she wouldn't mind if I got in by 10.30, I had been getting in between 10 and 10.15. So the conclusion I came to was that Laura was just trying to remind me that she was the boss. Later on in the day she told me Ben was annoyed with her because he thought she was the cause of my leaving.

Friday 11ᵗʰ March

Thank God I'm finished work and that horrible journey for a week. Laura had another talk with me today about not doing anything foolish – that herself and Ben don't like the idea of me leaving, and if I did go to work somewhere else and didn't like it would I go back to them and I could work shorter hours or a shorter week; didn't like to tell her she'll want to treat Jenny a bit better or she'll be leaving too. She even said she considered me a full-time worker I'd done so much in a week, so it makes you wonder why she wanted me in earlier in the morning. I do think the nicest of people, but when they begin to get on in business, get greedy. Got home five minutes before Bernie. As soon as he came in he was moaning about his wages, the firm have cut down on the bonus. He said some of the men had £17.00 less this week, and next week it would be worse. Didn't pay much attention to him, I always hear about the bad times but I never heard anything when he was working loads of overtime or got any extras. Ciarán had told me he'd be late home this evening as he was going to get his hair cut. Nearly had a heart attack when he did get in, he had got a skinhead. Was afraid to hit him in case I'd lose my cool and kill him, so I ordered him up to bed. He's in for a month except to go to Mass and school, hope they don't expel him. Can't let him serve Mass on Sunday – he looks so rough-looking with that haircut, you wouldn't think he came from a respectable home.

Saturday 12th March

Bernie's Saturday off. He brought me up a cup of tea at eight o'clock to get out of bed but I didn't budge until 9.30, I needed the rest. Once out of bed it was all go. Went to Tesco, got some very nice tiles (only 5p each) to put round the girls' wash hand basin. Also bought a set of chisels, getting ready for all the work I intend doing next week. Got lunch ready at 12.30, and before going out again at 1.30, I put a leg of lamb in the oven for Sunday's dinner. Went to Wickes, got some grouting for the tiles. Then myself and Fiona went to see Dan's new shop. I think he needs his head tested, never seen anything like it in all my life, it needed knocking down and building up again. He's supposed to come back to us to finish off the work in three weeks' time – if we see him in three months, I'll be more than surprised. After we left Dan's, we went to see Peggy Bowler; she moved last year. Her house is very nice, almost the same as our own but with a side entrance. She is having central heating put in and all new windows. Got back in time to give Terri and the other two ladies she works with a lift home. When we got home, Ciarán met us at the door to tell us the leg of lamb I left in the oven was burnt nearly to a cinder. I had forgotten to lower the gas; I get more stupid every day, think it must be old age, hope everybody enjoys burnt lamb. Asked Bernie to clean under the stairs before I went out – didn't do it, he was too busy watching telly. One day I'm going to lose my cool and throw that telly out the window.

Sunday 13th March

Went to eight o'clock Mass as usual. Ciarán didn't serve because of his haircut; every time I look at him, could murder him. Went over to the church again after the 9.30 Mass to see Eileen Buckley, wanted to pay her for the shower curtains. She was in great form after three days in hospital. The doctor told her the obstruction she has is more inflamed than diseased, so that's a relief to her. She is on a high-fibre diet. She has to go to hospital again in a month's time, please God everything will be alright then. When I came home, Bernie and Ciarán went up into the loft to lag the pipes, Terri weeded the front garden, Fiona sorted out the cupboards in her bedroom and I cleaned out under the stairs, the job Bernie didn't do yesterday. My mother, Lord rest her, must be turning in her grave – she would never let any work be done on a

Sunday. Cut off all the burnt parts of the leg of lamb and just about managed to get enough for four dinners. Terri didn't have any – didn't press her too much. She made a great job of the garden; at least the daffodils have room to breathe now. Couldn't inspect the loft, didn't want to risk life and limb climbing up there. If we do have a burst pipe I'll know it wasn't done right. Very worried about Ciarán going to school tomorrow; praying he won't be suspended over his hair. Dan's little girl was here tonight, she said she thinks he's a very brave boy to have got that haircut, thank God he didn't hear her. After he'd helped in the loft, he kept very much to his room – he knows every time I look at him it annoys me. I'll kill him if he's sent home from school.

Monday 14th March

Got up at eight o'clock intending to do so much today, but didn't feel a bit well so it took me a while to get started. So much to do I didn't know what to do first. Realised I needed a tile cutter, went up to Tesco to get one. They were £4.99, thought that a bit dear so went down to Wickes, got the same cutter for £3.49. Got home, had a cup of tea and started putting moulding on the skirting on the stairs. Had a bit of trouble getting it round the curve at the top of the stairs, but after soaking it in water and steaming it, finally managed to get it on. Was really quite pleased, it looked so well. Discovered I hadn't enough moulding, so went down to Wickes again, but they hadn't got what I wanted. Had to try a few places before I got it; this took up most of the afternoon. Just got back in time to get the dinner ready. After dinner, Bernie did some wallpaper stripping while I tried to do the curve on the other side of the stairs. Didn't succeed, spoiled a piece of moulding, have to get some more tomorrow. Mixed some timber dye: pine, oak, cedar and teak; if I run short later on, hope I can remember how much I used of each colour or I'll finish up with odd woodwork. Forgot to mention – yesterday (Mothers' Day) Fiona bought me a pine bread-bin, which I badly needed; Terri bought me two lovely slips from Marks and a bottle of sherry. Ciarán didn't get sent home from school thank God; had he been in the upper school he would.

Tuesday 15th March

Did another bit of running round this morning. Needed a plane, finished up buying two, one was £7.95, the other was tiny, it was only £1.95, I find the small one better. Had another go at bending the moulding for the stairs, but it was taking up so much of my time I had to leave it, plus the fact my hands were sore from trying to bend it. There must be a quicker way of doing it, wish I knew – with all the work I'm doing, doesn't seem much to show for it at the end of the day. Had to go down to Wickes for a strip-light tube. When I got home with it, discovered it was the wrong size, it was only 4-foot and I needed a 5-foot one. Didn't want to go back to Wickes again, so after dinner, Fiona and myself went up to Edmonton to get one, but the shop was closed so had to go down to Bruce Grove; was lucky to get one, the shop was just closing. Bernie filled a few holes in the timber tonight, to the usual moans and groans. He certainly doesn't suffer in silence, that's why I didn't want him to take a week off the same time as myself. Dan's son, James, came over tonight. I asked him was his father good at fixing phones, he said he didn't know. I said I hope he is because he has caught our phone under the radiator in the hall and we have to do all our phoning on the floor in the hall.

Wednesday 16th March

I have often heard it said, there are saner people locked up than there are outside, and I'm convinced I'm one of the ones who are not locked up but should be. Nobody but a complete looney would have decided to get rid of all the white paintwork in the house and stain everywhere with what I'm hoping will look like dark oak. What it will turn out to be is anyone's guess. Wish some level-headed, sane person had been around to give me some idea of the work involved, but I have yet to hear of anybody sane or otherwise ever doing this, which only goes to prove I must be the biggest nutcase of all. Threw out a suggestion tonight of getting rid of the banisters and having open plan, but it fell on stony ground – thought it would lessen my workload, but Bernie thinks it would increase the death rate. When we started this job, I jokingly told people it would be all done before next Christmas, but it's not a joke anymore, I only hope I'll keep till then. It would have been quicker and probably cheaper to have got all new timber. Started work early this morning, didn't even stop to have a cup of tea, yet when everybody came in this evening they asked me what I had done all day. Had to restrain myself from giving them a very rude answer, but that's the worst of this work – you can spend hours just cleaning off a piece of moulding, getting all the white paint out of the crevices. Dan came over tonight and fixed the phone. Himself and Colette were going out for a drink, only I was so dirty would have joined them and got stoned.

Thursday 17th March

Up at 6.30 this morning, not from choice but because every bit of me was aching, a runny nose and eyes. Went to the loo and got back into bed feeling very sorry for myself. Bernie brought me up a cup of tea and I took two tablets. After tossing and turning for a while, was just going off to sleep when Terri called me with another cup of tea. Could have done without it, but didn't like to hurt her feelings, so drank it and suffered on. Got up at 10.30 feeling completely drained. There was so much I wanted to do but hadn't the energy. Stuck nine tiles round the girls' wash hand basin and felt as if I'd been dragged through a mangle. Phoned Mary to tell her I wouldn't be able to go shopping tonight. She said she'd been phoning me all day but could get no answer – so much for Dan fixing the phone. Father Hegarty's in Ireland and she could have come over to help me do something in the house, but getting no answer she thought I was out. Told her to bring me some cabbage and whiskey – have to dose myself going to bed to try and get rid of this cold, can't afford to have a cold with so much work to do. After dinner, phoned Dan to tell him my life was becoming very dull as I wasn't receiving any obscene phone calls since he put the kibosh on our phone. Mary left at eight o'clock, couldn't drive her home, said she'll come tomorrow to go shopping. Dan came at 8.30 to fix the phone. Said his shop is subsiding; it's funny, that's how I feel about our house too.

Friday 18th March

Got up at 10.30, didn't feel as bad as I did yesterday. Had breakfast, then phoned the Head Office of the Leeds about my book, which they haven't returned to me. Said they couldn't return it as they haven't got it, it's still in their branch at Fore Street. Said a few words to them about their branch at Fore Street, was furious. At 11.30 my friend Mary Mac rang, told her I wasn't well, so she said she would come over, which she did at 12.30. Sat talking for a while. Then decided, with Mary's help, to stick a few more tiles round the girls' wash hand basin. Stuck nine more and broke three in the process. Had a cup of tea, then it was time to get the dinner ready. Mary came over to say she couldn't go shopping as June wasn't well and she had to get home to cook dinner for her, but she had some dinner with us before she went. After dinner, Terri, Mary Mac and myself went shopping. Had a letter from Mr. Peterson (head master) voicing disappointment over Ciarán's haircut. Said if he had it cut that way again he would be expelled. Phoned him, told him how upset his father and myself were over it, and that he was being punished by not being allowed out for a month and that he could also punish him in whatever way he thought fit. He said he was very glad to have our support and that Ciarán wasn't having a very pleasant time at the moment, as all the other boys were laughing at him. Can't say I feel sorry for him. Showed Jack my coconut out of which I'm trying to grow a tree, without much success. Told me I was doing it all wrong, have to get another coconut.

Saturday 19th March

Still not feeling well today, but had to soldier on. Put another few tiles round the girls' wash hand basin. It's taking ages to do, due to the fact it said to put matchsticks between each tile – what a performance – and to make matters worse they have stripes in them; wish now I had got plain ones. Had to go down to Wickes to get some more cement. It was packed there, they are going to run all the small DIY shops out of business. Had a bright idea of tiling the window-sill in the bathroom. Tried to get a tile edging but they only make them in one colour; I wanted white, so I'll have to have a rethink. After lunch, went out with Fiona to buy some shoes for her. She has a very long, narrow foot – after trying quite a few places we finished up getting them in Marks. Was nearly on the verge of collapse. Fiona had to ring Terri and tell her to come home on her own as I wasn't able to collect her, she also got the dinner ready while I had a rest and a couple of tablets. By the time dinner was ready, felt a bit better – in fact, well enough to eat a couple of cream cakes Terri brought home. We were all watching telly later on – that is, except Ciarán, when we discovered he had James up in his bedroom. We were furious, as we had told him he wasn't to have anybody in for a month. Bernie went mad with him and told him he's not going out for six months now – his hair will be down to his knees.

Sunday 20th March

All went to eight o'clock Mass, which Father Roderick said for my mother, Lord rest her – she was thirteen years dead in February. Had a record taking with the bingo this morning, £4.05. For the years I'm doing it, that's the most we ever made at the eight o'clock Mass, so things are looking up; it must be the fine weather which is bringing people out so early. After breakfast, did a bit of shouting and got everybody doing a bit of tidying up while I did some tiling in the bathroom. Did the window-sill with plain white tiles, it doesn't look too bad. The tile cutter I bought is really great, makes cutting very easy. Had my usual afternoon nap. Terri brought me up some potato cakes she had made for tea, they were very nice. Got up and had a bath then did some more tiling in the bathroom, this time at the back of the toilet, very pleased with it. Wish I had another week off work, there is so much more I'd like to do – don't get a lot of time after work. Had a phone call from Mary, she said June is very ill and won't let her call a doctor (I think she's got pleurisy), her doctor only lives a couple of doors away from her. I told Mary she should go and have a talk with him. June's sister wanted June to go to her, and she'd look after her (she lives in Sussex), but she wouldn't go, she's very headstrong. She's diabetic and on her own all day except when her cleaning lady comes in a couple of times a week. Still don't feel all that good myself, going to have a hot drink and two tablets.

Monday 21st March

Oh, how I hated going to work this morning, feel worse than ever. When I got in, Jenny told me she had only been in work two days last week, she also had flu and had the same aches and pains as myself. Laura told her to go out and have a look at the shops. I made a christening robe for Ben's brother's baby, beautiful lace with a satin slip. Laura is to be godmother, but she doesn't like the idea, as the baby is being christened into the Church of England and she is a Catholic. Ben and Laura are moving to a flat in Highgate on Friday, please God – they have their house in Essex up for sale. Lately they've only been home about one weekend every two months, the rest of the time they stay with Ben's parents in Romford. We had all sorts of weather today, hail, rain and sunshine, it has turned colder than of late. Ciarán didn't get home from school till near six o'clock, said he was practising with a pop group, didn't even know he could sing. He told me Mr. Peterson (his head master) had a talk with him today about his haircut and about his shoes. I insisted he wear his new shoes this morning, but what I didn't know was he had his trainers with him and he put them on when he got into school; he is determined to be a tramp, but thanks to his talk with Mr. Peterson he has agreed to wear his new shoes in future. Bernie put up some polystyrene tiles on the laundry room ceiling, did them very well.

Tuesday 22nd March

Against my better judgement, went to work today, but had such pains in my chest and back, rang the surgery and made an appointment to see the doctor at 4.45. Couldn't stand the pains any longer, so left work at one o'clock, got home at two o'clock, set the alarm for 3.00 and went to bed. Was just going off to sleep when it went off. Got up and cooked the dinner. Thought the girls would be in by the time it was ready, but they weren't, so left it in the oven. Left the keys with Leena in the shop and went off to the doctor. Gave me a prescription for antibiotics and a cough bottle, both cost me £2.60, that's how much prescription charges have gone up, £1.30 each item. When I got home, the girls still weren't in, but Bernie and Ciarán were waiting for their dinner. After dinner, took two spoonfuls of the cough syrup, an antibiotic, two painkillers and a cupful of hot sherry and was in bed by 7.30 – thought that should really kill or cure me, was feeling so bad… couldn't care less either way. Bernie said he'd do some sanding, but after ten minutes he gave up – must have been something more interesting on the telly. After about another half hour he started sanding again for ten more minutes. He came up later on, and I asked him why he didn't do any more sanding, and he said it's all finished. God, I could kill him, there's hours of sanding to be done and he thinks he can get it all done in 20 minutes, he hasn't a clue how to prepare paintwork.

Wednesday 23rd March

Just couldn't get out of bed this morning, pains everywhere. Fiona stayed home from school to look after me. She did a bit of shopping, then made me a cup of tea and an egg for breakfast. Felt a bit better by midday, and got up and finished tiling the window-sill in the bathroom. Nearly finished myself as well. Felt awful. Got back into bed at two o'clock and left Fiona to get the dinner ready. In spite of the fact I was dosed up to the eyeballs with tablets, I couldn't sleep. Mary rang at four o'clock to say she couldn't come over to see me as they were having visitors, but she would call tomorrow to go shopping. Could have slept after dinner, but it was like Piccadilly Circus with Fiona, Terri, Ciarán and Bernie – as soon as one left, the other came up. They seemed determined not to leave me on my own. Ciarán was telling me that himself and three other boys from school are forming a pop group. One plays the drums and the other two play the guitar. I asked him who the singer is, and he said, guess who? So between his haircut and singing there's no telling where this boy is going to end up. Then Terri was telling me about one of her teachers who is getting married and going to live in Austria. Fiona as usual didn't say a lot. Bernie came up and was telling me all the tales of woe from work and how bad the job is getting and how he thinks it might be better if he took early retirement after all.

Thursday 24ᵗʰ March

Bernie wasn't in work today, his firm is only working four days a week as a protest over men being made redundant. They sacked ten men this week who have a record for being late and taking too much time off. Bernie said he'd take the sitting room door out to the kitchen and burn the paint off it. I didn't feel too bad, so decided to go to work. When I got in, Laura said I was the last person she expected to see, that I didn't look very well. Didn't do much work as it's between seasons. Laura went off to the fashion show at Olympia. Kept feeling a little bit worse as the day wore on. By two o'clock I decided to come home, but there was such a heavy shower of hail stones I couldn't go till it finished at 2.30. When I got home, the kitchen and laundry room were in a terrible state where Bernie had been doing the door. The annoying part of it was he hadn't even got the paint off one side of the door. He said he couldn't get it off with the paint stripper, so he was doing it with the sander. Everywhere was covered in white dust, and he was in the dining room watching racing on the telly. When I gave out to him about it, he said he might clean it up when the racing was over. So, in between getting the dinner ready I had to wash all the chairs, cupboards and cooker, and mop out the two floors. When all that was done I was only fit for bed, so I went off leaving Fiona to sort out the dinner. Mary called to go shopping but I was too sick to go, she stayed until 7.30. Terri brought me up a cup of tea at nine o'clock.

Friday 25th March

Got up at 6.30 to go to the loo; my legs were so wobbly, there and then I decided the safest place for me was bed, so didn't go to work, stayed in bed all day. Fiona was off school at one o'clock; when she came in, made me a cup of tea. Later on, she got the dinner ready, I'm lucky she can cook. Terri stayed on at school for choir practice, anyone would think she could sing. Poured rain most of the day. Didn't know Ciarán had gone to school without a coat. He didn't have to wear uniform as it was the last day before the Easter holidays so he just put on jeans and a jumper. He's so stupid, won't be surprised if he gets a cold. Terri came in very upset over the teacher leaving to get married. Her friend Noreen gave her a nice pair of earrings for her birthday, which is not till the 4th April, but she won't be seeing her during the holidays. Bernie came up and said he's not going to work on Monday – didn't ask him why, not talking to him over yesterday. Then he was looking for paint strippers, so he must be going to have another go at that door. If the rest of them take as long to do as this one, I hate to think when this house gets finished. Don't seem to be getting rid of this flu, have pains all down both my arms this evening. Fiona cut and set Terri's hair tonight, it looks very nice. She's one of these people who can do anything she sets her mind to. Read the 'Tottenham Herald' today, they are closing down on the 7th April, will miss it for the local news.

Saturday 26th March

Got up at eight o'clock this morning just after Terri went to work, didn't feel all that wonderful but as we have got to eat, had to go shopping. Left Fiona and Ciarán in bed and Bernie still wondering how he's going to get the paint off that door. Went to Edmonton Green, didn't get back until midday just in time to get lunch ready. Lady Tottenham still in bed, Ciarán gone out, Bernie still doing the door between watching sport on telly. After lunch, the door and Bernie really getting on my nerves, so got the plane and planed the rest of the paint off myself. Mary rang to know how I was. Told her I felt awful, but I would bring Father Hegarty's sheets over which I had washed. Said she was going to confession in St. Edmonds, told her I'd call for her at three o'clock and go with her. Told Bernie to sand down the door while I was away and went off with Fiona to collect Mary. Went to the Maltese priest to confession; for my penance he told me to say the prayer at the foot of the cross at the bottom of the church, but the church being in semi-darkness and I not having my glasses, I couldn't see a word of that prayer. Mary said she thinks she has the words of it, so she'll write it out for me. Went to Edmonton Green again – Mary wanted to do some shopping there – then drove her home and arrived back just in time to collect Terri from Geary's, then home to get the dinner ready. The door Bernie had done looked worse than ever. Terri went to a birthday party and I went to bed at 8.30 feeling as if I'd been dragged through a mangle.

Sunday 27th March

A dreadful morning, pouring rain and very windy and cold, not many people at Mass. The bingo takings down a pound on last week in spite of the fact one lady bought a pound's worth. After breakfast, sanded the door Bernie had made a hames of [Irish – 'complete mess of'. Origin slightly uncertain, but hames are part of an agricultural horse's harness and easily put on the wrong way round]; was very pleased with it when it was finished. Changed my clothes and washed the sawdust off my face. Then Bernie, Fiona, Terri and myself went down to see Dan's shop. I still think he hasn't all his marbles to have bought such a place, it's in a dreadful state. The floors are parting company with the walls, the ceilings are caving in, and in the middle of it all he has a big Alsatian. He bought it from Battersea Dogs Home in case anybody breaks in. He's a bit annoyed with the dog, it won't bark at anybody, but I don't think he need worry – if anybody did break in they'd just take one look at the place and fly. Think it will take him about two years to sort that lot out, nevertheless he said he'll do the patio doors and brickwork for me next week, probably needs a rest from the shop. Ciarán went to Queensway market with James. Came back with white stripes up the back of his shoes, don't know what he's trying to prove. Fiona painted the mouldings on the cupboards under the wash hand basin in her bedroom, she is definitely a better painter than her father. Terri said she had a great time at the party last night.

Monday 28ᵗʰ March

Went to work today – Bernie didn't, he's on another one-day strike. It seems they are trying to throw the firm into confusion by not striking on the same day each week. I think they are doing the firm a favour – if they are trying to get rid of men, the next best thing is having them on short time. They are not working on Saturdays either – talk about cutting off your nose to spite your face. Katie was in work today, as she will be every day from now until she goes to nursery school. Ben and Laura moved to their new flat in Highgate on Friday. I asked Katie did she like her new home, she said it's lovely and I'll bring you there some day to play with my toys, I'm not going to hold my breath. Had a headache all day in work, so I don't seem to have got rid of that rotten flu yet. Bernie took Ciarán to Moulten today for a dental check-up, he has to have a few fillings, said it would cost £10.00 for a general anaesthetic. I got on the phone and told him I would prefer Ciarán to have a local anaesthetic, which costs nothing. Ciarán said since I am not paying £10.00 for him, can he have a new pair of shoes instead. When I got home, Dan was there, he's going to start the brickwork tomorrow. His wife phoned to tell him the dog wouldn't stop barking in the house – he won't bark in the shop, he's probably afraid the vibration might bring the whole place down on top of him, clever dog.

Tuesday 29ᵗʰ March

Wrote out a few Easter cards before going to work – left them for Fiona to get stamps and post them, but when I came home she said the Post Office was robbed and would be closed until further notice. Now I know where all the police cars were flying yesterday, had to pull into the kerb to avoid a crash. Dan started the brickwork today. Don't like it, neither does Bernie – maybe it will look better when it's all finished. Had a phone call from a designer tonight to know would I go and work for her at the end of April, she has a studio in Tottenham. She wants a sample machinist four days a week; Monday to Thursday, take home pay £80.00, and she said she'd pay my tax and insurance. It was funny, only today Laura asked me had I made up my mind about leaving, [and] I told her I felt so ill these last two weeks that I hadn't time to think about anything. Don't know how I'm going to tell her now that I am leaving. It's nearly a month since I answered the ad in the paper that the designer had in. She told me she was going away to Germany for a while and she'd get in touch when she came back, didn't really expect to hear from her again. It would be lovely not to have to do that journey to Primrose Hill every morning, nevertheless I'll be sorry to leave Ben and Laura, wish they hadn't moved so far away.

Wednesday 30th March

Had a letter from the Leeds this morning asking me to phone and make an appointment with the manager regarding my account. Phoned later in the morning and was told I could see him at 3.30 in the afternoon, which I did. He told me my new book was quite in order and what was shown in the book was what I had in my account. Told him according to my reckoning I should have £200.00 more. He said everything was done by computer and they did not make mistakes, told him I agreed but that the people feeding information into them did. Asked him what did he think of the whole situation regarding my book, he said to tell you the truth I am really ashamed of all the mistakes that have been made in it. But he was adamant that all was in order now. Told him

I had been given a receipt showing the amount in my first book when it had been sent to Head Office to be corrected, but I had mislaid it; he said there was no record of the sum I mentioned. We argued for over an hour. I opened my purse to show him the second receipt I had been given when my new book had been taken in to be corrected – when I discovered, folded up inside it, was the first receipt. I was delighted, because it proved everything I had said was right, but he was livid. He asked me could he have it to take a photocopy of it, which he did, now all the paperwork will have to go back to Head Office again. So I'm guessing heads will roll in the Leeds of Fore Street tomorrow morning.

Thursday 31st March

Got into work before anyone else this morning – Laura, Ben and Katie were late getting in. Now that they are living on their own, Laura is finding out what it is like to have to get Katie ready before going to work. Jenny is not in work, she has a bowel complaint caused by some infection she got from her holiday in Africa. Took some cakes with me – Katie was to have a tea party, but Ben took her out so that Laura and myself could get some work done. He needn't have bothered, because we didn't do any work. We spent the best part of the day discussing religion of all things. Laura is a lapsed Catholic, but I get the impression it worries her quite a bit and she is trying to justify herself for not practising her religion. Hadn't the heart to tell her I was leaving, will have to tell her after Easter. Mary came to go shopping. We were soaked with rain going from the car park to Tesco. Had to wait 20 minutes for a trolley to put our shopping in, never saw it so packed. Went in to see June, who is feeling much better. Took her my gas heater for her hall, but discovered it was broken due to the fact Bernie had forced the lid of the boot down on top of it – could kill him. When I got home he was feeling very sorry for himself, he thinks he's getting flu. Typical of him, just when I had planned with his help to do so much work over the long weekend.

April 1983

TIME FOR A CHANGE

Friday 1ˢᵗ April (Good Friday)

Terri brought Bernie and myself a cup of tea at 7.30 before she went off to work. Stayed in bed till 10.30. Bernie not in the best today, he has a cold and is feeling very sorry for himself. God forgive us all, we didn't go to the church. It poured out of the heavens all day and blowing a gale with it. I started making a cupboard for the laundry room, 8 foot by 30 inches wide, can have it up to the ceiling now that we have no multi-point there. Did a bit to it before lunch, then again in the afternoon, had to stop to get the dinner ready. Was hard at it again tonight when Leena, her husband and little girl came in with a great big chocolate gateau for me (Terri said they are over £6.00 to buy). She gave Terri an envelope and said it was for her and Fiona. Then they sat down and said they heard us playing Irish records last night and thought they were lovely, so Terri played them for them again. Talk about the mad Irish. There we were all sitting in the midst of all the rubble from the brickwork, dust everywhere, not even enough chairs for us all to sit on, and in the middle of it all, the record player going full blast. When Leena, husband and child left, Terri opened the envelope and in it was an Easter card and some money, it was payment for the girls helping her in the shop during the week. Was really upset over it, business is not very good, Terri is going to return it.

Saturday 2nd April

Couldn't move in bed this morning when I woke with the pain in my left arm, had to get Ciarán to put some PR spray on it before I could get out of bed. After breakfast, took two tablets, and after a while could move it a bit. Found it very difficult to drive with it, but had to go out to do some shopping. Tried to get some fire bricks, but all the builders' merchants were closed for the Easter holidays. Dan had got me some white-faced conti-board in Wickes, 8 foot x 15 inches, it was £3.30 a length. I was short of one length so I went to Halls of Edmonton to get it, cost £4.90 there so it pays to shop at Wickes. After shopping, did a bit of straightening out on the house (between taking tablets every few hours for the pain in my arm); it didn't look quite as chaotic when it was finished. Went off to collect Terri and her cakes. She had a beautiful birthday card and a £5.00 voucher for Boots that the ladies in Geary's had given her. She had also got a letter from a boy she'd met at the party last Saturday telling her he liked her very much and would like her to go out with him; I said certainly not, which took the wind out of her sail. Before we had time to argue about it, my friend Mary Mac and her husband called with Easter eggs, a box of chocolates for me and cigars for Bernie. Played a few

Irish records which Mary hadn't heard before. Had supper and they left just after eleven o'clock. When they'd gone, discovered Mary Mac had left her glasses here.

Sunday 3rd April

Went to eight o'clock Mass, which Ciarán served. Mary rang yesterday to say Dick Johnson said he could serve Mass if he liked now that his hair had grown a bit; it was well he did because none of the other boys turned up. Adam Kelly is away camping with the Scouts, God help him – between the rain and the snow I bet he'll be glad to get home. After breakfast, Fiona and myself set off for Wanstead with Mary Mac's glasses, knew she'd be at a loss for them. Dan had told us instead of turning for Walthamstow at the roundabout on the North Circular Road to go on straight, it was shorter – it wasn't. We found ourselves on the motorway for Harlow and had to keep going until we came to Loughton. We branched off there and got lost, my favourite past time [Vera's original]. Had to stop a man and ask the way to Wanstead, he turned out to be Irish, you meet them everywhere. He said he'd come in the car and show us as he was going to Woodford himself and it wasn't far from Wanstead, which was lucky for him and for us. When we eventually got to Mary's, Jack said she had just gone round to phone me about her glasses. [In the days before mobile phones, people were forced to try to contact each other using phone boxes placed on street corners, and could of course only dial landline numbers. Mary Mac would have had to have hoped that a) she could catch Vera in and b) the phone box hadn't been vandalised, a common occurrence]. Met her on the way back. Didn't go into her house – by that time I had to rush home

81

to get the dinner ready. Haven't got over the shock of Terri and the boyfriend when Ciarán tells me today he has asked Bernadette Wade to go out with him on Tuesday, and where was the cheapest place to bring her as he hasn't got much money. I was speechless, but when I recovered I gave him a bit of my mind. Bernadette will drop him like a hot brick if he turns up looking his usual dirty self. Can't get over these kids.

Monday 4th April

Was really pleased this morning when I woke to find my arm was much better and I could move it alright, thank God. Did some more work on the cupboard for the laundry room while Bernie stood looking on, he's a great help. Was hard at it when Leena came in with presents for Terri's birthday, she was 16 years old today, how time flies. Leena gave her a very nice brown handbag, a strawberry cheesecake and six bars of chocolate. Bernie gave her £10.00, Mary and my cousin Nan a fiver each, I gave her a long-playing record and a very pretty slip, Fiona gave her a box of envelopes and notepaper, which she'll find very useful as she must have about ten pen-friends in different parts of the world. Ciarán gave her his best wishes, which was all he could give as he had no money as usual, so with all she was very pleased. After Leena had gone, got the dinner ready. After dinner, had a rest for an hour then back to work again, wish I had married a carpenter. Told Terri if that boy (who wrote her the letter) can do any carpentry or gardening she can bring him home anytime. Can't for the life of me understand how Bernie can watch me doing things for the past 17 years and yet have learnt nothing, but as they say, there are none so blind as those who will not see – the only thing he wants to see is the television.

Tuesday 5th April

A mad rush this morning to get out to work. Terri had to go to work also, as they are short-staffed in Geary's. Ciarán got up before I went out, said he was going to see Bernadette at 1.30. When I got to work, nobody was in – Jenny didn't get in until 10.15 and Sam at 11.30. It was freezing cold – the central heating had been turned off for the long weekend; had to leave my coat on all morning. Laura, Ben and Katie didn't get in until one o'clock. Intended telling them I was leaving at the end of the month, but didn't get the chance. Poured rain on the way home. Was busy getting the dinner ready when I heard Ciarán coming in and running upstairs, thought it a bit strange and ran up after him. Well I nearly had a stroke when I saw him. He was like a drowned rat, and had on the jeans (which I was stupid enough to bleach) with zips stitched all over them, a green bomber jacket with writing all over it, a load of studs down one side, a load of badges and safety pins down the other side, at the back a pair of braces hanging down past his behind, and a pair of brown shoes with white stripes up the back of them. Ordered him to take them off at once. Showed them to Bernie when he came in, he nearly went berserk. I got a scissors and cut them up and put them in the dustbin, gave him a few whacks, and told him he's not going out for another month or getting any pocket money. I'm doing a Novena that nobody I know saw him in that get-up.

Wednesday 6th April

Told Laura when I went in this morning that I was leaving at the end of the month, she asked me had I a job to go to, told her yes, asked me a few things about it. Didn't seem too bothered about my leaving, wish now I hadn't been so worried about telling her, wasn't as important as I thought I was. Had to listen to a lecture from Bernie when I told him. He was on another of his one-day strikes today, so he took the door off the toilet to strip the paint off. He didn't put it back as it's not finished – the kids were horrified. They wanted to know, how could they go to the loo with no door on it? I told them they'd just have to tell everybody they were, and then keep whistling in case anyone forgot. After dinner, asked Bernie to saw one of the conti-boards for the cupboard door – wish I hadn't, he broke a piece out of it, and I had to run down to Wickes with it and buy another one. Was furious with him – he kept telling me I wouldn't be able to fit it in my car, but to prove him wrong I fitted it in so well, had an awful job getting it out – didn't tell him that of course. Managed to get the locks for the door of the cupboard today, have just to put them on now and put it up, hope to get it finished tomorrow night, please God. Terri's boyfriend rang tonight to know would she go to a disco in The Mayfair (for 15 to 18-year-olds) on Monday night. Asked me could she go, I said no, so she's gone to bed very upset.

Thursday 7th April

Had a very busy day in work having tea parties with Katie, had so many cups of coffee out of dolls' tea cups, which tasted so awful, that I had to take some bread soda when I got home; still, it was all in a good cause, it left her happy. Broke my driving glasses, my eyes are getting very sore – will have to get a new pair as soon as possible. Told Fiona to phone Mary and tell her I wasn't going shopping as I didn't like driving at night without my glasses, also wanted to finish my cupboard. She said she'd call over, as she had some sheets she wanted washed. When Bernie came home, he hadn't got the drill bit he was supposed to have got; couldn't finish the cupboard without it, so went shopping instead with Terri and Mary. Managed to get her home and back before it got dark. Was busy doing some work in the bathroom when the doorbell rang. Bernie shouted up that somebody wanted me at the door. I was amazed to see these two, almost skinhead lads. One of them said, "I'm Teresa's son, who works with Terri in Geary's, and this is Stephen", pointing to the other lad, "he'd like to ask you something". I said, "Yes", and he said, "Mrs. Byrne, will you let Terri come to a disco with me and some friends on Monday night?" I said I didn't know... "as I don't like your hair styles". I thought it invited trouble, but they assured me they were very respectable and would have her home by taxi at eleven o'clock. After a while, I said alright, hope I'm doing the right thing.

Friday 8ᵗʰ April

Was a bit late getting to work this morning, the traffic was dreadful, only Jenny was there when I got in. Laura and Ben had taken Katie to a private nursery to see would they take her in, starting on Monday. They came in at about eleven o'clock with the person who runs the nursery, she seems very nice and Katie seems to like her. She said she would ask the lady if I could come too. I think she will be a bit upset when she realises Ben and Laura won't be staying with her. Still, I suppose after a few days she'll get used to it. Ben gave me a very nice pair of black, silk trousers for Terri, they'll do her for the disco. They fitted her perfectly. She has a nice frilly, pink blouse which I made her, it will go lovely with them – now Fiona wants a pair. Terri said Teresa (out of Geary's) was furious with her son and the other boy Stephen for calling round last night. She said she had told him she didn't think Terri's mother would let her go out with him because he wasn't a Catholic (it's funny she should think of that, I didn't). He told her he'd go up and see the priest in the church, but when he went up, there was no-one there. I'm not a bit happy about her and this boyfriend, she has a lot of studying to do in the next few months and I don't want her neglecting it for this fellow. I asked her tonight was this fellow paying for her into the disco and she told me I was living in the Stone Age, that fellows don't pay for girls anywhere now. These kids really don't know what they are missing.

Saturday 9th April

Went to Gatebread Roby's this morning to get fire bricks for the sitting room fireplace where we are having the coal-effect fire. Got chatting to one of the blokes who works there, he told me he had to go to the police station to give them his car insurance, MOT and driving licence. He had run into a shop for a newspaper and left his engine running, a policeman came along and charged him, he even told him seven out of ten people don't know that is an offence. Little did I know then that I would also find myself in the police station today. After having got the fire bricks, myself and Fiona were driving down the Hertford Road when, coming to a bus stop, this bus pulled out in front of us flashing his right indicator. I slowed down to let him out, and all down the road his indicator was flashing. Fiona remarked he must have forgotten to turn it off. He pulled into another bus stop, still flashing the wrong indicator, and pulled out as quick because there was nobody waiting there. We came to the traffic lights at Montague Road, side by side, and I told him his right indicator was flashing. He said, what I thought was, it was broken, then he started making rude signs to me and pointing to his head, then I realised he was calling me a dope and saying I was touched. He stopped at Framway Avenue, so did I, and told him I wasn't a dope. He went berserk. Called me some filthy names and used a string of four-letter words, and told me if I didn't clear off he'd leave me lying flat in the road, so I reported him to the police.

Sunday 10th April

Poured rain all morning. Went to eight o'clock Mass. When I finished selling the bingo tickets, Dick Johnson came out and said there's a fellow smoking in the church and I'm afraid to say anything to him in case he's not all there and might turn a bit nasty. He asked me would I say something to him, as he mightn't mind a woman telling him. Was a bit wary after yesterday's experience, but as nobody, including Bernie, seemed inclined to do anything, I went in and told him very politely that smoking was not allowed in the church. The poor fellow, God help him, came out at once, he stood talking to us for a while in the porch. He was about 23 years old and didn't seem to be all there, he was very nice looking. I think he just went into the church out of the rain. Can't stop thinking of him all day, he looked like somebody who had no home. Leena told Terri this morning that a young lad stole a newspaper from outside the shop, Patricia (next door) saw him and gave out to him. Leena's husband ran out and caught him and brought him into the shop; he was going to ring the police, but Leena said not to as it was only 16p worth. Three lads went into their shop on Friday, held a knife to Leena's husband's throat and took all the money in the till. The husband ran after them, caught one and with the help of another man took him to the police station. He had £50.00 on him. He wouldn't tell the names of the other two who were with him. Leena is really scared in the shop on her own now.

Monday 11th April

Another of these nasty Monday mornings, pouring rain and gale-force winds. Katie was her usual talkative self, she really has a vivid imagination – a few zips wrapped up in a piece of cloth are her babies. She told me a whole rigmarole about how these babies waken her up in the middle of the night crying, "Mummy, Mummy, I want to go downstairs", and what she doesn't say to them isn't worth saying – she's really lost for somebody to play with. Fiona and Terri couldn't eat any dinner this evening, they were so excited getting ready for the disco, Fiona decided to go as well. I told them I'd give them and three of the others who were going with them a lift. Terri rang to tell them, but they said they'd rather all go together on the bus except Terri's boyfriend, who said he'd come in the car. He called for them at seven o'clock, and the first thing Bernie said to him was, "I hear you are going to be a plumber when you leave school?" I could have killed him, he always says the wrong thing. When I came back after leaving them to the disco, I filled up my new cupboard. I'm really pleased with it, it holds an ocean of things. I washed everything before putting them in, and Bernie dried. By the time we had finished, only had time to make a cup of tea and then down again to collect the girls. Terri said the boyfriend hardly spoke to her all night, he's so shy. Fiona never stopped raving about how lovely The Mayfair is.

Tuesday 12th April

My birthday today – got a bit of a shock when I realised I was a year older than I thought. The girls bought me a Yucca plant, Bernie gave me a tenner – he said he's very hard up with his four days a week and no overtime. Ciarán as usual had no money, as his pocket money has been stopped since the day he went out with Bernadette disguised as a skinhead. Didn't bother to mention in work what a very important day it was. Laura is starting to make jackets now, so was kept quite busy trying out new shapes. Jenny hadn't a lot to do so she went out to look at the shops. Ben took Katie out to one of the factories that do work for him. On my way home from work, went to the Leeds to get some money for Dan, he is going to do patio doors in the dining room – when, I don't know, as he hasn't even started on the fireplace in the sitting room yet. Phoned the Leeds, was furious when I was told they hadn't had time to sort my book out yet. Was so exhausted after dinner, went up to bed. My head was only on the pillow when I was fast asleep. At 8.30, Terri came up to tell me Leena was downstairs. Got up to see her. She gave me a really beautiful card and a shopping pad and pencil on a wooden board, I'll put it on the door of my new cupboard. Dan called tonight, said he'll start the fireplace tomorrow, won't hold my breath. Got the new fire today, the one that looks like a real coal fire.

Wednesday 13th April

Did some more jacket shapes today in work, Jenny said she thinks Laura is trying to get as many as possible done before I leave. Sue came in today, she's the new designer. Haven't seen her in over two years, she used to work in Brents, she's a very nice person. Herself and Laura went to see a cloth manufacturer. Before going out, Laura said to me, we put an ad in the paper for a machinist, if anybody should ring about it tell them the hours and money are negotiable and they could work full-time or part-time. I didn't feel very pleased with her, I've been underpaid for the last two-and-a-half years and now I bet they give the new machinist more money than either Jenny or myself are getting. Jenny is getting a bit fed up with things too. She asked Ben three or four times for her train fare and she hasn't got it yet. On my way home from work, went to the Black & Decker repair shop in Holloway Road and bought a new chuck for my drill; £8.95 it cost, it's cheaper than buying a new drill. Showed Bernie tonight how to strip paint off a door without burning the door and leaving it in a state. He said I did it so well I can do the rest of them, he just loves work and he's not joking about the doors. Dan didn't do anything to the fireplace today. He came over tonight to tell me he's going to start on it tomorrow, but I'm not banking on it. The telly man came tonight to fix the telly which packed up on Sunday, had to take it away. Left another one in its place which is better than our one.

Thursday 14th April

The usual mad rush to try and get to work a bit early, but the traffic was very bad and it will be worse next week when all the children go back to school. Laura had a phone call from a person today applying for the job as sample machinist. She spoke to her for a while, then told her to hang on and went into the office to talk to her on the extension phone – I suppose she didn't want me to hear what money she was offering. When she came back I said to her, if you'd like me to leave before the end of the month that's fine by me, and she said, that's very nice of you, I'll see how things go. I'm beginning to wonder if she's more anxious for me to go than I thought. Bernie said when people start to get on they don't want people around who knew them when they had nothing – he could be right. Had a letter from Ciarán's head master complaining about the shoes he wears. He's been going out with his new, black shoes, but only for my benefit, and before he gets into school he changes into the horrible, brown ones with the white-painted stripe up the back. There was a terrible scene when Bernie read the letter. Ciarán said he was leaving home. Mary and Fiona ran after him to bring him back. Don't know where he intended going, he had no coat on him or money. Things get worse here.

Friday 15th April

Phoned Dan this morning before I went to work, wanted to ask him if he was going to do the fireplace, but Colette said he was in bed, very ill, she thinks he has flu. God knows when the job will get done now. Jenny and myself were on our own all morning until Laura and Katie came in at 12.45. Ben went to see a buyer in Scotland and Sam was at one of the factories. Katie and myself had one of our tea parties while Laura was cutting out a jacket for me to make. Ciarán wore his new shoes to school but couldn't find his tie – he's impossible.

I took a load of skinhead posters off his bedroom walls and he was very annoyed over them. Bernie finished stripping the wallpaper off the bathroom tonight. I was hoping his eyes wouldn't light up with the bare wires that Dan left in the wall after he removed the electric wall-heater. Had a phone call from Ireland, from my cousin Nan. She thought there was something wrong because I hadn't written for a while. I wrote to her three weeks ago, she hasn't received it yet, don't suppose she'll ever get it now. When we got this house ten years ago, the doors were in such a state that we put hardboard on them back and front. Took the hardboard off the bathroom door and stripped all the paint off. I sanded it down tonight. Was delighted with the result, it's lovely to see the wood grain. The more I see of conti-board the more I love real timber.

Saturday 16th April

Got up at 9.30, had breakfast, then started stripping Ciarán's bedroom door. Took it down to do it on the kitchen table. Don't know what we'd do without the electric blow-lamp, it's great. Going to buy an electric plane next week, then I'll be all set up for my carpentry work. In the evening, went out with Fiona to do some shopping. One would think that shopping is a fairly dull routine, but with me it's more of an adventure. Went to Halls to buy some moulding – was talking, as I thought, to Fiona, but when I turned round, discovered it was a bloke about 23 years old I'd been chatting to. Apologised to him for mistaking him for my daughter. He gave me a funny look and said to Mr. Hall, "Do you want to serve my mother first?" Cheeky devil. Came out of Halls and was standing waiting to cross the road, which was packed with cars coming from the Spurs match. Armed with my eight-and-a-half feet of moulding, suddenly heard this terrible shouting, turned round to see this old man flying along on a bike, and to my amazement realised he was shouting at me. Was thinking he must be a nutcase when Fiona shouted, "Mummy, the timber!" Quickly stood the timber up straight, thus avoiding decapitating the flying cyclist. Still can't understand why he didn't slow down. On the way home, all the cars were going in the opposite direction to me – bit of a job dodging in and out to avoid oncoming cars. Thought I was doing very well till one bloke asked me, did I get my licence in a lucky bag?

Sunday 17th April

What a dreadful morning – pouring rain, it seems to wait for Sunday. Ciarán wanted a new bag for school, offered to drive him to the market to get one but he said he wanted to go with Adam Kelly. He came back at 11.30 soaked to the skin with this roaring red bag, trimmed with black. Could have killed him, but he said all the boys in school have bags like that. Adam didn't go with him after all, as he had to go to Mass. Did some more work on my door; they really knew how to make doors years ago, the grain on them is lovely and the moulding is made in with the door, not put on afterwards. They have six panels – three long ones on the bottom and three small ones on top, which I am taking out and putting muffled glass in instead, which will make the landing a bit brighter. Mary was telling Rose Cremmens about the state of our house, Rose said she'd have a nervous breakdown if her house was like that. It was funny really, because Helen Porter called on Friday night and I said to her I could have a nervous breakdown, but I'm not going to. It's the sort of thing that would drive sane people mad, so it must be that not being quite sane, I can take it. As I said to Helen, anybody coming here will just have to take me as they find me. Leena called to ask the girls to look after the shop while herself and husband went to a wholesalers. So, between watching telly, Bernie had to go in a few times to see they were alright – I was too busy working to go.

Monday 18th April

God, what a morning, pouring rain and freezing cold, what a change from Saturday – thought we were getting summer, or maybe that was our summer. Dan called before I went to work to tell me he'd start on the sitting room fire tomorrow, he doesn't look too well. A dreadful journey to work, be glad when I'm finished going to Primrose Hill. Quite enjoyed work today. Made some very nice jackets, was almost sorry to be leaving – that is until I heard Laura telling the production manager that Ben doesn't believe in giving people more money until they've proved their worth. I was furious. When the production manager left, I told her I had heard what she said and that Ben must rate me very low since I now had less money than when we were in North Road due to the fact that it was costing me more in petrol. She said Ben was talking about outdoor workers and that I was held in the highest esteem and how upset she was that I was leaving. She nearly had me in tears; nevertheless, I said a lot to her that had been on my mind for a long time, and about how much I resented her telling me off for coming in late since I never took a lunch break and did more work than she'll ever get out of another sample machinist, and that she'd have to pay her more money than I was getting. I was really annoyed.

Tuesday 19th April

Another wet morning, but not as cold as yesterday. Was late getting in to work, but I'm past caring now. When I got in, Ben was in the office with a buyer from Scotland and his wife, she was a very nice person. She was trying on one of the suits I made yesterday, it looked lovely on her. Laura and Katie weren't in until 1.30. Ben was supposed to have gone and collected them at 11.30, but he got tied up with another buyer from C&A. Jenny told me that after I had gone home on Friday a person called about the job as sample machinist, but she doesn't know if she took it or not. When I came home from work, Dan was working on the fireplace. Hadn't much time to talk to him, had to rush and get dinner. Ciarán had to get some fillings today, said he couldn't eat any dinner as his mouth was stiff but could he have a packet of crisps. After dinner, Bernie and myself stripped the paint off the girls' bedroom door, I did the mouldings and Bernie did the panels. It took three hours to do, we'll clean it up tomorrow night with paint strippers. By the time we were finished working, Dan had the best part of the fire finished, he had the fire working. I'm really delighted with it, it looks exactly like a coal fire. Wish I could have had one in the dining room. He didn't go until nearly one o'clock, he was washing the road at 12.30 where he had mixed the cement.

Wednesday 20th April

Very cold this morning – Bernie said when he was going to work at 6.40 all the cars were covered in frost – by the time I went out it had all thawed. Took me over an hour to get to work, it really is a boring journey. Was very tired after my late night. Katie had her doll in today, the one she calls Fiona. She said she was taking her to the church to have her christened, she is very entertaining. Jenny told me after I'd gone home yesterday another person called about the job as sample machinist. Later on in the day, I asked Laura when was the sample machinist starting, and she said there are two people she is going to try out and one of them is coming in today at 3.15. I hope she is suitable and starts on Monday, because I'm hoping to have a week at home before starting in the new job. After dinner, with Bernie's help, took the three top panels out of Ciarán's bedroom door and got it ready for the glass, think it's going to look great. Dan finished the fireplace tonight, but he's coming back at 11.30 to clean up the cement between the brickwork so we'll have another late night. Watched a boxing match on the telly tonight, Joe Bugner and some other bloke. I don't know who told them they could box, they were hopeless, I'd have done better myself. Even the audience were roaring, "What a load of rubbish" – couldn't agree more.

Thursday 21st April

The first day of spring, a really beautiful morning, very sunny and quite warm, a great improvement on the last four days, hope it continues. Got into work before everyone else. Ben and Katie came in a few minutes later. When I asked Ben where Laura was, he said she's gone to Paris. She never mentioned a word about Paris yesterday – talk about secret service. Jenny was very surprised when she heard that, as a designer she is supposed to go too. She told me she is going for an interview tomorrow at 12.30 for a new job, I hope she gets it.

Like myself, she is not being treated very well. I asked Ben how the sample machinist got on yesterday, he said it's hard to tell how quick a person is in a few hours. Apparently, she lives in Portsmouth, but is going to live with somebody in London and is looking for a job before she moves here. It seems they have decided to take her on, and she will start work on 3rd May, so there goes my hope of a week off before I go to my new job. Made a very nice suit today which Jenny designed, might make one like it for Terri. Fiona wants a navy, with a white stripe, fitted suit for her Confirmation, and a plain, white blouse with a Peter Pan collar with a navy bow tie, will have to stop work on the house to make them. Went shopping with Mary and Terri. Bought Ciarán a new shirt, 13½" collar, thought it might be too big for him but it fitted perfectly, which proves he is growing although I can't see it. Dan put a mahogany mantelpiece on the fire place, looks really lovely.

Friday 22nd April

Spring didn't last very long, it's back to winter again, very cold and raining. Was driving along to work quite unconcerned when I happened to look at my petrol gauge and discovered it was showing empty. Sudden panic to get to a garage before the car came to a standstill, drove for about two miles before finding one. Filled up the tank and was very surprised to find it only took five gallons. Turned on the ignition and discovered the gauge was still showing empty. Realised the gauge wasn't working, the needle seems to be stuck, so will have to be careful now I know and keep checking the mileage or I could come unstuck. Laura never mentioned a word about Paris, neither did I – she probably doesn't know Ben told me. Jenny didn't come in until two o'clock. When Laura went out of the room she told me about her interview. The name of the place is Wear Well, it's a huge, big place, beautifully done up. They are to let her know on Monday whether she's got the job or not, hope she gets it. Myself and Terri went to a jumble sale tonight in Windmill Road, Edmonton; I really went to look for some jackets to take patterns from, but I finished up with a lovely coat which fitted me perfectly and looked as if it had never been worn - only 10p, an Irish, hand-woven tweed jacket for 5p and six wine glasses with stems for 30p. Terri got a real suede top to wear over trousers for 5p and a linen jacket for 5p, so it was worth our while going.

Saturday 23rd April

Was up early this morning, had breakfast, then went off to Stoke Newington to a shop there run by a Jewish family, they sell all tailoring trimmings. Fiona wants a suit made out of men's suiting for her Confirmation. They hadn't got the material I wanted (navy with a white chalk stripe) but got in to chat with three Indian tailors who explained to me what part of a man's suit the various trimmings are used for, all very interesting stuff. Bought a few bits and pieces which came to £9.40. Came out and walked the half mile back to my car. Just about to drive off when I realised I hadn't got much for £9.40. Walked the half mile back to the shop and told the chap there I thought he'd over-charged me. He made up the bill again and sure enough he had charged me £3.00 too much. He said he was very sorry, he gave me the £3.00 and said, here, have these on me, and handed me four large reels of thread – was really pleased. Bought a very nice purse for Terri for £1.00 from one of the stalls. Went straight from there to Walthamstow market, which I walked the length of looking for the material, knew there was a man there who sold nothing but gents suiting remnants. The only piece of navy and white he had, hadn't enough in it to make a suit, but got a lovely piece of navy with a pale-blue stripe. Was hoping Fiona would like it, had visions of having to run back with it, but when she saw it she said, it's nice, which translated means she likes it. She's like 007, doesn't say much. Couldn't sleep when I went to bed with pains in my legs, not used to walking so much.

Sunday 24th April

A really lovely morning. All went to eight o'clock Mass except Fiona, who went to 10.30, which was a Mass for the boys and girls who are preparing for Confirmation. After breakfast, Bernie decided to clean out the shed while I was trying to put some shape on the dining room. Terri was helping her father with the shed to a non-stop flow of nagging and threats of what he wasn't going to do with anybody he found putting rubbish in the shed. I had to leave my work twice to run down with some stuff to the dump. The second time, Bernie came with me so that he could go to the off-licence on the way back. When we came back there was loads of things in the garden which had to go back into the shed. Terri went into Leena's and left her father going berserk because he had no-one to help him. He gave out yards to me for starting things and not finishing them – didn't bother to remind him that it was he who had started it, not me. I asked Ciarán and Adam Kelly to give him a hand. When it was all finished, Bernie said Adam is worth three men, thought it better not to say that I thought he was worth three Bernies. Adam said the dining room looks lovely with the brick work. It does look better now that we got rid of some of the rubbish out of it, so when we get the patio doors [and] paper and paint it, I think I'm really going to like it. The two girls went into Leena's this evening and Bernie brought me my tea up in bed after my nap, wonders will never cease.

Monday 25th April

Raining again this morning. Left for work earlier than ever and arrived in late – really fed up with that journey. Making jackets all day, which I love doing. Laura is making sure she gets her autumn range together before I leave, the new sample machinist won't have a lot to do when she comes except copy what I have already done. After work, tore down to Jones Brothers to get some blouse material for Terri and Fiona, when I got there was very annoyed to discover they were closed, forgot they close all day Monday. Was late getting home, the traffic was terrible. After dinner, Bernie said he didn't feel well, he thought he was getting a cold, so he sent into Leena's for some Lemsips and went to bed with orders to bring him up some tea at supper time. Cut out two patterns for the girls' blouses. Terri likes frilly things but Fiona is strictly the tailored type, she wants a white blouse with tucks each side the button stand and a Peter Pan collar. Terri taped the Eurovision Song Contest on Saturday and James called over tonight to hear the songs; don't know how on earth Bernie slept with all the racket going on, but he did. After supper, was feeling very tired and looking forward to going to bed, but Terri wanted to see 'The Day of the Triffids' on telly. It didn't start until 11.30 and I, stupid enough, stayed up with her – I need my head tested, never saw such a load of rubbish.

Tuesday 26th April

Very tired this morning thanks to the Triffids. Really didn't want to go to work, but thought I'd better make the effort as it's my last week. A beautiful morning, very warm and sunny, which did make me feel a bit better. Jenny hasn't heard yet whether she's got the job that she was interviewed for last week, but she phoned about another one and they've asked her to go for an interview. She's really annoyed with Laura, she found a list on her table with all sorts of instructions on it. At the top of it was that her hours were from 9.30 till five o'clock, and if she went out to see the shops she was to come back and do sketches of what she'd seen, and always cut out samples with the wrong side of the material together (although she cuts out samples, it's not part of her job). I can't remember all that was on the list, but Jenny said there wasn't one word about her having a lunch hour or tea break. Can't understand Laura at all, it really does seem the more you do for people the more they want. She'll find it hard to get anyone to do as much as Jenny. Went to Jones Brothers and got the material for the blouses – white for Fiona and yellow for Terri (her favourite colour). No work done on the doors again tonight. Bernie went off to bed with some more Lemsip. Dan's little girl asked me was Bernie sick, I said yes, sick of work. I worked on some patterns for the girls' jackets. If Bernie is doing the dying swan tomorrow night, I'll cut them out.

Wednesday 27th April

Took Fiona's dolls' pram into Katie this morning, staggered up the stairs with that and my bag, which weighed a ton, thought to myself, I need my head tested carrying such heavy loads, but looking at her face when she saw it made it worth the effort. She was delighted with it. Don't think Ben was too pleased, he said she'll be running into everything. Later on, he took her out with him, and she wanted to bring the pram in the car. While they were out and I was waiting on some work to be cut, I made a mattress, a pillow, a pillow-case with a frill of lace, and a quilted cover, also with a frill of lace round it. When she came back and saw it, she said, "Oh, my God". Ben said, there's not much work done when I'm out; was tempted to say, you'll get less work out of your new sample machinist, but thought better of it. Bernie still doing the dying swan – went to bed early with his Lemsip, but not before he had seen Alex Higgins get through to the semi-finals [famous Irish snooker player, known as 'Hurricane' Higgins for his fast-play style. He was world champion twice and won several other titles and helped popularise the game. Snooker had record viewing figures in the 1980s]. Cut out Fiona's blouse, went to great lengths cutting out a pattern for it, when I had it all done she said she didn't like the material, but like it or not, that's what she's having, you couldn't please her. Terri is so different, when I ask her what she'd like, she first says, "Whatever you like". When Fiona and Ciarán had gone to bed, I opened a box of Terry's Dairy Milk which Mary Mac had given me at Easter – wish she hadn't, Terri and I gorged ourselves.

Thursday 28th April

A real headache getting to work this morning, never saw so much traffic in all my life. Sam only lives one-and-a-half miles from Primrose Hill, and he said it took him over an hour to get there. Jenny said the tube station was almost empty. She reckons that, as most people have tomorrow and Monday off, they brought their cars to work today and are going straight from work away for a long weekend. A beautiful day, really warm. Bernie said we are to have a heatwave in May, hope he's right. Katie started nursery this morning. Laura stayed with her for about an hour, then later on Ben went and brought her home. When she gets used to it, she'll be there from nine o'clock until five in the evening. Poor thing, when she came back she didn't speak for a while, I think she was suffering from shock, but after a while she was her usual talkative self. Mary called to go shopping. I left her home afterwards, but didn't go in to see June – had to rush home and cut out three skirts, which I want to overlock tomorrow in work before I leave. Mary's going to Ireland on Monday. Father Hegarty has been called home to Cork – his sister is dying, God help her. When she goes, he'll be the only one left of his family – his two brothers, also priests, are dead, one was killed in an air crash. Dan called tonight to tell me he'll do the work he left undone on Sunday.

Friday 29th April

Bernie didn't have to go to work today – his firm, along with a lot of others, have an extra day's holiday this year. He said he was going to get a haircut, and when he came back he was going to do the doors, but when I came home from work, he was sitting watching snooker on telly. My friend Mary Mac had come over and had made him a cup of tea. My last day in work. Laura wasn't in when I arrived, she had taken Katie to nursery. Ben called Jenny into the office, and when she came out she was very annoyed. Ben had told her that her tax had gone up by £3.00, which means instead of getting a raise, she's now worse off. Made a couple of jackets, then did some overlocking on

Fiona's and Terri's skirts. Laura didn't come in until two o'clock, she had stayed to lunch in the nursery. Ben gave me my wages and said I wasn't entitled to any holiday pay – was a bit disappointed. When I was leaving, Laura gave me a beautifully wrapped box and a bunch of red roses. Was dying to get home to open the present. Was really delighted when I did, it was a lovely cut-glass rose bowl. After a very fine morning, it rained all afternoon. After dinner, showed Mary Mac how to use the paint stripper; only intended doing one panel of a door, but she kept insisting I do more until I finally ended up with one side of the door completely stripped. After everyone had gone to bed, stayed up to watch snooker on telly, was sorry to see Alex Higgins beaten by Steve Davis.

Saturday 30th April

A beautiful morning. Got up early, needed some moulding to put round the glass in the bedroom doors, went everywhere looking for it, finished up in Finsbury Park. Got my electric plane today, it has a bag on it for collecting the shavings. Took me quite a while to assemble it and fix the handle on, I expect to get the woodwork done twice as quick now. This was my day for selling flags for the Crusade of Rescue. I usually stand at the corner of Worcester Avenue and catch the Spurs crowd as they pass. The girls used to come with me, but as Terri is working and Fiona was helping in Leena's, I had to go on my own. Spurs were playing Liverpool, so decided to try my luck on the High Road, which was packed with supporters, so I took up my stand at the top of Paxton Road. Found myself amongst all the ticket touts, who kept giving me funny looks, but after a while four of them came over to me and bought some flags. A few coppers passed by, but they didn't take a blind bit of notice of them. Two old ladies asked me how I was doing, and told me they'd been out this morning selling the flags and now they were off to see the match. You'd think they'd be more inclined to go home and put their feet up. I stood there for two hours, and my legs were aching so much I had to keep standing like a stork, resting one leg and then the other. My hand was sore from shaking the box. Two blokes were coming along and one said to the other, "I'm going to buy a flag from the old lady". I nearly gave him a belt of my box.

May 1983

Sunday 1st May

Pouring rain this morning, it seems to wait for Sundays. Father Roderick said Mass. Father Hegarty has been called home to Ireland – his sister has taken a turn for the worst and is only expected to live a few days. Mary is also going home tomorrow for a few days. Adam Kelly, Ciarán, and another lad he goes to school with, went off to Petticoat Lane this morning; came home at two o'clock, you'd think they'd fallen into a river they were so wet. The sun will have to be splitting the trees before I'll let him go there again. Was talking to a lady after Mass who was selling tickets for a benefit dance to send a man called Brian Walsh to Lourdes, I said I never heard of him, she said he's my husband. It seems they lived in the parish years ago and left to go to some other part of England to start a business. They were only there a few months when he got a kidney complaint and couldn't run the business. He's so bad now he can't even be put on a kidney machine. He's a convert and his wife said he is an example to everybody. He has such faith and has great devotion to Our Lady – that is why she is so anxious to get him to Lourdes. And we think we've got troubles.

Monday 2ⁿᵈ May (Bank Holiday)

Intended having a lie-on this morning but Bernie woke me before eight o'clock with a cup of tea, which I could have done without, especially as I couldn't get back to sleep after drinking it, so got up and tried out my new electric plane. It's really very good, but will need a bit of practice to use it properly. Worked on one of the doors until one o'clock, then got dinner ready, after which I went to bed for my well-earned rest. Later on, Terri brought me up a cup of tea and told me herself and Fiona were going to a disco in The Mayfair. Terri washed her hair and I set it for her, it looked very nice. Took them down to the disco just after seven o'clock. Ciarán wasn't in when we left, but I wasn't too worried because I thought he was in Adam's house. I was amazed when I came back to hear Bernie talking to Judy on the phone, she had rung to know was Adam in our house. She was annoyed when she heard he wasn't, as he hadn't been home to his dinner. I went round to her and we drove round looking for them – couldn't find them. Was leaving Judy home when we spied Adam coming along the road. When Judy asked him where they'd been all day, he said down the marshes. It seems they found a tent there and just sat there talking as there was nothing else to do. Judy said they probably thought they were soldiers. Well, the outcome is the two of them are confined to barracks for a couple of weeks. Collected the girls from the disco, Terri said her nice hairdo didn't do much good, nobody asked her to dance.

Tuesday 3rd May

Woke at 7.50 this morning, thought the house was very quiet, was amazed when I realised the kids were still in bed – they should have been on their way out to school. Jumped out of bed and shouted to them to get up and ran down to get breakfast ready while they were getting washed and dressed. When they came down, I went upstairs and dressed myself and said I would drive them to school – we all left the house at 8.25. Got the girls there by 8.45, then thought I'd take a short cut to Ciarán's school – that was my undoing. We got lost (the story of my life), and finished up in Whetstone, didn't seem to bother Ciarán. As a matter of fact, when I looked at him through the front mirror he was mumbling under his breath and throwing his eyes up to the sky. I think he was praying we'd never get to his school, but we did eventually; after going through Cockfosters, Barnet and Southgate we found ourselves back in Enfield at 9.30. Ciarán said it wasn't worth his while going in, but I thought half an hour late was better than the whole day off school. Felt like going back to bed when I came home after my hectic morning, but instead worked very hard sanding down. Fiona and myself started on a high-fibre diet today – I'm hoping to lose two stone, please God, hope I can keep it up. Fiona wants to lose half a stone, I fancy her chances better than mine. Phoned Laura today to thank her for the lovely present they gave me. She said the new sample machinist is ok.

Wednesday 4th May

Terri left for school at 7.30 this morning – she had to be in by 8.15, she is doing an exam in home economics and it starts at 8.30. Prayed hard she'll pass, please God. Spent my day sanding down and planing. Got some sawdust in my right eye. Had to go to the school to collect Terri and all the things she had cooked for the exam. For starters there was cauliflower soup, then a quiche Lorraine with English salad and mayonnaise, and a jam and fresh-cream sponge. Very nearly abandoned my diet. Did cheat just a little bit – Fiona and myself decided to have a bit of quiche Lorraine and salad for dinner, it went down a treat. After dinner, my eye was giving me lacko. [We can find no reference to this word anywhere, though Vera used it often. In context it just seems to mean 'annoyance', or 'trouble'. No amount of research or asking Irish friends or family has revealed its use by anyone but Vera, so we assume it is one of her 'made up' words – she had a vocabulary that included some words that she seems to have invented]. Dr. Bernie said if I didn't go to Moorfields and have it seen to, a film would form over the sawdust and that could be very serious. So, on his advice the girls and myself went off to the hospital. There were about 20 other people there before us. When I told the nurse I got it planing timber, I didn't know she was going to put it on the record. While we were waiting, a woman came out and said that the doctor stuck a needle right into her eye. The next minute we heard a blood-curdling scream come from the surgery, everybody turned a paler shade of green. Just when I was thinking of slipping out quickly, I was called in. It turned out there was no sawdust in my eye, but what had been there had scarred my eye. Came home, my eye full of ointment and a big white pad over it.

Thursday 5th May

Was very relieved this morning when I woke to find my eye an awful lot better, thank God, but had a dreadful headache. Stayed in bed until

10.30. Got up, had my high-fibre breakfast – All-Bran, sultanas, an egg and a cup of tea. For lunch had the cauliflower soup Terri made yesterday and 8oz of baked beans and half a grapefruit, felt like a stuffed pig. Did some more sanding down, hoping to work it off. For dinner, Fiona and myself had some salmon and a salad. Bernie and Terri had Shepherd's pie while Fiona and I looked on longingly. Bought the 'Evening News' to look for a job. There was an ad for a sample machinist with an 802 number, which is south Tottenham – rang to make enquiries. A very nice man answered, and after a few enquiries on both our parts he asked me would I come in on Friday and make a sample. They make children's wear, which I'm not all that keen on doing; however, told him I'd go on Friday. Really don't want to go to work so quickly, I've so much to do in the house plus the two suits for the girls. Had to phone Dan tonight to tell him the central heating, although it was turned off, was still coming on. He came over at nine o'clock, he was very upset. Colette's best friend had committed suicide – she was an Indian lady with a married daughter and one 13 year old. Lord have mercy on her, she must have been very unhappy. Bernie bought a new lawnmower. He put a plug on it tonight, and if anybody had used it they'd have been electrocuted.

Friday 6th May

Was up at eight o'clock this morning trying to make up my mind whether to go to this new job for an interview or not, but as I don't like making promises and not keeping them decided to go, which I did. Was pleasantly surprised to see the design room, it was really lovely, so bright and big, overlooking south Tottenham High Road. There were two designers there and one sample machinist, a lady called Doris, who it turns out is a friend of another lady I worked with some years ago. Made a skirt while I was there. The boss said he had to see two more applicants and he would phone me on Monday or Tuesday to let me know if I had the job or not. Hope I get it, as I really think I'd like it there and it would be so convenient for me, it only took me ten minutes to get there. When I left there, did some shopping, came home and made some cauliflower soup for my lunch. Had just finished when there was a ring at the door – was amazed to see Father Hegarty. He was looking for motorists to take the children who are making their Confirmation to Totteridge tomorrow. He also asked me when Mary was coming back from Ireland. He said she told him if she wasn't back by Friday, I would cook a dinner for him on Saturday. I'm going to kill that Mary when I see her. Phoned June tonight to know was she back – thank God she was, wasn't looking forward to cooking for Father Hegarty.

Saturday 7th May

Went over to the church with Fiona, loads of people with cars there, so my services weren't needed. Mrs. McClusker said she would take Fiona in her car and look after her very well, I said you better or I'll be up to you, she said I know you will. She really looks well since her retirement. Went into the chapel house to see Mary. She was annoyed at the price of things in Ireland. Dorrie, who she stayed with, paid £14.00 for a leg of lamb – it would cost less than £7.00 here – and three pieces of cod cost £3.75. Stayed chatting to her until nearly midday. Went home and got lunch ready. Then went off to pay my gas and electric bills, £110.95 for gas and £78.95 for electric. Have to pay my phone bill on Monday, that's £33.95, they all come together. Then went up to Edmonton Green to do some shopping, but had to stay in the car for quite some time it was raining so bad. Went into Woolworths to get some cheese. Had just got it when there was a terrible commotion. Four black youths went charging out of the shop (think they had stolen something) – they knocked a poor old lady right down on her back and kicked another lady on the leg, they were both very shocked. I'm afraid I didn't keep to my diet tonight, had to have one of Terri's cakes. Fiona said she had a lovely day in Totteridge.

Sunday 8th May

All went to eight o'clock Mass – raining as usual. Afterwards, took Adam, James and Ciarán to Queensway market. Bought Ciarán a flying jacket, told him if he writes on it, I'll take it from him. Bernie was in a tidying mood this morning so we made two trips down to the dump, then to the off-licence. Only Terri, Bernie and myself at dinner, the other two were missing. Colette had gone to visit a friend, so Fiona took Sally to the park, then had her and Tina here for the rest of the day. Went for my usual afternoon nap. When I got up, helped Bernie to put all the doors back on the rooms, even though they are not finished; decided I will just take them off as I'm doing them, because I'll have to stop working on them while I make Terri's and Fiona's suits. Was cutting out the lining for Fiona's suit when Leena called. She had a terrible mishap with her pressure cooker a week ago, it exploded. I had an almost new one in the shed, so I sent Terri in with it today. She was delighted with it, but she said she would have to ask her husband could she have it – apparently, he said no, and that was what she came in to tell me. He is a very hard man, and she has a terrible life with him – God help her, she is so nice. Dan called for Sally, told him that although our central

112

heating is turned off, it still comes on – it could only happen to us. Said he'll fix it tomorrow.

Monday 9th May

Oh God, what a day. Got up early thinking Dan was coming over to fix the central heating which he had turned off but was still coming on. He didn't come, so said a few prayers for him. At 10.30 the phone rang, it was the nurse from Fiona's school to tell me Fiona wasn't well and would I come and take her home, which I did. Was shocked when I saw her, she looked so ill. Prior to that I had spent an hour and a half trying to get my old machine to work so that I could make the girls' suits. I haven't used it for over two years, finally got it to work. Brought Fiona up her lunch, which to my surprise she ate. Made the jacket of her suit. In the afternoon, she was in such pain I phoned and made an appointment to see the doctor. Saw Watson at 5.30, he prescribed tablets. When she took one of them she was violently sick. When Terri came in from school she went into Leena, who was dressing her up in a Sari for the fancy dress disco at The Mayfair. Took herself and Helen down there. Had another phone call from the new job I had applied for to say I had got it – was really delighted, as I feel I'm going to enjoy working there. Fiona got so bad, took her up to Middlesex hospital. The doctor examined her and said she had an acute appendicitis and they would operate on her at once. Then another doctor examined her and said it wasn't appendicitis. In the end, they said they would keep her in overnight for observation. She was very upset. I didn't get home until three in the morning, Bernie was still up. Both very upset over Fiona.

Tuesday 10th May

Felt very exhausted this morning. Phoned the hospital to enquire about Fiona. The nurse said she had a comfortable night, but she didn't know if she was being allowed home as the doctor hadn't been to see her yet, and I could only visit her between three and four o'clock. Went back to bed. I was so tired, didn't get up until one o'clock. Got the dinner ready for evening, phoned the hospital again to see were they letting Fiona home, but was told they were keeping her in for another 24 hours at least. Took her up a night dress and dressing gown. She was fast asleep, didn't like to wake her as I knew she must be very tired too. She is in a ward with three, very old, incontinent women; one of them, who is 89 years old, keeps shouting all the time. Was pleasantly surprised to see Angela Kileen was the nurse in charge there. Had brought up some orange juice, but she said Fiona was only allowed drinks of water, no food at all. Tomorrow they will start her on a small amount of food – if she has no ill effects after it, she can go home, but if it disagrees with her, they will take her down to theatre and open her up. I'm very worried, but please God it won't come to that. When she eventually woke up she looked an awful lot better than she did last night, and was quite cheerful telling me all about the old lady that keeps shouting, but when Bernie and myself went up tonight to see her, she was very depressed and cried a lot when we were leaving – really upset me. Would feel depressed myself in a ward with such old people. Needless to say, I'm praying hard she'll be fit to come home tomorrow.

Wednesday 11th May

Rang the hospital this morning to know if Fiona was being allowed home. The nurse I spoke to said she didn't think so, but wouldn't know for sure till the doctor had been to see her. Did some machining but my heart wasn't in it, very worried over Fiona. Phoned later in the day and was told she was definitely not being allowed home. Went up to see her at three o'clock and found she had been moved along with the three old ladies into another ward – the ward they'd been in was being done up. However, Fiona was in great form and didn't seem too upset over not coming home. Said she was dying of hunger, and gave strict orders to bring loads of food and her clothes for going home tomorrow, hope she's not disappointed again. Had a bit of a job getting back up to her tonight, Spurs were playing Manchester and the traffic was chaotic. Took her up a salad and three slices of bread, she said she'd have a midnight feast. I asked Angela Kileen if it was alright for her to have it and she said yes. While we were there, the lady who brings the patients' night-time drinks gave Bernie and myself a lovely cup of tea and said it was really dreadful to have Fiona in a ward with such old people. I explained to Angela that if Fiona was coming home tomorrow, I wouldn't be able to call for her until after three o'clock, as I was starting in a new job and couldn't very well ask for time off my first day there; she said I could call for her at any time. On the way home, Bernie went to pay his union fees and left me outside for half an hour, wasn't very pleased with him.

Thursday 12th May

Before setting off for my new job, rang the hospital – couldn't believe my ears when the sister who answered me said she didn't think Fiona would be allowed home today, that after all she was only one day on solid food, and that it was better to keep her in for another day to see how she gets on than have me running back to the hospital again with

115

her. I had to agree with her, but I didn't know what to do – whether to go to the job or not – but then I thought if they do keep her in I can't go to see her until three o'clock, so I decided to go to work. Was glad I did, it kept me from thinking too much about Fiona. Can't get over how slow the pace is there, after all the mad rushes with Laura and Ben. Had a phone call from Ben on Wednesday to know would I do some work for them at home. Had to tell them I couldn't, what with going up twice a day to see Fiona in between trying to get things ready for her Confirmation. Left work at three o'clock, got up to the hospital by twenty past. Found Fiona all dressed and packed, ready to come home, a big smile on her face. When we got home she ate half a packet of cream crackers and cheese while I was getting dinner ready. Then had her dinner, came to six o'clock Mass with us, and then over to the chapel house for the last class before she makes her Confirmation. Although she doesn't look too well, she seems to have quite recovered.

Friday 13th May

Felt a bit guilty this morning going to work and leaving Fiona on her own. Told her to stay in bed as she seemed very tired. Only took me quarter of an hour to get to work – a bit of a difference to Primrose Hill. The designer I'm working for is called Jo, short for Joanna, she is very nice. The other designer is Lizzie and her sample machinist is Doris, they are both very nice and friendly. There is just the four of us in this great big room, which overlooks south Tottenham High Road, everything in it is so neat and tidy. We have a morning coffee break and an hour to our lunch in which we can do our own work. I overlocked a pair of jeans for Ciarán today and Doris cut out a dress for her daughter. Everything is so relaxed here, so different from my other job. A man came in today, shook hands with me and said, "I'm Mr. Abrahams". Jo told me afterwards he's our boss. He said he'll have a chat with me next week. Really think I'm going to like it here, everybody is so nice. An Irish woman came up from the factory underneath our room. She told me she comes from Dublin and is years over here. She has a sister or a brother in nearly every part of England. She said her mother had 21 children and she couldn't even have one – she seems a real hard nut. When I got home, Fiona had tidied up the house. She had stayed in bed until eleven o'clock. She looks a lot better today, thank God, eating all before her, hope it won't do her any harm. After dinner, made her a white blouse to go with her suit, also made Ciarán's jeans. I love the bright evenings for sewing. Terri brought home two boxes of chocolates and cards from Fiona's school friends.

Saturday 14th May

Finished off Ciarán's jeans this morning, after that did some more bits and pieces. Was so busy today everybody got their own lunch ready. Spurs were playing today, so waited until three o'clock to go shopping with Mary and Fiona, it's the last Saturday before her Confirmation. Really wanted to get her a pair of shoes, but she couldn't see anything she liked under £27.00 – she has very expensive taste our Fiona. Didn't feel like paying that much, as I have to buy a pair each for Ciarán and Terri. The nicest shoes she tried on were in Marks and they were only £10.00, so she'll probably get a pair of them during the week. She tried some hats on in BHS, they looked really lovely on her. They were £12.00 and £14.00, a bit dear I thought for one hour because

I doubt if she would wear it again. In the end, we didn't get an awful lot for our few hours of shopping. Bought a jumper for Ciarán which Fiona said he'd love, but when he saw it he said he wouldn't wear it, so will have to change it some day when I get time. Apart from that just bought some underwear for the girls and myself. The price of things is really terrible – a bra, a pair of tights and panties for the girls came to £5.00 each. Got into the thick of the Spurs crowd on the way home. The police were directing the traffic, wish they'd leave it to the traffic lights, they cause more chaos. Got home just in time to collect Terri from work and gave her work mates a lift home.

Sunday 15th May

Another dreadful Sunday in more ways than one, poured out of the heavens all day, started just after we came out of Mass. Took the girls, Ciarán and Adam Kelly down to Queensway market. Thought I might get a pair of shoes there for Ciarán, but all we got was very wet. Came home, had breakfast and, God forgive me, did a bit of sewing. Then at midday Bernie and myself drove down to the off-licence – was just pulling in to the kerb when the next thing there was a terrible bang and we were thrown up on the pavement. Thank God there was nobody passing at that time or they'd have been killed. A bloke behind us had crashed into the back of us – the funny thing was I didn't feel a bit shocked. We got out of the car, as did the bloke who crashed into us, he was a young lad. He said he was terribly sorry and not to call the police, that he would pay for any damage done. I said, there's something wrong, isn't there? He said yes, this isn't his car, it belongs to a friend, and the friend wasn't insured for somebody else driving his car. The next thing, two policemen, who were just passing, stopped and asked did I want to make a charge. I said no, it was alright, that the lad had agreed to pay for the damage done to my car. The whole boot was bashed in and the side wing, also the rear lights. We exchanged names and addresses and the lad said he'd phone me tonight, which he did – told me to have the damage estimated tomorrow and he would pay for it. Hope I'm not being too trusting.

Monday 16th May

Didn't think I'd be able to use my car, but having checked to see if the indicator lights were working alright, tied the boot lid up with a piece of wire and set off for work. Arrived there without mishap, didn't dare bring it into the firm's car park, it would really have lowered the tone of the place, so left it in a side turning. Really like my new job. Did some machining there during my lunch hour, which is a great help as I am way behind owing to Fiona being in hospital. Doris, the other sample machinist, wasn't in today. She's attending the doctor for a sore throat, which she's had for quite some time. Left work at three o'clock and was home at 3.15. Had the dinner ready too early – will have to get used to being in that much earlier and time it better in future. After dinner, cut out a blouse for Terri and made it up, [and] also cut out her suit. Was just having a cup of tea at nine o'clock when the phone rang, it was the bloke who had crashed into my car. Told him I had taken my car to a garage in Lordship Lane to have the damage estimated, didn't add that I'd been soaked to the skin and scared out of my wits with the thunder and lightning while there, and that it had cost me £4.50 to be told that it would cost £320.00 plus to have my car repaired – the labour charges alone on it would cost £205.00. I think he nearly had a heart attack, he said he thought

119

it would cost about £100.00. I finished up telling him I would try another garage tomorrow.

Tuesday 17th May

Had a really nice day in work, like it very much. The only thing I really miss is Laura's and Jenny's precision-cut patterns. The designer I work with now doesn't put nips in anything, I have to keep asking her what seam allowance is on everything. I'd love to show her how to cut a pattern, but she might think I'm trying to tell her how to do her job – apart from that she is a very nice person. The other designer whom Doris works for seems to really know her job. She is a very positive type person, very gay and cheerful. She is married, but values her independence a lot – a real women's libber. On my way home from work in the pouring rain, took my car to another garage on the High Road to get another estimate. When the man there saw it, he said it was a write-off, meaning that what it would cost to repair would be more than the car is worth. He reckoned it would cost £550.00 to put it right; it only cost me £600.00 when I bought it. I told him what had happened on Sunday and he said I was mad not to go to the police and charge that bloke. He was very nice, and after chatting to him for a while he said if I got no money from the bloke he would do a cheap, tidying-up job on it for me. Later on, I took it down to Murphy (the mechanic) and he also said I was mad not to go to the police. He said I've no hope of getting money out of that bloke; otherwise, he also said he would do a job on it for £200.00. When the bloke who did the damage phoned tonight, Bernie told him what the other garages had said. He said he couldn't possibly pay that amount of money. Bernie told him if he didn't pay £200.00 by Friday he was going to the police.

Wednesday 18th May

Did some more machining and pressing for myself during my lunch hour – hope this job lasts, it really suits me down to the ground. Doris's designer, Lizzie, said to me today there's some material out in the cutting room (which is next door to our studio) and you can have whatever you want of it. Went out to have a look – could have taken loads, but didn't want to be greedy, just took four suit lengths. One of the cutters said to me, you'll have to do an odd job for us now and then, and if you know any nice girls we are two eligible bachelors looking for wives. After dinner, decided to go shopping, as I wouldn't have time tomorrow as I have to go to bed early to be up at 4.30 to take Ciarán to his school by 5.45, he is going on a day trip to France. Was just getting into the car with the two girls when three lads came over to me and one of them said, are you the lady who had the crash on Sunday? I told him I was, and he said he was the one who owned the car the bloke was driving. He asked me would I let them take the car, and his friend who worked in a garage would repair it. I said I didn't think so, that I wanted a good job done on it. However, as I was in such a hurry, told them to go and talk to my husband about it – thought, he'll tell them where to get off. Couldn't believe my eyes when I got back to find the three of them in the house and Bernie chatting them up as if they were old friends. He said to me, these lads are going to fix your car; I said, no they are not, but it was four to one and in the end off they went with my car, said they'd return it on Sunday. If they don't, God help Bernie.

Thursday 19th May

Waited nearly half an hour for a 149 this morning and paid 40p to get to south Tottenham, bus fares are outrageous. Had a visit from my boss today. He wanted details as to when I was born, where my husband worked and how many children I had. I was hoping he wouldn't ask their dates of birth as I usually have to do a bit of mental arithmetic whenever anybody asks me that. After work, stood for another half hour waiting on a bus, but had a very nice chat with an Irishman at the bus stop. Told me he's 40 years over here, comes from Wexford, went home to Ireland for the Pope's visit. Works for the council here, was doing some painting on a flat in Tottenham, and was going to Wood Green to collect his wages. Got on the bus with the Irish lady who works in the factory (whose mother had 21 children). It turns out she lives in Willoughby Lane. Had a good laugh with her on the bus over husbands – she has one like mine, who sits down while she does all the work. Pouring rain again today, there seems to be no end to it. After dinner, got Ciarán ready for France. He had a shower, and came down with his neck and face filthy – gave him a good scrubbing up. He is staying the night in a school-friend's house, whose father will take them to school in the morning and bring him home tomorrow night (I should say morning). Filled his bag with four ham rolls, four Mars bars, three packets of crisps and three cans of Coke, a packet of biscuits and a flask, which his friend's mother will fill with tea. Bernie, the girls and myself tidied up the house and bunged everything into the shed, the house now looks less like a builder's yard.

Friday 20th May

Fiona's big day, or should I say night, since she won't be making her Confirmation until seven o'clock. Herself and Terri didn't go to school today, they had appointments to have their hair done at two o'clock. Left Fiona in bed this morning when I went to work, but Terri was up at seven o'clock and went in to help Leena in the shop. I really love my new job, especially as I got my first week's wages today. I have £90.00 a week, paid £12.00 insurance, and got a tax rebate as I'd been out of work for nearly two weeks, so finished up with £91.16. Worked during my lunch hour so that I could get off at two o'clock. Just missed a bus as I came out of work, expected to have to wait half an hour for the next one when a car drew up beside me – it was Leena's husband, I was really delighted to get a lift home. Did some shopping in Marks and got home just a few minutes before the girls, then Mary Mac came. Just cooked rashers, eggs and sausages for the dinner. Then a mad rush for everybody to get ready, had to be in the church before seven o'clock. Leena's husband made two trips in the car to take us over – took their little girl with us, couldn't believe it when I heard her singing some of the hymns, she had learned them in school. When we came out of the church after the Confirmation, which went off very well, Leena and her husband were waiting outside to take us home. There was a reception in the school, so we took them round there with us. Then home. We had a chicken and ham salad which I had prepared earlier. Had a very pleasant night. Then Fiona, myself and Mary, who was staying the night, sat up waiting on Ciarán to come from France.

Saturday 21st May

Vaguely remember Terri giving me a cup of tea before she went off to work, was too tired to drink it. Ciarán didn't get home until 2.45 this morning. By the time he gave us an account of his day in France it was nearer to four o'clock before we got to bed. He brought back two bottles of shampoo for the girls, they were about a litre full, so they must have been very expensive. It seems he bought me a bottle of perfume, which he left on the boat – maybe it was just as well judging by the shampoo, his taste in toiletries leaves a lot to be desired. He wasn't very impressed with Boulogne, said it was a dump. Didn't drag myself out of bed until 12.30. Had lunch, then Fiona and myself went to Wood Green on the W3. Took the jumper which I had bought for Ciarán last week to change it. Hadn't got the sort he wanted, so got my money back. Bought a cardigan for myself, a size 16. When I got home and tried it on it was miles too big for me – was quite pleased, it means I have lost a bit of weight. Also bought a pair of shoes for Ciarán, they were also too big – not a very successful shopping trip. The blokes who had taken my car were supposed to call today to let me know how things were going. When they hadn't called by eight o'clock I rang the one who owns the car. He made all sorts of excuses for not coming, like they couldn't get the parts needed to do the car. He said he had spent his day looking for them, and the car won't be ready by Sunday as promised. I was really annoyed, I feel I've been taken in. He didn't seem a bit concerned, a completely different attitude to Wednesday. I finished up telling him if he didn't have the car ready by Monday, I was going to the police, but I hope it won't come to that.

Sunday 22nd May

Everyone up bright and early this morning – no car to take us to Mass, so it was shanks's mare [Vera's version of 'shanks's pony'. The shank is another name for the lower part of the leg between knee and ankle] for us all. Bernie set out at 7.20 because of his gammy legs, Ciarán at 7.35 and myself and the girls at 7.45. Went down Worcester Avenue, haven't been down it for years. A certain house doesn't look the same. The front garden has been paved over and the door looks as if a bad machinist

124

had painted it – paint all over the glass, altogether very dull and drab, felt a touch of nostalgia passing it. A really beautiful morning, the first dry Sunday in weeks. Arrived at the church to find Bernie selling the bingo tickets. Just before the bell rang for Mass he was fussing, trying to lock the money box to put in the case which I take into Mass with me. He was taking so much time over it, I told him not to bother – that I didn't think it likely I'd be mugged going up the aisle. After Mass, one of my regular customers (a very comical Irishman) said to me, I got my bingo tickets from your husband, I think he's on the … and he made a sign as if playing a fiddle – when I told Bernie he roared laughing. A very uneventful day after that, until tonight when I went to have a bath and discovered there was no hot water – phoned Dan, who had called last night with his friend to fix the central heating, which although it was turned off was still coming on. Whatever they've done with it, the heating is off and so is the water – he came over and fixed it. I hope he doesn't decide to move, because only he knows how to work this central heating.

Monday 23rd May

Really miss my car, you'd grow old waiting on buses here – waited 20 minutes this morning. Had a very nice day in work – quite like making children's clothes now. The designer I work for says she'll have to put me on a go slow or I'll be catching up on her – if I go any slower I'll be static. We are getting quite a nice range of things together: skirts, trousers, blouses and jackets, now all it needs is a good rep to go out and get orders on them. Went into the car insurance place on my way home from work. The man there told me if I reported the accident, although I'm not claiming from them, I would lose my no claims bonus and I wouldn't get it back for months or maybe not until next year. He suggested I didn't fill in the form until I got my car back, and if the work on it was done alright, there was no need to report it at all. The car didn't arrive at 5.30 as promised. Bernie and myself kept ringing the bloke on and off up to eleven o'clock, and kept getting very evasive answers; in the end I was so furious I told him I was going to ring the police, which I did, only to be told there was nothing they could do about it for a while as I had given the car to those people legally. I would have to write to the bloke telling him I wanted my car back within two days or I would charge him with theft. If he didn't return it then the police would take action. I'm really sick over the whole thing.

Tuesday 24th May

Another long wait for a bus this morning, after killing myself rushing to get ready for work, as none of us – apart from Bernie who had gone to work – woke until eight o'clock. Gave Ciarán a quick cup of tea and packed him off to school, but when I went up to the High Road to get my bus, he was still waiting on his bus – told me later he didn't get into school until 9.15. I was also late getting into work. When I told Doris I hadn't got my car back, she was very upset. She said to give her the bloke's phone number and she'd ring him. Having rang him so often I knew his number off by heart, but I told her I couldn't remember it, I didn't want her to get involved. I was sorry I told her anything about it because it really worried her. Bernie worked until 5.30 this evening, didn't get home until six o'clock. After dinner, we were sitting giving out yards about the bloke and the car when Fiona came running down the stairs and said the car is here. We nearly all got caught in the door rushing out to see it. Out of it stepped a tubby, little man, behind him, in the car which had crashed into mine, was the bloke we had spent last night phoning, he was all smiles, and introduced the other man as the one who had done the work on the car. It really looked lovely, much better than before the crash. They also had done the MOT on it. I paid them the cost of the MOT and we all parted good friends.

Wednesday 25th May

Felt a bit strange driving to work this morning, gave every other car a wide berth in case they'd scratch my new paintwork. When I told Doris I'd got my car she positively beamed, she said she was greatly relieved. Made a dress for myself at lunch hour, very plain and straight with elastic in the waist. When I got home from work I fitted it on – I looked like a floating bog. [It is definitely 'bog' in Vera's original. It manages to be very funny while almost impossible to envisage, and even better spoken out loud]. Took the elastic out of it. Put it on later to show the girls and Terri asked me, when was the big day, so that really put me off it. Wish I could stay on a diet. Bernie worked late again tonight. After dinner, my friend Mary Mac and her husband Jack called. They brought me a lovely tree for the back garden, I don't know what it's called but it's got a lovely red flower on it. Now all I need is somebody to dig a big hole so that I can plant it, will probably have to do it myself. After Mary and Jack had gone home, Dan came over to tell me he will start work on the patio doors tomorrow, please God, so I'm to expect the house to be a bit disrupted – seeing as it's been a bit disrupted for the last six months, I don't think anybody will notice the difference. Can't see this house ever getting back to normal. Haven't done any work on it for the last few weeks, was too busy doing things for Fiona's Confirmation. Will have to get cracking on it again. Had a phone call from my cousin Nan tonight, wanted to know if I minded if she came over in August, told her if she didn't mind roughing it, it was all right by me.

Thursday 26th May

Doris wasn't well today in work – she doesn't think she'll be in tomorrow; neither will her designer – she's going away for the bank holiday weekend, so there will be only me and my designer in tomorrow. Started on another dress for myself at lunch hour. Doris cut out a jacket for herself, she is making a lot of clothes for her holiday in Jamaica. She is going in September to look for a house there, and next year is going home for good, she is very unhappy living here. When I came home from work, expected to see Dan here, but he wasn't, but signs that he had been here. The door and the windows between the dining room and the extension were knocked down – he had done a good job of tidying up. The dining room looks so bright, it even looks well without the door, but hope the weather doesn't get any colder or we'll be blown out of here. Went shopping with Mary and Terri, then left Mary home. Went in to see June, who isn't well – she looks very bad. She is diabetic and has bronchitis, and all the tablets she's taking is upsetting the balance of her body. She goes to a specialist in Harley Street – Mary went with her on Tuesday to see him. It cost her £40.00 for a few minutes, hope he's worth it. While I was there an Irishwoman called to see her – she was telling us the parish priest at her local church had an operation on Tuesday for cancer of the stomach, he is only 46 years old and is not expected to live, God help him.

Friday 27th May

Bernie hadn't to go to work today, Terri hadn't to go to school either, she had the day off because of her exams. I got up so early that I got to work by 8.45; my designer didn't get in until 9.20, the bus she travelled on had an accident with a motorist. She is going to Devon for the weekend to visit her parents. She is going by coach, which has a buffet and a toilet on it. It's a journey of four hours and costs £12.00 – by train with no buffet takes three hours and costs £19.50, the coach also has a video. Wish I was going away for the weekend too. Got home from work to find the house all tidied up – Terri had been busy, and Bernie had mowed the lawn and planted the tree Jack had given to me. Dan hadn't come over, so nothing further had been done to the patio doors. If the extension was made of brick instead of timber, wouldn't have doors there at all – quite like it as it is, except it would be too cold in the winter. After dinner, myself and Terri went off to visit Connie – her husband died in March, she lives in Enfield. She has two lovely daughters – the eldest is a chartered accountant and was married eight months ago, the youngest is still at university, she is studying music and is a great violinist. She gets a 100% grant from the Borough of Enfield, so she must be good. Needless to say, Connie is very upset and lonely since her husband's death, but is coping quite well. Stayed with her for an hour and a half. Peter came in to use the phone, theirs is out of order. He was telling us he has a cousin dying of cancer, 52 years old.

Saturday 28th May

Wanted to go to Walthamstow, Wood Green and Edmonton Green this morning, but the rain was just pelting down so instead boned and stuffed a half-leg of pork for Sunday's dinner, hoping by the time I'd finished the rain would have stopped, but no such luck, it was down for the day. Dan came at midday to do the patio doors. Leena's husband asked Fiona to help in the shop while he went to buy a new cash register, she wasn't too pleased as she wanted to come to Wood Green. Told her I'd wait for her, so got lunch ready. Then took herself and Helen to Wood Green. Took back the cardigan I'd bought in Marks last Saturday, thought I'd get my money back but there was such a queue of people waiting to get their money back that I couldn't wait. While there, bought Ciarán a V-neck jumper with cables. When he saw it, said he wouldn't wear it, he wanted a plain one, there's no pleasing that child. Changed his shoes also, and true to form he didn't like the ones I got instead, but like them or not, he's going to wear them. Left Fiona and Helen in Wood Green and went to Edmonton Green. Had ordered a record there two weeks ago called 'No Charge'.* When I got home, Dan had the patio doors up. Really pleased with them, they look great. Will look better when the wall round them is plastered. Collected Terri and co. Return of Fiona, who told me Helen had her ears pierced in Wood Green, a pound including earrings, hope she doesn't regret it.

* 'No Charge' – Johnny Cash (1975)

Sunday 29th May

Very cloudy morning, but at least the rain has stopped, thank God. Ciarán had to serve Mass on his own, nobody else turned up. Left himself and James down to Queensway market. After Mass, the girls and myself went to Wickes, bought a dimmer switch for the dining room.

Have 3 x 100-watt bulbs there – find it a bit glaring by times. Bernie mowed the lawn on Friday, so took two bags of grass clippings down to the dump. Then Fiona, myself and Bernie went down to see Dan in the shop. Couldn't believe the transformation seen there. He had made a mahogany banister and hand rail in the flat above, four bedrooms and a kitchen all beautifully done up, all fitted carpets and central heating. There's still a lot to be done in the shop, but he's hoping to let the rooms soon to get in some money. Even the dog has improved – he now barks. At least he barked mad at Bernie – that's why he didn't see the shop, he was afraid to pass him. Dan came over to do some work after dinner, I was having my afternoon nap. He came back after tea – Bernie gave him a glass of whiskey, and that finished the work. Later on, Ciarán and the girls went over to his house to watch some video tapes. Bernie and myself watched 'Everyman', a very disturbing programme. When the girls came back we watched 'Cabaret', which I have seen twice before but is still one of my favourite films apart from 'Oliver'.

Monday 30th May (Bank Holiday)

Bernie brought me up a cup of tea at 7.30, tried to go to sleep afterwards but just couldn't, so got up and sorted out some cupboards. Dan is going to sell some second-hand stuff in the shop. At the moment he is not making any money, so he's prepared to try anything – he's going to have a stall outside the shop to see how he gets on. Sorted out quite a lot of clothes and ornaments, hope he gets rid of them. Bernie and myself took some of them up to him this morning, and he called for the rest of them tonight. Not a bad day – cloudy, but at least it didn't rain, which makes a change. Had a nap this afternoon, woke up feeling awful. Had a terrible pain all down my left arm and leg – thought, this is it, this is where I have a stroke. When I came downstairs, said it to Bernie about how bad I felt – he didn't even hear me, he was too busy watching telly. Hope I can remember to ignore him when he tells me he doesn't feel well. Fiona and Helen went to The Mayfair tonight. Terri didn't go, she's having a lot of trouble with spots lately, but it's her own fault, she eats all the wrong things, she never stops eating sweets and cakes. Peter collected Fiona and Helen from The Mayfair as I didn't feel up to it.

Tuesday 31ˢᵗ May

Had to remind myself this morning it was Tuesday and not Monday, it felt like the usual Monday morning feeling after the weekend. Had no bother getting to work, the traffic is so much less when the children are not at school. Had a nice easy day in work – made another dress for myself in my lunch hour, I had it cut out for over a year. The boss came in and asked me when I was taking my holidays (thought he wanted to get rid of me), but it was just that he didn't want Doris and myself to take our holidays the one time. My designer suggested I take my holidays the same time as her, but he said he'd rather I didn't as I could help the other designer as she has quite a lot of sealing samples to do (When a buyer buys a design and places an order with the company concerned, the company then sends the buyer three sealing samples, which are tested for wear and durability; when the sealing samples are approved by the buyer, the order goes into production, and everything must be done the same as the samples). In the end, I told the boss I'll take my holidays whenever it was convenient for him, as we weren't going away. He said great, so he'll let me know later in the week when I can have them, I don't mind if it's in October. Thought I'd do some work on the house, but didn't feel up to it, have got out of my stride what with Fiona's Confirmation and the bank holiday, so cut out a pair of curtains for Dan's flat instead.

June 1983

GROWING PAINS

Wednesday 1st June

Very tired this morning – awake half the night with the dreadful storm. It was really frightening, thunder and lightning for almost five hours, thought it was never going to stop. Everybody was up except myself, thought if this is the end, I want to die in bed. When I got to work, the main topic of conversation was the storm, it seems nobody in London slept last night. The strange thing about it was, it didn't seem to do an awful lot of damage. Not a very nice day, showery. Left a note for Bernie last night to put 50p each way on the Guns of Navarone [betting on the Epsom Derby horse race]. He came in fifth, at least I got a good run for my money. Was very sorry to hear while listening to the race that Caroline Bradley had died suddenly while taking part in show-jumping. She was a great horse woman, only 37 years old, Lord rest her. Bernie varnished the beauty board which Jim had put up for us some years ago in the kitchen, it looks really nice. I tried to do some work on the house but my heart wasn't in it. Dan did the patio doors today. I'm very pleased with them, they make the room so bright. Ciarán was very upset tonight because he wasn't allowed out – he didn't come in last night until ten o'clock, said he was in a friend's house, so once more he's C.B. – confined to barracks, he never seems to learn. I don't know whether I feel more sorry for him or myself. My God, the problems of growing up and of the parents looking on.

Thursday 2nd June

Terri had to go to work today so called her at 6.50. Got back into bed. The next thing I knew was her telling me she was late and it was 7.50. A mad rush, but managed to get to work by 8.55. Had a nice day there. Did some shopping on the way home and indoors by 3.20. Terri was in her bedroom revising for her exams, Fiona was next door in Leena's helping in the shop. Got three different dinners ready. A salmon salad for myself and the girls, steak for Bernie and pork for Mary, who came at 4.30. I have to wait until Ciarán comes in to know what he's having for dinner as he doesn't eat the same as anybody else. We all went to six o'clock Mass in St. Edmunds except Ciarán, who had been to nine o'clock Mass in the morning. It was raining so bad, got soaking wet just getting into the car. After Mass, went shopping in Tesco. Bernie came too but stayed in the car park, said he was too tired to walk round Tesco. Dropped him off on the way back, then took the shopping to the chapel house, then took Mary home to June's, who looks better than she did last week, thank God. When we got home, Bernie was going berserk over Ciarán. He had come in with a load of badges and stickers over his jacket. Tempers were really frayed. Ciarán crying and Bernie raving like a mad man, he really doesn't try to understand his son. When he had gone to bed, had a talk with Ciarán, tried to explain to him how concerned we are about him.

Friday 3rd June

Was supposed to call Fiona early this morning, but she was up before me – said she was going to Wood Green to look for a Saturday job, wished her luck before going off to work myself. Got there in less than ten minutes, very little traffic on the roads. Had a nice day at work. A bit disappointed when I got my wages to find I hadn't been paid for the bank holiday Monday, I suppose I'm not there long enough to qualify. Called to South on my way home from work to pay my rent, which has gone up, and also to give him three dresses which I had shortened for his wife, but he wasn't in his office. Then went to Dewhurst in Park Lane to get some meat and was home by 3.30 to find Fiona beaming – she had got a job. The first place she went to was a dress shop, the lady she saw there complimented her on her appearance and said she was very well presented (she had on her Confirmation suit) and that she was looking for a Saturday girl and thought she'd be very suitable; she asked her to call back on Monday as she was very busy at the moment. She then went to Boots, saw the manager there who said they were looking for Saturday staff; he also said he thought she'd be very suitable, but she would have to apply in writing (that's the rule of the store). From there she went to a shoe shop. The manager there said he was very busy and would she come back in half an hour, which she did. He asked her a few questions, the outcome of which is she is starting in the morning at 9.00, and he told her she can come in any day during her school holidays.

Saturday 4th June

Couldn't get out of bed this morning I was so tired, due to the fact that I didn't get to bed till after three o'clock. Stayed up to see the late film, which was the greatest load of rubbish I've seen for a long time. Would have gone to bed earlier only I was too tired to get up. [In other words, she was so tired that she couldn't get herself out of her chair to go to bed]. The film didn't end until 1.30, after which I was dragging myself wearily upstairs when all of a sudden there was a terrible banging on the front door. Shouted for Bernie to get up and see who it was. Followed him down the stairs with Fiona behind us and Terri and Ciarán in the rear. Bernie, in the toughest tone he could muster, shouted, "Who's there?" and a voice answering him said, "Please let me in, I'm being attacked!" When the door was opened, the young lad almost fell into the hall. He was 19 years old and had been attacked by two other 19-year-olds, who had demanded money from him. They beat him and took £2.00, which was all the money he had on him. Phoned the police, who arrived one-and-a-half hours and six phone calls later. It turned out the boy who was beaten was epileptic. His parents live in Wood Green, and for some reason (which I didn't learn) he lives in a hostel in Hornsey. He said he'd been seeing his girlfriend home – she lives in Northumberland Park – and the two lads who attacked him live in a rehabilitation centre in Northumberland Park. It seems this is the third time they have stolen money from him, and are to appear in court on one of the charges. Never a dull moment here, just wish these things didn't happen in the middle of the night. Fiona came home from her new job, foot-sore and weary, but she said she loved every minute of it. She gets paid monthly and gets commission on anything she sells. She gets 15 minutes break, morning and afternoon, and an hour for lunch. It's a very posh shop and they sell very expensive shoes.

Sunday 5th June

A really beautiful morning, so warm (I wore a suit to Mass) – hope it's the beginning of summer and not just a flash in the pan. Bernie mowed the lawn this morning, he's preparing it for sitting out in, and going mad because Dan left bricks and rubble in it. He wanted me to take them down to the dump, but I think my car has taken enough abuse, everything is dumped in it, so I am not very popular at the moment. With so much to be done in the house, the least of my worries is the garden – I don't get time to sit in it, not so Bernie, who spends every sunny day there. Not a very exciting day, for which I suppose I should be grateful. After dinner, the two girls went in to look after the shop while Leena and her husband went to the Cash & Carry. Ciarán went out with Adam. I went up to bed for my afternoon nap. Couldn't sleep with the noise of the telly, shouted to Bernie to lower it but got no response, so came downstairs to find him fast asleep and the telly at its highest pitch, enough to waken the dead except him. It was with great pleasure I woke him up and lowered the telly. Went back to bed, read a book until Terri brought me up my tea, after which I got up and spent the night cutting out blouses and skirts for the girls, which I'll make in my lunch hour in work. From tomorrow, I really must get started on the house again if it is to be done before Christmas, please God. Had my hair cut and permed yesterday, cost £15.50, nearly had to give Bernie the kiss-of-life when he heard the price.

Monday 6ᵗʰ June

Late getting up this morning but still managed to get to work by five to nine. Was waiting on work, so the designer I work for asked me had I any of my own work to do. When I told her yes, she said, well you can do it while I'm getting something ready for you, so made a blouse for Fiona. We were all passing out in the design room except Doris, who felt cold, so couldn't open the window between us. Was glad to get out at three o'clock into the air, but when I got into the car it was like an oven. Stopped off at the chapel house to give Mary the sheets I had washed for her on Saturday. Hated cooking dinner, it made the kitchen so warm. After dinner, decided to tile two walls round the bath. Bernie came up to help but just stood looking at me working, prayed I wouldn't lose my cool and tell him where to go, however he did tidy up afterwards. When we came downstairs it was like bedlam in the kitchen, with six kids in along with our own all sitting round the table drinking tea. Everybody is brought into our house – really fed up with it, we never seem to have a night to ourselves. Bernie keeps saying, wait until the new carpets go down, this is all going to stop. Dan told me on Saturday night he'd finish off the work next week; gave him a set of keys so that he can get in during the day time but he didn't come today.

Tuesday 7ᵗʰ June

Another very warm day, didn't do a lot in work. Doris is still complaining of feeling cold but we did open a window. In spite of the heat there was a very strong breeze blowing, which blew some of my work off the machine – it was really lovely. After work, went up to Tesco in

Edmonton Green to get some more tiles. Was nearly strangled carrying them to the car, a hundred tiles is no mean weight. When I got home, felt really exhausted. Was surprised to find Terri in, she'd been let off early from school – she is doing her exams and finished them at one o'clock. When I told her I was really whacked, she said, you sit down and I'll get dinner ready, I didn't need much persuading. As the weather is so warm we just had a salad, so there wasn't a lot of getting ready on it. After dinner, went upstairs to rest for half an hour. Bernie was working late so got up when he came in. I did some work on the bathroom – this time he didn't bother to stand watching me, he wasn't in the best of form; neither was I, so tempers were very frayed. Finished working at 9.30. Came downstairs to find all the kids drinking tea in the kitchen again – might as well talk to the wall as talk to my kids. Had a few more words with them when I got them on their own. After supper, watched a very interesting film, a true story about a young boy called David who is eight years old and so far has had 52 operations on his face.

Wednesday 8th June

Another scorching hot day, thank God, I really love this weather. Doris wasn't in work, she had gone to a funeral, so we were able to open all the windows. Made a sample for her designer as my own designer hadn't a lot for me to do. Made a dress for Terri in my lunch hour, she was very pleased with it when she tried it on. When Fiona came from school she was all sunburnt. She said her art teacher didn't feel like working so they all sat out in the playground sunbathing – and these teachers think they are hard done by. The sun did nothing to affect Fiona's appetite, she ate ten potatoes with her dinner and was looking for more when Bernie was having his dinner; much as I love potatoes myself I could never eat that many. After dinner, did some more work on the bathroom, Bernie as usual looking on. Asked him to file a tile which I had cut uneven; he wasn't too pleased, he has no patience whatsoever. Didn't get a lot done tonight as most of the work entailed having to cut tiles for awkward places. Bernie gave up looking at nine o'clock; I didn't get finished until 9.45. Was relieved when I came downstairs to find there were no kids in except our own, they must have got the message. After supper, watched the final part of the film which started last night about the boy called David; it was a lovely story, very touching. After that, watched some terrific dancing on the programme 'Come Dancing'. Too tired to get up and go to bed.

Thursday 9th June

Had to get some petrol on my way to work, it's a fortnight since I bought any and since my petrol gauge isn't working was afraid to take any chances. Being short of ready cash, only got two-and-a-half gallons – £4.50, a bit of a difference towards when I was working in Primrose Hill, then I was paying £10.00 a week to get to work. When I got into work, my designer (Jo) told me two of our bosses had looked at the range yesterday evening and seemed quite pleased with it. It was Mary's birthday yesterday, so when she came this evening to go shopping Ciarán and the girls gave her a Replay pen which she was very pleased with as she said she's always wasting notepaper through making mistakes. I gave her £10.00, I couldn't think of what to buy her. Terri prepared dinner again today, she's very good. She did her English Literature exam today, she is hoping to do very well, please God she will. It won't be for the want of trying, she's been studying so hard for the past few weeks.

When we left Mary home after shopping we went in to see June. She was giving out about her gardener, whom she'd had a row with and isn't coming to her any more. She said her lawn badly needs mowing. Her garden is more than twice the size of ours, with three apple trees and two pear trees. She was so annoyed about it that the two girls said they'd mow it for her, which they did – she was really pleased with it. On the way home I bought some chips and we had them for our supper. Bernie said he'd wait up to hear some of the election results, but he finished up fast asleep.

Friday 10th June

Left Terri in bed this morning – she hadn't to be in school until 12.30 to do her biology exam. Another beautiful day, thank God. Had a very nice day in work, just made a couple of children's skirts. The other designer (Lizzie) gave me a lovely sample skirt, fully lined and beautifully made by her sample machinist. I gave it to Terri, it fitted her perfectly, she was thrilled with it. It's a fine wool with lovely colours in it. Doris told me they sell all sorts of skirts in the factory (underneath us) for £2.00 each, so I'll be having a few of them; you couldn't buy the material for that price, not to mention the time spent cutting out and making them, so I like my job a little bit more each day. Made a white, straight skirt for Fiona in my lunch hour; she'll wear it to her new job tomorrow. Bernie gave her £10.00 yesterday, an early birthday present, out of which she bought a nice pair of red sandals – her feet are still sore from last week. Bernie had a burst of energy after dinner, he went out and dug up half the front garden, said he'll do the other half tomorrow. I won't hold my breath. Ciarán sketched a jacket tonight which he wants me to make for him by the 20th of next month, he's going to Clacton with the school. He's really marvellous at drawing – he'd make a terrific designer, but at the moment all he's interested in is being a punk, but I cramp his style too much for his liking. He just won't conform, I don't know where I went wrong with him. Dan called tonight, gave me a bottle of whiskey as a peace offering for his not coming over all week, said he'll come over next week.

Saturday 11th June

All off to work this morning by 7.45 except Ciarán and myself, who had a lie-on until 9.30. Got breakfast ready for both of us and then went to Marks to get my money back on the cardigan I bought and which would fit Finn MacCool [a mythical giant from Irish folklore], also the jumper for Ciarán that he didn't like because it looked too respectable-looking on him and he so much wants to be a punk. Came home just in time to see him going off with Henry, who's in the same class as himself in school. I then went off to Walthamstow, got some very good bargains there. Got some white cotton jersey, five yards for £1.00; they have jackets made from it in Marks for £7.00 – there is only one yard of material in them; I also got some in a lovely shade of red and blue. Bought some material for two dresses for Terri and some for myself, so I'll be very busy for the next few weeks. Went to Wickes on my way home and discovered the tiles I've been buying in Tesco for the bathroom are £1.50 less there. From there went up to Edmonton Green and got some denim for Ciarán's jacket. As I was driving along, thought, how on earth did I manage before I had a car? When I got home, made another pair of curtains for Dan's flat, then went off and collected Terri from Geary's – it's all go here on

Saturdays. Fiona was very tired when she came home from work, but at least her feet weren't sore, thank God. She sold the most miscellaneous today, which includes polish, insoles and heel grips. The other sale girls told her the manager would be very pleased with her. Dan came over at ten o'clock to tell us he'll finish the work next week.

Sunday 12th June

Raining this morning, a bad day for Father Hegarty and the people going to Aylesford, there were three coach loads. Bernie did some gardening and we took the rubble down to the dump. Couldn't believe what I saw, there was such a tail-back of traffic all waiting to go to the dump – the recent fine weather we've had seems to have got everybody working. Ciarán and Adam went to Queensway market, it's their favourite haunt, don't know what the attraction is. It turned out really fine and warm later in the morning. Fiona spent the afternoon sunbathing, I went for my usual nap. When I got up, had a bath, then from seven o'clock till eleven was spent cutting out T-shirts and jackets for the girls from the material I got yesterday; but while I'm doing all this there is nothing getting done in the house. Had a letter from a cousin in Ireland, she said herself and her husband would like to come over for a week or so, she also said I'm sure your house must be lovely by now; we all roared laughing when we read that. Our house is in such a state, between the jobs Dan has started and not finished and the things I have started and haven't got time to finish – between the two of us we've made a right mess of this house. Wish I could put the clock back, I'd be very happy with what I had. I always thank God for the gift of being able to do things, but sometimes I wish he hadn't been so generous to me, or even been a bit more generous and made me rich so that I didn't have to go out to work and had time to indulge in all my talents.

Monday 13th June

These Monday mornings come round so quickly. Ciarán cooked his own breakfast before going off to school – two fried eggs and two slices of toast. When I went into the kitchen, had trouble seeing him through all the smoke – will have to teach him how to cook eggs without smoking us out of the house. Terri had a maths exam today; she thinks she's done alright, hope she won't be disappointed. Great excitement in work today – all the bosses in to look at our children's range. One of them had taken snaps of his ten-year-old daughter in some of them, they really looked lovely on her, so hopefully they'll get lots of orders on them. I can't keep track of all the bosses, there seems to be more chiefs than Indians, but at least they are all very nice. My designer, Jo, is very pleased, as up to now nobody has taken much notice of what has been made, which wasn't very encouraging for her. I really like my job, and it's great getting so much of my own work done during my lunch hour, it saves having to open up my machine at home, which is nearly at the end of its days, plus the fact that the machine in work is twice as fast. After dinner, did some more tiling in the bathroom while Bernie sat looking at me, there mustn't have been anything he wanted to see on telly.

Tuesday 14th June

Felt very stiff this morning, getting too old for going up and down a ladder, wish I had married a handyman. Terri had another home economics exam today, she hadn't to be in school until 11.45. Could do with a few lessons in home economics – every week my food bill gets higher; still, it would be worse if we weren't able to eat, and from what I hear the cost of living is twice as high in Ireland. Had a nice, easy day in work, thank God. Nearly hung out the flags when I came home, Dan had been over and done the steps of the patio doors. He had gone by the time I got in – God knows when he'll come again to finish all the other bits and pieces, I think he's fitting my work in between his shop and other jobs he's doing. Terri prepared dinner today – just a salad, but at least it gives me a break and it's nice to have dinner handed to me. Thank God for her and my easy job, because once I get home I never stop working. I go to bed exhausted and get up the same way. Ciarán went over to Adam's this evening, so at least we didn't have the usual crowd of children here tonight, for which I was thankful. I went up to the bathroom to do some more tiling, with Bernie taking up his usual position sitting down to watch me. Told him he could be doing some grouting, but he didn't like the way I asked him so he went downstairs in a huff and sat watching telly for the rest of the night, leaving me asking God to grant me patience.

Wednesday 15th June

Terri brought me my usual cup of tea in bed, in spite of the fact she didn't have to get up early this morning as she has no exams today and hadn't to go to school. Got up just in time to get Ciarán's breakfast ready. As he was going out the door, had to call him back to wash himself, he's a dirty little devil. Everybody keeps telling me he'll change when he gets older, hope they are right. Heard in work today they were selling skirts off cheap. Got one each for the girls, lovely material in them, pleats all round and fully lined, £4.00 each. The girls were delighted when they saw them. Tried to get some for myself, but all the size 16s were gone. They sell for about £17.00 in the shops. Bernie not in the best of form when he came in from work, so gave him his dinner and went up to do my tiling, feeling murderous. Bernie came up later with his boiler suit on, one would think he was going to work, but not he. The boiler suit was in case I let tile cement drop on him. Please God, when this house is all finished and I have time to have a nervous breakdown, the first thing I am going to do is get a large tub of cement and push Bernie's head into it for all the times he has sat on the toilet watching me doing the tiling. Nipped my thumb and one of my fingers with the pinchers while shaping a tile, really painful. Feeling very sorry for myself and hard done by.

Thursday 16th June

Terri had a general science exam today, she said there wasn't one question on the paper that they had studied so she hasn't much hope of a pass. She was home from school by 12.45. She did a great job of tidying the bathroom, which was pretty bad with chippings and broken bits of tiles all over the floor. Made a jacket and T-shirt for Fiona in my lunch hour. When she saw them, all she said was, they are nice, which is about all one can expect from her, she is a proper what's it [Vera's original: 'whotsit']. Mary called to go shopping. Gave her a letter and some money to give Eileen Buckley, who is going to Lourdes in the morning; Father Hegarty is also going. Would love to be going with them – maybe next year, please God. Left Mary home after shopping, went in to see June. She is still not very well, and was all the time complaining about a pain in her thumb which keeps her awake at night. Left there at 8.45. When we got home, I discovered I had left my purse in June's. In the meanwhile, Mary had rung Bernie to tell him she would take it down to me tomorrow, but as I had quite a lot of money in it and I didn't want to give her the responsibility of it, there was nothing for it but to go back to June's; the two girls came with me.

Friday 17ᵗʰ June

No school for Terri today, so she went into Leena's early to help in the shop. Doris's designer asked me to do a try-out for a bridesmaid's dress she is making for a friend, I did it during my lunch hour. She gave me a box of Cadbury's Roses; I was really annoyed with her, told her I didn't need payment for doing a turn. Bought another skirt from Harry (one of the bosses) for June's sister, he said he'll have some autumn ones for sale in a couple of weeks. Had my friend Mary Mac to dinner this evening. She watered the rose trees and the rest of the plants in the back garden. I planted some silver leaf last year and now it seems to be taking over, silver leaf everywhere. Jack (Mary's husband) gave me a tree for the front garden last year, it is really beautiful, now covered in white flowers, everybody passing remarks on it. When Jack came later on tonight he brought me two more plants – one is called, the Mother of Thousands, it has a very dainty, white flower. The other one I can't remember the name of, it has a lovely, pink flower and the leaves look like wax. Dan came over at nine o'clock to case in the pipes in the bathroom, said my tiling was very good. Told me he's having a lot of trouble letting his rooms over the shop. Said when he was going he'll come over in a week's time to do another bit of work, really getting this house done by degrees. Mary and Jack left at 11.30.

Saturday 18th June

Ciarán was very upset this morning, said he needs a job as he owes money for dinners he had in school last week – anybody listening to him would think I starved him. He'd like to have school dinners every day, other kids try to avoid them but he has to be different. Asked him did they serve Cornflakes (as that is mostly what he lives on), he said no, chips and sausages – sounds very exciting. However, it's agreed he can have school dinners until he gets tired of them. Went to Walthamstow market, spent £15.00 on material for the girls. Will give it a miss for a while, I have enough cloth now to keep me busy for a few weeks. Went to Edmonton Green, and in spite of all my good intentions bought some more material there. I've decided not to go out next Saturday because I'm sure to come back with more material. Took the sheets over to Mary. Dick Johnson was there drinking coffee, so I had a cup too and a piece of cake. With Father Hegarty being away, Mary was not very busy, so I stayed chatting until two o'clock. Went home and did some cutting out until it was time to collect Terri. Had dinner ready just before Fiona came in from work, foot-sore and weary, in spite of which she loves her job. She heard today they take in a thousand pounds on Saturdays. Today she wore a red, V-necked T-shirt and jacket to match, which I made one day in work last week; she said one of the customers told her they looked very nice on her.

Sunday 19th June

A really beautiful morning, even at seven o'clock really warm. Everybody up early due to the fact they all went to bed early last night. Father

Roderick was very annoyed at Mass this morning, he didn't even give a sermon. A child at the back of the church never once stopped shouting and carrying on, it was really disgusting, I don't know how her parents sat through it all. Ciarán asked me yesterday, what would I do if he dyed his hair, I told him I give him the hiding of his life. He said I was old-fashioned, that John O'Brien's mother was letting him dye his hair. I went back to the church after the 9.30 Mass to do the bingo, as Charlie Dougan is in Lourdes. I saw Judy there and asked her was Mary O'Brien going queer, letting her young lad dye his hair. She roared laughing and said Mary's in Lourdes and she'll kill him when she comes back. It was with great pleasure I told Ciarán when I got back. So we mothers are not very popular at the moment. Fiona lay in the garden all day sunbathing. Don't think she'll get much sleep tonight, her skin looks very sore, but you can't tell her anything, she knows it all. She's gone to bed smothered in cream. Terri lay out for a while and turned quite red but she said it did her spots good. Don't know if it did Bernie any good, but he lay out in it all afternoon while I had my afternoon nap.

Monday 20th June

Horrible Monday morning. We all slept late – that is, except Bernie, who never fails to wake at his usual time due to the fact he always goes to bed early. The usual mad rush for Ciarán and myself. Terri didn't have to go to school (no exams today) and Fiona couldn't go, her sunburn was so sore. Didn't waste much sympathy on her because everybody told her not to lie in the sun too long. Couldn't believe it was so cold this morning after yesterday's heatwave, however the sun came out later in the day and by the afternoon it was really a scorcher. Hadn't a lot of work to do today, my designer went to see some buyers. At 2.30, Harry (one of our bosses) asked me would I stay on a bit late and make a skirt for Lizzie (Doris's designer) which was needed urgently. Finished by 3.30 and was home by 3.45. The girls had the house all nice and tidy, Terri had even mowed the lawn. Got dinner ready. Bernie wasn't home until 5.20, he's off at 4.30 on Mondays but he doesn't believe in rushing. After dinner, did some more tiling in the bathroom, it's taking ages to do. It's having to cut the tiles for awkward places that takes up so much time. Bernie was his usual unhelpful self. To make matters worse, I have a sore thumb; I cut it with a tile last week and it doesn't seem to be getting better.

Tuesday 21st June

Another quite cold morning, but like yesterday it turned out very warm in the afternoon. Didn't do a lot in work, but made three T-shirts for the girls in my lunch hour, which is the busiest time of the day. Doris can't get over how fast I can do things – whatever I bring in to do, I always get finished, pressed and all ready to wear. Terri had to go to school today for two-and-a-half hours, she was home by 12.30. She did a bit of shopping for me, which saves me from stopping off on my way home from work. The girls and myself had our dinner early, as Bernie was working until 5.30. Ciarán didn't arrive home from school until 6.30. He had two hours' detention for not handing in an essay he got for homework, he was very indignant because he hadn't been given 24 hours' notice for the detention. He was twice as indignant when I wouldn't allow him out for not doing his homework. He said he forgot, so hopefully being confined to his bedroom will help to remind him. Did another bit of tiling after dinner. Getting cheesed off with it, it's so tedious cutting tiles for around pipes. Dan had cased in a pipe; when I started tiling over it, discovered he had written on it, 'Vera, don't put large nail through this or you might burst the pipe and it will cost you a lot of money to have it fixed!' Wouldn't mind what he wrote if only he'd finish the work.

Wednesday 22nd June

When I went into work this morning Harry said he wanted to have a few words with me later on. I went on up to the design room and discovered nobody was in, Jo and Doris are always in before me. Just when I was wondering what was wrong, Harry came in and said, "We let Jo go last night". He said, "she wasn't very good". All I could think of saying to him was, "Oh, I feel so sorry for her", which I did because they gave her no hint that her work wasn't alright – on the contrary, they gave her to understand she had a free hand there. He said a few more words, and I said, "What you're trying to say is, you don't need me now?" "Oh no," he said, "we would like you to work for Lizzie (Doris's designer) until we get another designer, we are interviewing one on Friday". Told him that was alright. Later on, when Lizzie came in, she said she didn't know if she could keep two sample machinists going. I told her not to worry – whenever she hadn't enough work just to tell me and I'd take a day or two off; she went and told Harry. He came up later on and said thanks very much Vera, but when Lizzie has no work for you, would you mind doing production samples until we get the new designer? Told him I didn't mind. So for my day just made one skirt for Lizzie, and at 2.15 Harry brought me up four production samples. The girl who usually does them is going on holiday next week. Didn't feel quite so happy in work today. A very bad car crash on our road tonight – nobody hurt, thank God, but both cars very badly damaged, one of them brand new.

Thursday 23rd June

Gave Ciarán such a telling-off before he went to school this morning he annoyed me so much, he is getting so cheeky. He doesn't seem to care how late he is for school, I don't know if this is part of his growing up – if it is, I don't like it. Worked on the production samples today, didn't like doing them one bit, much prefer to do original samples. Lizzie went out with Harry at 10.30 to see a buyer with Jo's range. While they were out, Doris and myself discussed religion, Doris is a Mormon. When Lizzie came back at two o'clock she told us that the buyer didn't like Jo's range at all, said it was too out-dated, so she has cost the firm a lot of money and all for nothing, not even an order on one garment. Terri's first day of her holidays and she was asked to go into Geary's, so she had to be up early as usual – she really needs a rest, and to make matters worse Leena came in tonight and asked her would she go into the shop at 6.30 tomorrow morning. When Leena had gone, Fiona said she would go in until 7.45 so that Terri needn't get up so early. Fiona's birthday today, she got some nice presents. Terri bought her a watch, from Leena diamond earrings and a T-shirt; Mary gave her a fiver. One of her school friends gave her a £5.00 voucher for Woolworths, another friend gave her three lovely china figurines of ladies, Bernie and myself gave her money, and Ciarán, true to form, gave her nothing. He never has any money, spends it all on himself. Saw June, she is not very well at all, her breathing is very bad, God help her.

Friday 24th June

Was two minutes late for work this morning. Lizzie asked me to cut out a sample skirt and make it up; when I had it finished, Harry gave me some more production samples to do. During my lunch hour, made a jacket for Fiona. Jo came in to get her wages and collect some things she had left behind, said to her it must have been a shock to be told to go so suddenly, she said yes it was, especially as Harry had told her earlier in the week that her range was very good. There were two phone calls today from college leavers looking for jobs as trainee designers, so they'll have no trouble replacing Jo. Harry's father came in today, asked me how I was getting on, he seems a very pleasant person. Fiona was delighted with the jacket when she saw it, she wants something new to wear every time she goes to work. She gets paid a month's wages plus commission tomorrow – said she is going to give me half of whatever she gets, but wants a lot of clothes made. Typical of Fiona, throwing a sprat to catch a salmon. Bernie was late getting home this evening, he's off at 3.30 on Fridays but he didn't come in until 4.45. He said things are getting worse in his firm. They want to employ the workers on a hire-and-fire basis and they have given them three months' notice, [and] that they have drawn up new contracts which all the workers must sign before September. The workers have responded by putting a ban on overtime, so Bernie won't be working tomorrow. Things are really getting worse here. Thatcher really meant it when she said she wants to go back to Victorian values.

Saturday 25th June

Didn't go to Walthamstow this morning, thought I'd do a bit of tiling. Took the sheets over to Mary, then went to Marks, and then up to Edmonton Green, where I met a young girl I used to work with, she used to cut out the samples for Laura. The firm sent her to college one day a week to learn designing, but all she was interested in was machining. She often asked me to show her how to do things during our lunch hour. She even, with a little bit of help from me, made her sister's wedding dress. It was lovely seeing her after such a long time, we stood chatting for half an hour or more. She's still mad about machining (she has an office job now) and makes all her own clothes, but she said I'm going to make her wedding dress for her. Collected my bread on the way home, and told Terri I wouldn't call for her in the evening as I'd be too busy tiling. Set to work when I got home, Bernie as usual watching the racing on telly. Stopped at five o'clock to get the dinner ready. Ciarán came in wanting his dinner in a hurry as he was going out again. Told him to have a bath and wash his hair first, which he did. Said his friends were calling for him. Nearly had a stroke when I saw the friends. Told Bernie to go out and see them and not to let Ciarán out with them. When Bernie saw them he was furious. I didn't get a good look at them, but he said one of them had a long beard and a mop of wild-looking hair and looked about 24 years old. There was a terrible scene, Ciarán cried for the night. When Bernie had gone to bed, he told me they were a pop group and he (Ciarán) was the singer, but he sang his swan song tonight.

Sunday 26th June

A beautiful morning, got to church just as Mass was starting, so Ciarán couldn't serve – luckily Adam and Henry were there. A black priest said Mass, nobody could understand one word he said, he's here on holiday from South Africa. There were two coach-loads of people at the church going to Walsingham. After Mass, myself and the girls went down to Wickes to buy some more tiles – 75 in a box for £11.99, much cheaper than Tesco. Came back, had breakfast, which Fiona cooked. She's in great form since she got paid yesterday, £52.00 for four Saturdays. She gave me £25.00 and bought a very nice, leather handbag in the shop where she works, they have a sale on. The handbag was £19.00 reduced to £10.00, and with staff discount she got it for a fiver. She also bought a nice purse. You'd think she had won the Pools she was so excited with the money she has. Bought bars of chocolate for everybody and wanted Terri to go to Queensway market this morning, but Terri wouldn't go. Did a bit of tiling with Bernie's help till it was time to get dinner ready. After dinner, went for my usual nap, and later, while still in my nightie, did some more tiling again with Bernie's help. The bathroom is really beginning to look nice, everybody is very pleased with it. Hopefully it will be finished this week. Felt sorry for Ciarán stuck in all day, he is his own worst enemy.

Monday 27th June

Everybody annoyed this morning, that is everybody except Ciarán, because we had no hot water – don't know what's gone wrong with the water system. Fiona went into Leena's to wash her hair before going off to school. As Terri hasn't to go to school, she went in to help Leena in the shop. Hadn't a very cheerful day in work. Lizzie and Doris seem to be suffering from Monday morning blues; myself feeling very tired after my busy weekend. Harry asked me to make a production sample. When it came to putting the waistband on, the skirt was 28.5 inches and the waistband only 26 inches. Told Lizzie who had cut the pattern, she said take some more in on the pleat and I'll alter the pattern later. Had that been Laura she would have altered that pattern immediately. Tried to phone Dan at the shop when I came home from work to tell him about the water, but could get no answer. Later on, Colette told me his phone is out of order, she said she'd tell him. He called over at ten o'clock but he didn't know what had gone wrong. Said it could be any number of things and he'd come over tomorrow and have a look at it, praying it won't be a big job. Ciarán in his room all evening, am really worried about him. He used to be so good, don't know what to make of him, he has changed so much.

Tuesday 28th June

All moans and groans again this morning from the girls because of no hot water, good thing it's not winter or we'd all have something to moan about as we'd have no heating either. Lizzie seemed in very bad humour today. She was quite rude to Doris three times – felt really embarrassed listening to her, don't know how Doris kept her patience. During lunch hour, made a skirt for Terri and helped Doris cut a pattern for a dress she's making for a friend. When I came home from work, found Dan had fixed the water; he had also taken the radiator off the wall in the bathroom so that I could tile behind it. So as soon as I had my dinner, I got cracking on it. Had quite a bit done before Bernie came home from work. When he had his dinner, he came up to help me, but by that time I felt really too tired to do any more, but he seemed so anxious to help that I soldiered on. Sat down once and had trouble getting up again, every bone in my body aching from getting up and down the ladder. Mary rang to tell me June is very bad and is going into hospital tomorrow, was glad to hear that because she certainly wouldn't get better at home – she doesn't even eat the right food for a diabetic. Dan called over at 10.30 just as we were all getting ready to go to bed, he said the reason we had no hot water was, there was air in the pipes. Thought he'd just put the radiator back in the bathroom, but he said he'd do it some other time.

Wednesday 29th June

Lizzie wasn't in work today, she phoned in to say she wasn't well. Doris said she couldn't understand her rudeness to her yesterday, that she has never spoken like that to her before and she thinks she wants her to leave because I know so much more than she (Doris) does about the work. She was so upset, she said she's thinking of leaving. I told her if she leaves, I'll leave too, and perhaps it was because Lizzie wasn't feeling well she was rude to her, although I don't think there is any excuse for rudeness. However, in spite of all that we had quite a nice day, until Harry came in at 2.30 and asked me would I stay a bit late and make a sample which was needed in a hurry. Dropped everything and started on it, [but] when it came to putting on the waistband discovered, like the one I made on Monday, it was 2.5 inches too big – Lizzie hadn't altered the pattern. When Harry heard about it he was very upset, because they had cut 1,000 skirts to that pattern and they are all made up in bundles ready to go out to other factories to be made up. Had to leave at 3.30 because we were all going to six o'clock Mass in St. Edmunds. Bernie was working until 5.30, but he got a lift up to the church and had his dinner when we got home. Ciarán had been to Mass in school, so had told him he could go over to Adam's rather than leave him in the house on his own. Later on, went over to

Judy's to collect him, only to be told he wasn't there; had a cup of tea with Judy, whom I haven't seen for a while, we swapped stories about our erring sons. Got home to discover Ciarán had been in a friend's house up the road.

Thursday 30th June

Lizzie was in work today and seemed in much better form, very glad for Doris's sake. She interviewed a couple of designers for the children's wear section, but she wasn't impressed by them. Later on, she said to me, I think you could do that job. Told her I probably could, but wasn't keen to do so. When Harry spoke to her about the skirts which were coming up too big, she said she had cut two patterns for them and they had used the wrong one, so they will have to put a note with each bundle telling them to take more in on each pleat – I'm sure the production workers are going to be very annoyed with that. Just before lunch hour, Harry came in again to wish us a happy weekend as he won't be in tomorrow, he was going into hospital this evening to have four wisdom teeth out. He has beautiful teeth, but his dentist thinks he'd be better off without those four, which haven't even come through yet. When I was leaving work, Lizzie came out after me and said she wanted to talk to me about Doris, that she didn't think she could cope with her work and what did I think. I told her I thought Doris was a very good sample machinist. Got the impression had I said otherwise she would have sacked her. So Doris was right when she said Lizzie wanted her to leave. Went home feeling very upset, don't think I'm going to feel as happy in my job as I was. When I left Mary home tonight after shopping, she phoned June in hospital to know how she was. She is in a private area because she is a member of BUPA and it will cost them £800.00 per week for her stay there. She is starving with hunger because the food is so bad, she can't eat it. She got her tea this evening in a plastic cup – she is really furious and unhappy there, God help her.

July 1983

A HEATWAVE

Friday 1st July

Very busy in work this morning finishing off 15 production samples. Another designer came for an interview, said she lives just round the corner, she seems a nice, cheerful sort of person. At the moment could do with some cheering up, very upset over Ciarán. Had a letter from his school about the number of lates he's had, and it seems he had detention one evening and walked out before he had finished it. I rang the school, but the head master was not there. Mary Mac came to dinner, and while getting it ready [I] had a phone call from Father Sullivan. He said he had a talk with Ciarán today, and Ciarán told him he wasn't called early enough in the mornings to get to school on time. Told him that wasn't true and that I was very worried about the company Ciarán is keeping. I asked him about this boy called David, he [Fr Sullivan] said he didn't think he was a bad child but he had got into bad company. Told him I was thinking of going up to see David's mother; said he thought that was a very good idea. So myself, Mary Mac and Fiona went to see David's mother after dinner. She was out, but spoke to his father, who is a very nice man. Told him I didn't like the people his son had introduced my son to. He said he didn't know them, and [we] made David take us to one of them. Had a few words with him, told him to keep away from Ciarán. On the way back, met David's mother, who is also a very nice person; was shocked when she told me she thought (before she met me) that Ciarán came from a dreadful family because of the way he dressed.

Saturday 2nd July

Ciarán was very upset this morning, said since I wouldn't let him be with David he had no friends. Adam Kelly had gone somewhere with John O'Brien, so took him out and bought some new clothes for him. Got a very nice blazer for school in Marks, £17.00 – would cost £30.00 in Keevans, two Fred Perry T-shirts and a pair of trousers, the lot cost over £40.00 – that cheered him up a bit. Then took him over to Mary, where we met the South African priest who's staying there for a couple of weeks – he had just come back from Ireland. You'd need an interpreter to understand what he was saying. He is trying to raise some funds for his parish in South Africa. Took Mary up to Edmonton Green to do some shopping, said I'd leave her home; Ciarán didn't want to come so left him home first. When we got to June's, her two sisters and their husbands were there, they had just come back from the hospital after seeing June. Said there's a slight improvement in her, although her feet are still very swollen and she's not eating, but at least she's in the best place, she'd never have got better at home. Was late getting home, got caught up in a carnival in Wood Green. Was too late to collect Terri;

luckily I had got my bread earlier or she'd have had to carry it all home. After dinner, washed my hair and was in bed by 9.30.

Sunday 3rd July

The girls didn't come to eight o'clock Mass this morning as they were going to Aylesford. Ciarán was also going, but he had to serve Mass first. The coach was going from the church at nine o'clock, so after Mass just had time to rush back for the girls and take them to the coach. They had got all the grub ready and were ready to go. After breakfast, Bernie and myself had a quick tidy round in the sitting room as Mary had stayed the night and had slept on the bed settee there; she also stayed to dinner. We had a lovely, peaceful day. I went up for my usual nap. Mary brought me up my tea, after which I had my bath. Did some cutting out before the children came back home. The girls came in first, said they had a marvellous day. Just when I was about to send Bernie out to see what was keeping Ciarán, heard him coming downstairs (nobody had heard him coming in). He was dressed in his school clothes; when I asked him where were the clothes he went out in, he said they were in the laundry room. When I saw them I nearly went mad. They were soaking wet – shoes and jeans and underpants and T-shirt. Adam had thrown bottles of water over him in Aylesford. I was so furious, I jumped in the car and took them over to show Judy. She called Adam and gave out to him. He gave her such abuse, I nearly died. If Ciarán spoke to me like that I'd kill him. Adam is a real pup.

Monday 4th July

Went to see Ciarán's head master this morning, meant to get there by 8.30 but got lost on the way, as usual – didn't get there till nine o'clock. However, chatted to Mr. Peterson for nearly an hour. He said they were taking a very serious view of the fact that Ciarán was very resentful that he had got two hours' detention while other boys only ever got one hour. He said in that case he should have come and told him and he would have sorted it out. Told him I had seen David's parents on Friday night. Didn't get to work till 10.40. Nearly died with the heat there, the temperature must have been up in the eighties today. When Ciarán came home from school he said Mr. Peterson had spoken to him, also Father Sullivan. He seemed much happier than he's been for a long time, thank God. He said he's not going to be a punk anymore, and Mr. Peterson said he should look for a paper round, it would give him an interest. He didn't even ask to go out this evening, he's gone off Adam after yesterday. He's a lonely child, he hasn't got a decent friend. He said he's going to turn over a new leaf and keep himself very clean – that I'll have to see to believe, he's allergic to soap and water.

Tuesday 5th July

Ciarán was up bright and early for school this morning, hope he can keep it up. Another scorching hot day, very hard having to work in it. Made a nice sample jacket in work, then did a bit of cutting out for Lizzie. After work, went to Hackney to get a skirt pleated for Fiona, she is clothes mad. All she talks about all week is what she'll wear on Saturday in her new job. Phoned Mary when I came home, she'd been to see June last night, said she seems a bit better and the swelling in her feet was caused by water. After dinner, went up to do some tiling; haven't done any for a few days, it's been much too warm for that sort of work. Bernie came up to help, but after a few minutes threw a tantrum and went downstairs and sat watching telly for the night. I was furious – everybody was sitting down while I was killing myself, I gave them all a piece of my mind. Leena's husband asked Ciarán to do a sign for the shop, he is great at sign writing. Later on, he had a headache and went to bed early. When I went up later to go to bed he called me into his room and said he had good news and bad news. The good news was he came third in science, he beat eight boys in the top band (he's in the middle band). The bad news was he came last in maths. He seems to have a mental block where maths is concerned, will have to get him a tutor.

Wednesday 6th July

Harry went today to have the stitches taken out of his gums, he hasn't been able to eat since he had his wisdom teeth out on Friday. Didn't have a very happy time in work today. Got a skirt to make with a pleated waistband; made loads of them when I was working for Laura in crêpe-de-sheen, but this one was in a heavy crêpe – wouldn't believe how different it was to make. The skirt itself was pretty straightforward, all the trouble was with the waistband. Had nearly finished pleating one when I realised it was too small, so Lizzie had to cut me a new one. It took me almost four hours to make, usually make four skirts in that length of time. In production, the waistbands will be processed so the machinists won't have any problems. During lunch hour, started on a denim jacket for Ciarán. Took it home to fit on him this evening, he's very pleased with it and it really suits him. There's a lot of work on it with all the double stitching and fancy work on the pockets, but should finish it tomorrow, please God. When I came home from work Terri handed me a parcel. When I opened it, it was a box of my favourite chocolates, Black Magic. There was a card with it, with 'Sorry' written on the front. When I opened it, written inside was, 'Dear Mummy, Sorry for upsetting you, from Ciarán, Fiona, Terri and Dad'. That was Terri being her usual kind self, the other three knew nothing about it. Another beautiful day. At 4.30 Terri hung out washing in the garden, just then I saw Minnie (the cat) flying like a mad thing out of our garden and through all the other gardens. About 20 minutes later we had a most dreadful thunderstorm, the lightning was really frightening. Didn't stop till half an hour later, heard on the telly the lightning killed a man.

Thursday 7th July

Was stopped by the police this morning on my way to work, they were taking a census of all the cars that go down Northumberland Park and Park View Road. I was asked where I lived and where I was going, I heard it was something to do with the new road they are going to build, and which will run from Angel Road straight up to the North of England. Got a very strong smell of petrol in my car; was a bit nervous driving it, kept all the windows down. Didn't get Ciarán's jacket finished. Had to do two samples which were wanted in a hurry, worked part of my lunch hour. Killed with the heat again today. Leena's husband had an accident with his car. He took the cap off the radiator to put water in it and the boiling water inside burst out, scalding his chest, arms and face. He was taken to hospital and returned swaddled in bandages. He'll be off work for two weeks. Leena was worried about the morning papers for the customers which he collects every morning at six o'clock. I offered to go for them, but he said he thinks he'll be well enough to get them. So Terri stayed to help Leena tonight, while Mary, Fiona and myself went shopping, after which we set off to visit June in hospital. The car was really struggling up Hornsey Hill when all of a sudden it stopped dead – realised it had run out of petrol. We left it and went to a garage a few hundred yards away. There were five Greek lads there who were more interested in Fiona than my car, one of them said I had a beautiful daughter; I told them I had a nicer one at home. Was trying to get the petrol I had bought into my car when a police car came along. Two policemen got out and did it for me. Didn't get to the hospital until 8.30.

Friday 8th July

Thought it safer not to use the car because of the petrol leakage. Phoned Murphy (the mechanic), [who] said it was dangerous to drive it, and a new petrol tank is expensive, and he couldn't do it until Monday. Got the bus to work. Very hot and bothered, the heat is dreadful. Did a few production samples and finished Ciarán's denim jacket at lunch hour. Also made a loose dress for myself, hope it will keep me cooler in this heat. Sweated buckets while getting dinner ready while everybody else was relaxing and sipping lemonade. Vowed I'm not going to cook any more dinners while this heat lasts – from now on we are going to live on salads except on Sundays. This evening, Leena's husband said he'd take a look at the car. Said he didn't think the petrol tank was leaking, thought it could be something else. He took a look under the bonnet and discovered the petrol tube was split, asked me for a scissors, cut the split piece off and connected it back on. It all took about three minutes, I was delighted. Didn't know what I was going to do without it tomorrow, wouldn't have been able to go out. After dinner, did some tiling while Bernie did some grouting. Realised I wasn't going to have enough tiles to finish the bathroom, so Ciarán and myself went down to Wickes to get some more. While there, asked if they had any vacancies for boys on Saturdays or Sundays, but was told they only employed 16-year-olds, Ciarán was very disappointed. When we got home, didn't feel like doing any more tiling, so cut out a pattern instead. Had supper and watched a film on telly.

Saturday 9th July

Was delighted to have a letter from Jenny this morning, she is very pleased with her new job and has twice as much wages as she had in the old job, so it seems we both did better by leaving. Ciarán had to go to the upper school this morning to keep the cricket score in a match they were playing, it was part of his detention for walking out on the other detention he was given. I went to Walthamstow market for a change. Bought some material for myself, three lovely pieces which will make a dress and jacket, £1.30 each. Went over to see Mary before going home. Had a chat with Father Roderick, then Dick Johnson came in for his usual cup of coffee. Mary told me June's sister, Rose, and her husband are up for the weekend. They are hoping June will be let out of hospital on Monday, and they will take her back to Sussex with them for a couple of weeks. They did tests on June on Friday and discovered she has a hernia in her chest for which there is no cure. Told her she will have to eat every two hours and she mustn't talk while eating, which will be very hard on June. Bernie wanted us all to go to the Dogs [Walthamstow Dog Racing Stadium] tonight, but after being on my feet all day I didn't feel like going, so he took Ciarán and John O'Brien with him. The girls and myself were watching telly when James (Dan's son) called with the dog.

The poor thing was dying of thirst; gave him a dish of water which he lapped up with gusto. Mary gave me a load of meat for him, I'm sure he thinks it's his birthday.

Sunday 10ᵗʰ July

Quite cool and fresh this morning, really nice after all the heat. Father Roderick said the eight o'clock Mass. Afterwards, had a chat with him about the Stations-of-the-Cross which some man out of the parish is painting. It has taken weeks to do one. It is very well done – brown around the outside, and the figures were done in different colours, but I preferred them as they were. Asked Father Roderick what he thought, he said he didn't like them either way. Ciarán went up Petticoat Lane with John O'Brien, who bought a pair of fluorescent pink socks; hope Ciarán doesn't want to start wearing them too. Bob, our Jamaican neighbour two doors away, did a service on my car today. Gave Bernie £20.00 to give him, but he wouldn't take anything for doing it – will have to buy him something. Everybody set to work today to put some shape on this house; we seem to be always putting some shape on it but it still looks as if a bomb has hit it. After my bath tonight, did some cutting out – a dress for Mary to make before she goes to Rome on Saturday, a skirt for a lady who works in Geary's – she's also going on holiday on Saturday – and a dress for Fiona, who is going to Brighton on Thursday with the school. Couldn't believe after such a cool start to the day we finished up having the warmest day yet since the heatwave started. Dan called over tonight, said he'd be over tomorrow to do some work, told him that had a familiar ring. Not going to hold my breath – Dan's promises are like pie crust, made to be broken.

Monday 11th July

Thought I was going to be on my own in work today, Doris didn't come in until 11.30, she'd been in the bank about her account. Lizzie came in at 12.30, she'd been in the West End to see some cloth rep. A terrible effort to work today, the heat was really oppressive, 86 degrees. Sweated buckets, and according to the forecast it's to reach the nineties tomorrow, not looking forward to it. Would be lovely if we didn't have to work. Nearly hung out the flags when I got home, Dan was there finishing off some of the jobs he had left undone. He sat down when I came in, and after having a chat, left saying he'd be back tomorrow. Fiona didn't go to school today, she couldn't sleep all night with her head itching. When I looked at it this morning she had a rash all over her scalp. Told her to go round to the doctor, which she did. She got some Betnovate scalp liniment, said she has dermatitis, hope it gets rid of it. Only have a few more tiles to put up in the bathroom. Intended finishing it tonight, but I was so exhausted with the heat couldn't be bothered. To my surprise, Bernie went up and did some grouting while I cut out a couple of dresses for myself. Terri was in Leena's since seven o'clock this morning helping in the shop. Leena's husband was in such pain last night from his burns that he had to get out of bed at one o'clock in the morning and go to the hospital. After waiting there one-and-a-half hours they gave him some sleeping tablets.

Tuesday 12th July

Didn't sleep very well last night because of the heat, so didn't feel exactly on top of the world this morning. Really an effort to get ready for work, but was quite pleased when I did get in to find there was a nice breeze coming through the window where I sit, so I didn't feel as uncomfortable as I did yesterday. It's funny, Doris felt hotter today than yesterday. She had Harry put a curtain on her window to keep out the sun. Said she wished she was back in Jamaica – although the temperature is a lot higher, it is more shaded and not as oppressive. Made a dress for Fiona during my lunch hour – plain, white cotton, with a very full skirt, no sleeves and a low, round neck back and front, so she's all set for her trip to Brighton on Thursday. I got strict orders not to forget to get her loads of grub to take with her. Terri spent her day in Leena's as usual, she looks as if she'd need to sit in the sun for a while to get a bit of colour in her face. Cut Ciarán's hair tonight, it has got quite thick since he had the skinhead. Forced myself to do some tiling tonight, have to put up about seven more and that will be it, all done, thank God. Bernie as usual sat on the toilet watching me. Terri mowed the lawn and did some weeding, she's the only one who bothers about the garden. Ciarán went over to John O'Brien's to play tennis.

Wednesday 13th July

Was on my way to work this morning, about 200 yards from my firm, when all of a sudden my car stopped and refused to go any further, it had run out of petrol right at a bus stop. Got out and asked Harry had he a can I could put petrol in, but he hadn't – told him what had happened. He said I should have put a note on it, otherwise the police may take it to the pound. Ran back to the car, wrote out a note saying I had run out of petrol and was gone to get some. Luckily the nearest garage wasn't too far away, but when I got there they had no cans to put it in. Finished up having to pay £5.75 for a proper petrol can and £2.00 to fill it up. Must say the can is very handy, it has a tube on it which goes right into the fuel tank. Finally got in to work exhausted from the effort but mostly from the heat, which is really beginning to get to me, it was 92 degrees again today. Mary came over this evening – made her a dress in my lunch hour, she was very pleased with it. She left at about 7.30. Didn't drive her home, couldn't face getting into the car, it's just like getting into an oven. Stuck up a few more tiles, my heart wasn't in it, much too warm for work, feel I'm growing old doing this bathroom. Was so tired decided to go to bed early. Was in bed by 10.30 when Dan came over; had to get up to talk to him, said a few prayers for him.

Thursday 14th July

Got some petrol on my way to work this morning – six gallons cost me £11.03, barring any leaks should last me a fortnight. The design room was like a Turkish bath. Bert, one of the bosses, came in and said he'd get a fan at the weekend; probably be snowing on Monday. Made a skirt during my lunch hour for Peggy, a lady Terri works with in Geary's. Told Terri if she asks how much she owes me, to tell her two small fresh-cream cakes, which she duly arrived back with. Fiona went to Brighton today with the school. She was up at 5.30 washing her hair and dolling herself up. She brought enough food to feed the five thousand, think she was going to feed all on the coach. Mary came to go shopping, and also to borrow a case for Rome. The best one we have has two zips round it but no lock. Found a padlock which held both zips together, hope she doesn't lose the key. Terri as usual came shopping to Tesco with us. They had a sale in their Home & Ware department. Was really mad when I saw the petrol can I had paid £5.75 yesterday for £3.00, so these garages really rub it in. Went in to see June, who's home from hospital – her sister didn't take her to Sussex after all, she said she lives miles from a doctor, and if June went into a coma she could die while waiting for a doctor, so she is staying till Mary comes back from Rome. June looks a lot better, but won't do what the doctors told her. Her sister is really annoyed with her.

Friday 15th July

Another sizzling hot day, up in the nineties again, but when I got to work there was a lovely cool breeze coming through my window where I sit, but had to close it when I started to make a skirt out of fine material, it was blowing everything all over the place. Made a dress for myself in my lunch hour. When I got into the car after work the steering wheel was so hot it burned my hand, will have to get a cover for it tomorrow. When I got home I felt really flattened with the heat. Terri was sitting watching a film on telly with Leena's little girl. Sat down with them, hadn't the energy to get the dinner ready. It was a film called 'On the Beat' with Norman Wisdom. It was very funny, really enjoyed it. Had dinner ready by the time Bernie came in. He went straight upstairs and changed into his shorts before having it, he's anyone's fancy in them. Did a few more tiles tonight. Had a phone call from my cousin, Nan Kavanagh, she is coming over on the 29th of the month. Mary came to stay the night, she's off to Rome in the morning for a week. We were having our supper at 9.30 (me in my nightie) when there was a ring at the door. Terri answered it. Heard her saying, "Hello Father" – realised it was Father Hegarty. Shouted to him not to come out to the kitchen. Quickly got a dressing gown on. Sure he must have thought us a right lot here, me in my nightie and Bernie in his shorts.

Saturday 16th July

Oh God, what a really horrible, stinking day I've had. It started off with Mary and her trip to Rome. She left here at 8.50, said they were starting out at ten o'clock sharp from the church for Gatwick airport; five of them were going, one of the women's daughters was driving them all to the airport. At 9.30, discovered she had left her keys here, including the key of her case. Phoned the chapel house to tell her I would take it over to her. Got into the car, had only gone a few yards up the road when I realised I was losing petrol fast. Had a look under the bonnet and discovered the petrol tube was broken. Left the car and ran back to get Ciarán to take the keys to Mary. Leena's husband fixed the car and I went over to the chapel house at 10.15. Was amazed to see Mary still there – it seemed nobody had turned up. Finished up collecting Hanna Mulligan and another lady and bringing them to the church. In the end, the lady whose daughter was taking them to Gatwick didn't arrive till 11.15. When I got to Marks to get some chicken portions for dinner, they were all sold out. Took Ciarán up to Dan's new shop, which he opened today – that's when my troubles really started. When I got into my car (which I had parked outside the Town Hall) and started her up, drove a few yards when the smell of petrol nearly killed us. Got out and discovered the petrol tube broken right off, couldn't even find it. Went back to Dan. Colette drove me round trying to find a shop that sold them, finally found one. Came back, connected it up, started up the car but not a gig out of it, no petrol. Back into Colette's car to look for a garage, finally found one which was open, filled up my new petrol can, back to the car, but even with petrol it wouldn't start. Tried everything, to no avail. Colette drove me home, by now it was seven o'clock. Got dinner ready. Got Bob to take a look at my car, who eventually discovered the cause of the trouble was, I had connected the tube wrong.

Sunday 17ᵗʰ July

A beautiful morning, not too warm. Saw Judy, Michael and the children at eight o'clock Mass. Thought since they were at early Mass they must be going out for the day, but when I spoke to Judy afterwards, she said no, they were out early because Michael was going down the marshes to get some plants from a friend who has an allotment there. We chatted so long, Michael and the children had gone, so gave her a lift home. Cut out some patterns after breakfast, Fiona thinks I've nothing else to do but make her clothes all the time. Bernie and myself aren't speaking. Told him off for leaving a beer bottle and glass on the new fire I paid £400.00 for. He's so unreasonable, he really gets on my nerves. I'm getting very, very sick of his tantrums, I'd want to take my words out and look at them before I say anything to him [one of Vera's characteristic expressions]. It's not as if he's too particular of what he says to me, but I'm expected to put up with that and say nothing. In spite of everything, had a nice afternoon nap – got up feeling very rested. Cut out some broderie anglaise tops, skirts and shorts for the girls. Leena called in to give Terri some money for helping her in the shop all the week. Terri would like to take her out to a film and supper, but I don't think her husband would let her go.

Monday 18ᵗʰ July

Woke this morning with a lovely breeze blowing in through the bedroom windows. Thought, thank God, fresh air at last – not that the air in any part of London is fresh, but it felt lovely after all the dreadful heat. Terri had to go to work in Geary's in the afternoon, one of the ladies is on holiday. She went in to help Leena in the shop this morning. Poor Leena isn't feeling well since somebody shot her in the back on Saturday night with an air pistol. She had taken Terri to an Indian festival and it happened when they were coming out of it. Thank God the pellet didn't go right through her, otherwise she would have had to have had an operation; as it was, she was three hours in hospital on Saturday night. Didn't do a lot in work today, Lizzie can't keep up with two sample machinists. They had no luck yet with their ad for a pattern-cutter/grader. Told Harry I'd take tomorrow off, but he said he had some things he wanted me to do. When I got home there were two letters for me – one was the phone bill, couldn't believe my eyes when I read the other one. It was an order to serve on a jury and a £400.00 fine if I hadn't got a very good excuse for not doing so. I'm always telling my children not to judge people, and here am I being asked to do exactly that – what do I tell my kids now? Laura and Ben called tonight, they were on their way to visit Ben's parents. They have a lovely new car, Katie was fast asleep in the back of it. They all looked lovely, very tanned. Laura is very excited about going to New York at the end of the month, said she hasn't a thing to wear. Told her I'd run up a few things for her if she was stuck.

Tuesday 19th July

Another nice, cool morning, thank God – the sun didn't come out until evening. Ideal weather for working in, not that I did a lot today. Harry gave me four production samples to do, Lizzie's having a hard time trying to keep Doris and myself going. When I got into my car after work, started her up; was backing out of the car park when I got a dreadful smell of petrol, got out to investigate and discovered my petrol tube had slipped off, lost a lot of petrol. Had to go into the factory, and asked the forelady if she had anything I could tie it up with. She gave me a little metal ring that holds the flex of the irons, it done the job grand. ['Grand' is an Irish catch-all for 'great, very well, sure, ideal' and so on]. This car is like a lethal weapon, I take my life in my hands every time I get into it. Called to Dan on my way home, bought a few bits and pieces from him. He said business is very slow; I suppose that is to be expected, it takes time for people to get to know he's there. Told me his dog is having an operation on Monday for a lump on his back. After dinner, tiled round the wash hand basin in the girls' bedroom. Didn't like the others I had put up, the new ones look really nice, they are a shade lighter than the wash hand basin. Got fifty tiles but hadn't enough to finish it, will have to get some more tomorrow. Bernie scraped the ceiling in the bathroom ready for painting, we are still not talking.

Wednesday 20th July

A very dull, cloudy morning but I am not complaining – it's cool, that's the main thing. Made a couple of samples today and a white, box-pleated skirt for Fiona in my lunch hour. Doris had a phone call from her daughter, she's having husband trouble. She said she was going to leave him and her two children, but Doris told her she couldn't leave the children; she's very upset over it. She [Doris] said if she [Doris] had money she'd tell her [daughter] to leave her husband and take the children with her. She [Doris's daughter] is a chemist and could get a job anywhere, but of course she can't work with two young children – we all have our problems. Went to Hackney on the way home to collect two skirts I had left to be pleated. Then I went on to Wickes to get the rest of the tiles for the girls' bedroom, which I finished after dinner. Leena came in while I was doing it, she said she thought tiling was a man's job, I told her so did I, but after she told us a few stories about how badly treated women are in India, I didn't mind so much doing a man's job in England. Ciarán went to Clacton today with the school, he didn't get home until near nine o'clock. Said he had a great time, they spent the day in Butlins. Said he helped another boy win £13.00 on the slot machines and then gave it all back again. Had a phone call from June tonight, she wants me to get her some shopping tomorrow evening, Ciarán wrote the list on the wall in the hall. Gave him a clout when I saw what he had written, for toilet paper he had bog wrap and for tissues he had snot rags, he thought he was funny, I didn't.

Thursday 21st July

Quite cool this morning, had to wear a cardigan. Harry gave me some production samples to do. He asked me did I really want to take holidays, told him I was hoping to have a fortnight in October when my children were back at school so that I could have a good rest. He then asked me could I not take them earlier. At the moment they are having trouble getting a pattern-cutter, which means it's hard for Lizzie to keep two sample machinists going. It will be alright in September because Doris is going to Jamaica for a month. Told him I had a problem about September, that I had been asked to do jury service; asked me to bring in the forms I had got and they would write a letter to the court asking for me to be excused. Not really fussy when I have my holidays as long as I have a bit of peace and can come and go as I please without having to be at somebody's beck and call. The two girls came shopping with me tonight, then onto June's. Her sister, Rose, is staying with her while Mary's in Rome. Her husband had come up today from Sussex where they live, he is staying until Sunday to take her home. She said she'll have a nervous breakdown with June – she expects to be waited on hand and foot, she is worn out with her. She has got her a home help who'll come in two mornings a week, I don't know what she'll do for the rest of the week while Mary's at work. I think June is a very sick woman, much worse than her sister realises. Bernie put some Sandtex on the bathroom ceiling, said it needed another coat.

Friday 22nd July

Quite warm this morning, didn't need a cardigan. Couldn't get into the car park, there was a dustbin cart blocking the entrance, had to park on the road. Lizzie wasn't in today, she left yesterday at one o'clock to go to Bristol, she is matron of honour at a friend's wedding on Saturday, so Doris and myself were on our own. I made a sample which Bert had cut out. Doris started on a jacket which a freelance pattern-cutter had done the pattern for; it was so bad Harry told her not to finish it, I'd have done the pattern better myself. Made a broderie anglaise top for Fiona in my lunch hour. Just when I finished it, had a dreadful pain in my stomach; thought I was going to pass out, but thank God after a while I felt alright. When I left work, went up to Herodes, couldn't believe it when I heard they were closing down; feel very sad about it, loved going to their sales, always bought curtain material there. Geary's, where Terri works, is also closing down, along with all the other shops on that block, and Bruce Grove is going to finish up a ghost town. Marks and Spencer are gone also, together with the Co-op and several other shops. Woolworths said they'll only be there for another year or so.

After dinner, felt so tired I had to go to bed. Got up after an hour, and with the help of the girls had a tidy round the house, was quite pleased with the result. Was always wishing I had a hot-press, but now I'm not so sure, everything gets pushed into it. Cleared it out tonight and gave strict orders that nothing was to be put in it except for towels and sheets, how long that will last is anyone's guess. Dreadful rain tonight and thunder and lightning, terribly warm – it seems we are going to have the hot weather back.

Saturday 23rd July

The weather forecast was very wrong about today. Last night they'd said the temperature would be up in the eighties, but it poured rain up till 1.30 and was quite cool. Got soaked getting in and out of the car when I went shopping. Mary had asked me to get some chicken portions in Marks for the priests. Took them over to them, then went to Godfrey's to buy a soap dish and toothbrush holder for the bathroom, those two items in chrome cost £8.20. The toilet-roll holder to match was £11.50, will make do with the one I have, which is also chrome. Thought I'd buy a longer towel rail, but they don't make them longer than the one I have. I think I paid less than £4.00 for it a few years ago, now they are £33.50; have a little bit more respect for my one now. Want a new bath panel, the cheapest they had (which were plastic) cost £16.50 plus VAT, so I have decided I'm going to tile the hardboard one which is on the bath. I have a lot of tiles over so it won't cost anything, and I'm sure it will look better, not to mention last longer, than the plastic one. When I came home, put up the soap dish and toothbrush holder, prayed to St. Anthony [prayers are directed at St. Anthony for minor intercession like lost objects and help around the house] I wouldn't crack the tiles drilling the screw holes. Got them up without any mishaps. Mary came home from Rome at 11.30 with presents for everybody – a beautiful pair of gold earrings for Terri and a lovely, big doll dressed in traditional costume for Fiona, a book on Roman history for Ciarán, a bottle of whiskey for Bernie, and a very nice ornament and bottle of brandy for me, so if the going gets too rough I can always take to the bottle.

Sunday 24th July

Was really tired this morning after my late night with Mary, didn't get to bed till two in the morning. It was alright for her, she didn't have to get up early – they all got Mass yesterday in Rome for today, but I had to be up at seven o'clock; I felt punch-drunk when Bernie called me. When we came back from Mass, Mary was up having breakfast. Yesterday, Leena asked Bernie and myself if we'd look after the shop while they went to Southend for the day, so when we finished breakfast, Bernie went in to learn how to use the till. They left at about 11.30, Terri went with them. They would have taken Ciarán and Fiona but they didn't want to go; Fiona went up to London with some school friends. Mary stayed to dinner. I spent my time between getting dinner ready and running in and out of the shop to see if Bernie was coping alright, and if he wanted to go to the loo. Took him in his dinner and a couple of bottles of beer. He seemed to be really enjoying himself, chatting up all the customers. Mary went home at four o'clock. I popped in to see if Bernie wanted anything, then went off to bed to have my afternoon nap. Was so exhausted, didn't waken until seven o'clock; when Bernie came up, he wanted his tea. Got up and got it ready. Just as we were having it, Ciarán and James came in – gave them some beef burgers and fried bread, made them wash up afterwards. Then Fiona came in starving, in spite of the fact she had just had dinner in a friend's house. Later on, Bernie and myself counted the day's takings, which came to £160.00, Leena was really pleased. They had a lovely day, she hasn't had a day away from the shop in eight months.

Monday 25th July

Everybody up early this morning except Ciarán – Terri had to go to work all day and Fiona went in to help Leena in the shop. I never felt less like going to work, still feeling the effects of Saturday night. At least it's still nice and cool, which makes it easier for work. When I got in, nobody was in the design room – then I remembered, Doris had gone to the hospital to have an x-ray. Lizzie was a bit late getting in – thought it was because of the wedding she went to on Saturday, but apparently not, she's having husband trouble and didn't get much sleep last night, she wasn't in the best of form. Doris came in at 11.15. I had just finished making a sample when Lizzie said I have no work for either of you. Harry came up and asked Doris would she do some production samples for him, but she said she'd rather go home as she didn't feel so well. He asked me would I mind doing some overlocking for him as three of his workers weren't in, I said alright. At one o'clock, went up to the design room to have my lunch with Lizzie, she said Doris better watch it or she'll be out. Puts me in an awkward position – if they do sack her she'll think I've taken her job. When I got home, phoned Mary to know how June was (her sister went home yesterday), she said she wasn't well at all this morning. When she took her in a cup of tea (before going to work) she was being sick and hadn't slept very well during the night. I then phoned June, and she could hardly speak her breathing was so bad.

182

Not one of her so-called friends (who all live nearby) called to know if she was alright. God help her, wish I lived a bit nearer to her, she shouldn't be left on her own.

Tuesday 26th July

Nice and cool this morning. After the girls had gone to work, went in to see Ciarán, who was still in bed. He said he was going to be very bored all day. Asked him why didn't he go next door and keep Leena company in the shop – said he would, so on my way out told Leena, she was very pleased. Lovely driving to work this morning, not a lot of traffic on the roads, everybody seems to be on holiday. Neither Doris nor myself had much to do in work, so when it came to going home I asked Lizzie did she want me in tomorrow. She said Harry would rather I'd come in because if they were short staffed I could help out in the factory. On my way out I met Harry and asked him about the letter he was to have written to the court. He told me to give him the forms and he'd get it done this evening as time was pressing on. Did a bit of shopping on the way home. Went into Fine Fare in Bruce Grove, haven't been in that shop for years. Wasn't in a hurry home, as nobody would be home to dinner until nearly six o'clock and we were having a salad, so called to Dan's shop to see how his dog was after his operation. Poor thing, he seems very weak, which I suppose is to be expected. Colette and the children drove to Liverpool today to catch the ten o'clock boat to Ireland. Bought a few bits and pieces from Dan. Business is not very good, but he said he got a few second-hand things, put them outside the door and within minutes they were sold. Told him when he got that shop that I thought a second-hand shop would do well there, but he's keen on having a DIY shop.

Wednesday 27ᵗʰ July

Oh God, another dreadfully hot morning – sweated buckets before I even went to work. Thank God I didn't have a lot to do, only cut out and made one sample skirt up to lunch hour, then made a very nice, royal-blue jacket trimmed with white for Terri. After lunch, got four production samples to make – so hot and sticky couldn't get interested in them. The sun hardly shone all day, just a dead heat all the time. Drove straight home after work. Ciarán was out. Salad again today, much too hot for cooked meals. So while I was waiting for everybody to come home to dinner, cut out two dresses for Terri. She was the first in from work and looked dreadful, she hasn't been well since her outing with Leena and her husband on Sunday. She's a very bad traveller, and having a go on all the things at the funfair didn't help. Told her she shouldn't go to work tomorrow, but she said she couldn't let them down. After dinner, Bernie wanted to paint the bathroom window, but told him to forget about it, it all needs filling and sanding down, which he doesn't believe in doing. I would have to do that myself, he would slap the paint on over humps and bumps. Wanted to put some shape on the house before Nan comes from Ireland on Friday, so got everybody working – everybody except Fiona, who said she'd do her share tomorrow as she's not working. Only I hadn't time, I'd have killed her – even though Terri's sick as she is, she did her share. Going to hang out the flags, even Ciarán cleaned out his room, browbeaten into it by Bernie.

Thursday 28ᵗʰ July

Stripped all the beds before going to work and left the sheets on the washing machine for Fiona to do, said she'd clean upstairs as she hadn't to go to work. Still doing production samples, as Lizzie has no work for me. Another very hot day, lovely if we didn't have to work. Made a dress for Terri during my lunch hour. She's still not too well, had pains in her stomach this morning, but she insisted on going into Geary's, she hasn't had a rest since the school holidays. When I got home from work, Fiona came out of Leena's and said she had done all the cleaning, but when I got indoors I discovered she hadn't done any washing – was really annoyed with her. Mary came over to go shopping; asked her how June was, said she's not well at all, still being sick when she eats. She had to get the doctor in to her on Tuesday night – he wanted to drive her in his own car to the hospital but she wouldn't go. After shopping, decided to take my shopping home before leaving Mary home – the weather is too warm to drive far with things like butter, lard and sausages. Fiona came with us to June's. While going along in the car, asked her had she made the beds, said she hadn't. I hadn't been upstairs since I'd come in from work, but I got a funny feeling about Fiona and her cleaning. When I got back and saw the rooms upstairs I nearly had a heart attack – they were in a dreadful state, she had done absolutely nothing. Could have killed her. Insisted on her doing them, took her nearly three hours.

Friday 29th July

Dreadful heat again this morning. Fiona and Terri went off to work and Leena asked Ciarán to help in the shop. He was up bright and early, he wanted to see Reg (the milkman) about helping him on Saturdays. He got the job, which pleased him very much. Did some production samples in work and made another dress for Terri in my lunch hour. Made no delay on my way home from work, as my friend Mary Mac was coming to dinner, but first we had to go to Euston station to collect Nan (my cousin from Ireland) who's spending two weeks with us. Well, we set off at about 4.15 and arrived at Euston at 4.50. We went round in circles looking for a parking space but had no luck, so parked right outside Euston station. At five o'clock Mary Mac went in to meet the train while I stayed in the car. Just as she left, one of those horrible traffic wardens came out of the station and walked straight over to me. I made a very quick getaway, but came unstuck with all the one-way streets, finished up near Trafalgar Square. 25 minutes later, and cursing all the traffic wardens, I finally got back to Euston station expecting to find Mary and Nan waiting for me, but there wasn't a sign of them. Swearing what I wouldn't say to them if they had gone home without me, I ran into the station just in time to see both of them coming out of it. The train had been 20 minutes late, lucky for all of us. Was really flattened by the time we got home, the temperature was in the nineties.

Saturday 30th July

Had to have Dan over first thing this morning – couldn't unlock the patio doors. Just took him a few minutes to fix them, it's a good thing he lives so near. After breakfast, took Nan to Walthamstow market. The heat was unbearable, had to keep stopping to rest – it was well up in the nineties again today. We went into Marks and stood under their air conditioning. I asked a woman who was standing there, how do you like this weather? She said, I don't want anybody to hear me saying this, but I've never felt so bloody miserable in all my life. One good thing about this heat, it has people talking to each other. Took Nan over to see Mary in the chapel house. Father Hegarty asked me what I thought of the Princess Michael of Kent situation. Told him I thought it dreadful that she should be received back into the Church in spite of the fact her children were being brought up as Anglicans. He said he was going to a discussion on it and he wanted to know what people thought, he seems very worried about it. [In 1983 Princess Michael had her second marriage blessed by Pope John Paul II, taking her new husband's name. As Prince Michael is a member of the British royal family, and as the Act of Settlement 1701 prevents any Roman Catholic from succeeding to the throne, their children are raised Church of England, not Roman Catholic]. I finished up telling him that it looks that even in the Catholic Church there is one law for the rich and one for the poor. Ciarán was up at 6.30 to help Reg, he wasn't home till 3.30. Reg gave him £4.00 and a lady gave him a 10p tip, so his hopes of getting rich quick were dashed. Still, he seems to enjoy it and it will keep him out of mischief for a few hours. He gave me £2.00 out of it and went off to Wood Green to buy some punk records, which is pretty stupid since our record player is broken.

Sunday 31st July

Felt a few drops of rain on our way to Mass this morning – still very, very warm. Thought I smelt petrol in the car, so after Mass left Terri to sell the bingo tickets while I went out to see was my petrol tube alright. When I went back into the church, Bernie said Father Hegarty was looking for me. He is still worried about what people think of Princess Michael of Kent, he said a few words about it at Mass. I think it would be better if he'd said nothing, I'm sure some people haven't even thought about it. When I did see him, told him I had car trouble, so he came out and fixed my petrol tube. Poor June went back into hospital yesterday – she is not getting better, God help her. So Mary came to dinner today, and after it herself, Nan and the girls went off to see June. They found June on the verge of going into a coma, they had to get a nurse for her. So much for going private, she is not being treated very well there. Coming home on the W3, the driver stopped the bus and ordered them off because he wanted them to pay an adult fare for Fiona – he wouldn't believe she was only 15 years old and was very abusive to them, but they wouldn't budge and the other passengers gave out to him for holding up the bus. When they came to getting off at Northumberland Park he tried to close the doors before Fiona could get out. I think she'll have to start carrying her birth certificate with her she is so tall, and she really does look older.

August 1983

VISITORS

Monday 1st August (Bank Holiday)

The girls didn't have to go to work today, so everybody slept late. Terri made breakfast while I was getting ready. Rang Harry to tell him I'd be a bit late in. Got in by 9.15 – hardly any traffic on the roads which helped. Didn't do anything interesting in work, but during my lunch hour made a nightdress for June. She is not eating anything, so thought I'd take her the nightie when I go to see her tonight. Believe we had a dreadful thunderstorm during the night, but thank God didn't hear a bit of it, but did appreciate the cold weather it brought – I think everybody was delighted with it. Still very cloudy this morning. Nan and Terri went to Wood Green and had lunch in BHS. Then they went and booked for a coach trip to Margate tomorrow, Fiona is going with them. Ciarán is the only problem – I don't like him being on his own, all his friends are on holiday so he's rather at a loose end. Mary, Nan, Terri and myself went to see June tonight. Two of her sisters and a niece were with her, they came up from the country this morning. June was very bad. Five doctors examined her under anaesthetic today, one of them told her sisters she was seriously ill. We didn't stay very long with her, the nurse said she wasn't well enough to have visitors. When we got home, discovered my car lights wouldn't go off. Leena's husband had a look at it and said the wiring was gone. He fixed it so they turned off, but will have to get new wiring and a switch tomorrow.

Tuesday 2nd August

It was really very cold this morning. Everybody up early, except Ciarán, for their trip to Margate. The weather didn't look very promising so they all brought their woollies with them. Nothing to do when I got into work. Asked Harry if he'd like me to take next week off but he said no – if BHS gives them the orders they are expecting, we'll be very busy next week. Thought he was going to give me production samples to do, but Lizzie said she wanted me to make a sample jacket; I was very glad, getting a bit cheesed off doing production samples. When I got home from work, phoned Mary to know how June was, she said there was a great improvement in her today and all the nurses were making a great fuss of her. She said she thinks it's due to the telling-off I gave them last night for not looking after her properly, they hadn't been a bit nice to her when she was in before. Ciarán had a pretty lonely day. He stayed in bed until midday, had something to eat, then went to Wood Green. When I came in from work he was upstairs playing records. Nan and the girls didn't get home until nine o'clock, they'd had a great day in spite of the rain and cold. Nan wasn't feeling too well and couldn't eat anything but Fiona pulled up for her [meaning, ate enough for the both of them] – she had rashers, an egg, and black and white pudding which Nan had brought from Ireland, and several slices of bread.

Wednesday 3rd August

Left everybody in bed and set off for work quite early, but arrived there 20 minutes late. When I got to Park View Road the traffic was at a standstill. Made a detour to get out onto Chestnut Road but that was worse, had to get in the queue. With stopping and starting finally got to Broad Lane 40 minutes later and discovered the cause of the hold up, there had been an accident. There were police everywhere. Saw one of the cars involved, it was so bashed up, doubt the driver could have escaped with his life. That's the second accident I've seen on the one-way system in the last two days. Spent a boring day in work, not much doing. Lizzie had a freelance pattern-cutter helping her. When I came home, Terri told me they had all stayed in bed until 11.30. Herself and Nan went out to lunch, then sat in Pymmes Park for a while. Mary called for some nighties I had washed for June, she had been to see her last night. Said she had spent most of the time out in the corridor, as June didn't seem well enough for visitors. Her two sisters were there. Mary said she wasn't going to the hospital tonight, then after a while changed her mind and went. Told her to phone me afterwards and let me know how June is, which she did at nine o'clock. Said one of June's sisters had seen the specialist today and he told her June has about one week to live, I was stunned. I knew she was very bad but I thought she'd last longer than that. Very upset, but I suppose if she's not to get better, it's better if she goes quickly.

Thursday 4th August

Nan and Terri were up early this morning, they were going to Madame Tussauds. I had a clear run to work, hardly any traffic on the roads, so arrived quite early. Made two sample skirts. Later on, started on a jacket which the freelance pattern-cutter had cut out, but couldn't put it together – the lining didn't match up with the outer part at all, I'd have done it better myself, don't know how they get these jobs. Lizzie was really annoyed. She said she's going to get him to alter it on Monday when he comes in. Was very upset and annoyed when I came home from work to hear from Fiona that Ciarán had borrowed a bike and had gone to Wood Green with David, the boy that all the trouble was about a while ago. I phoned his mother to know if he was there; she said no, that David wasn't allowed out. She thought I was lying when I told her he had called for Ciarán. I was so furious at Ciarán defying me that I got all his punk records and T-shirts and put them in the dustbin. Mary came to go shopping, we were to go and see June afterwards; left her home first with the shopping, and while we were there one of June's sisters phoned from the hospital to say they were staying in the hospital as June had deteriorated – they didn't think she'd last much longer. Mary said we wouldn't go see her as all her family were there. Mary phoned me at 11.15 to say the sisters had come home. The doctor had given June a sleeping tablet and they didn't see much point in staying.

Friday 5th August

Woke to the sound of the phone ringing at 7.45, it was Mary to tell me June had died last night at 20 past 12. Was really stunned, couldn't believe she'd go so quickly, Lord have mercy on her, but thank God she didn't last too long in pain. It was well Mary rang or we'd all have been asleep yet. Cut out and made a jacket in work. On the way home called into Mary in the chapel house. Father Hegarty came in and said he had a letter for me from Cardinal Hume [then head of the Roman Catholic

Church in England]. It was all about Princess Michael of Kent being taken back into the Church. Of course, it wasn't for me, but to be read out at all the Masses on Sunday. Mary said June's family were all very upset, as they weren't expecting her death so soon, but that is always the way – no matter how long a person is ill, their death always comes as a shock. What I find so hard to take is the fact that June was so neglected in the hospital. Ciarán is annoyed with me because I got rid of all his records. Told me he's not giving me half his wages this Saturday, now I'm really going to feel the pinch – I really hit him where it hurts. Just when we were about to have supper, Father Hegarty and Dick Johnson called to give me the letter. On the top of it he had written, 'Dear Mrs Byrne' and at the end, 'Cardinal Hume'. I told him about the house meetings we used to have, he didn't approve of them at all. Said when the new church hall is finished, he will have some meetings there.

Saturday 6th August

Everybody up bright and early this morning for work. Ciarán went off with Reg on the milk round. I left Nan in bed and went out early to do some shopping. When I came back, she was up and finished her breakfast, so we went off to pay my bills: phone, gas and electric – set me back well over £100.00, which of course was a lot less than my last bills. Then we went off to Ridley Market, it's years since I've been there. Got some good bargains, but was very tired walking round, so we went to Percy Ingalls for a cup of coffee, never saw such a scruffy place. When we came home, Bernie said Mary had phoned, so phoned her back. She said June was being buried on Thursday, please God, leaving at 3.30 from her house – said she'd come to dinner tomorrow. Phoned June's sister, Rose, who is staying with her husband in June's house. She asked me was Mary coming to me for dinner tomorrow, when I said yes, she seemed disappointed. I asked her why, and she said herself and one of her sisters were going home to Sussex tomorrow to get some clothes, as they hadn't brought much with them and they would be staying there till Monday – her husband wasn't going and she was hoping Mary would cook him a dinner tomorrow. Met Mary later on in Edmonton, told her what Rose had said, so she doesn't know if she'll be coming to dinner after all. Went to Herods for the last day of their sale, bought a few odds and ends. Fiona came from work, she could hardly walk, a piece of metal had gone into her ankle. She had pulled it out, but it swelled up and was very painful. Took her to the hospital. They dressed it and gave her a tetanus injection.

Sunday 7th August

Father Roderick said the eight o'clock Mass, seemed a bit confused, made two mistakes. He didn't mention the Cardinal's letter. They were left at the bottom of the church for anybody who cared to take one, don't think many people bothered. Had a record takings with the bingo tickets, £4.85, things are looking up. Terri, Ciarán, Nan and myself went up to Petticoat Lane after Mass. Bought three pieces of material to make trousers for Ciarán. He was disappointed I didn't get red material, he is still hooked on this punk business. He left us and said he would get the bus home; didn't know he was going to buy a punk T-shirt – if I can find where he's hidden it, it will go the way of the others. While I was out, Mary phoned – phoned her back, said she wasn't coming to dinner after all. June's two sisters had gone to Sussex, so herself and June's cleaner were moving things around to make room in the dining room for a meal they are giving to the people who attend June's funeral, which is on Thursday at 3.30; will have to arrange to leave work early. Fiona is still limping on her sore leg, but it didn't prevent her from going to the Turkish house up the road to spend her day – just came home in time for dinner and then back out again. Really enjoyed dinner, which was Irish corned beef which Nan brought over. Bought a watch for Fiona up the Lane, but she annoyed me so much didn't give it to her, she will have to improve a lot before she gets it.

Monday 8th August

Hated getting out of bed this morning, I felt so tired. Didn't sleep too well last night, woke nearly every hour, however managed to get to work on time. Dennis, the freelance pattern-cutter, came in and did a couple of patterns and left at 1.30. Doris and myself started on a bundle of production samples, getting cheesed off doing production samples, they are so boring. Doris was complaining about all the clothes she has to make for herself before she goes to Jamaica in September, but if she didn't make so much for other people (and she knows how to charge them) she'd have plenty of time to do her own. Was really glad to get home from work. Fiona had been busy and had the house nice and clean, she even cleaned out the cupboards in the kitchen. Mary came this evening. She said June left all her money and her two houses to her youngest sister Rose, so a few noses are going to be knocked out of joint. The three other sisters don't know yet – would love to be a fly on the wall when they find out. It seems before she died, June's mother made a will leaving the house to her because she was the only unmarried daughter, but on her deathbed the sisters made her change her will and leave the house between all of them. They wanted June out of the house so that they could sell it; in the end she had to get a mortgage to buy it, otherwise she'd have been without a home. They all got their share of the money, and June had to scrimp and scrape for years to pay back the mortgage, then she opened a café and made loads of money.

Tuesday 9th August

Left everybody in bed this morning except Terri, who went in to help Leena at 7.30; gave me a cup of tea before she went. Wish I could have stayed in bed myself, still very tired, the result of staying up late to watch Vincent Price in one of his horror films, a load of rubbish it was too. Got to work at 8.50, Doris was doing some of her private dressmaking. At about 11.30, Harry brought up three bundles of production work for us to do as there are no samples cut. He said they'll do you for the rest of the week, then he said he'd see us tomorrow. At about 12.55 Doris took out some of her own work to do, she was showing it to me when in walked one of the directors, I nearly died. He asked her what she was doing; she said, I was showing Vera something I'm going to make in my lunch hour. He said you have no right doing any of your own work here, these are our machines and if you want to use them for your own work you have to ask permission. You are not earning the money you are being paid. I felt terribly embarrassed. Doris told him not to shout at her. When he was gone, she said only she has a few weeks to go till her holiday and she needs the money, she'd leave now. I had a dress to make for Nan but I couldn't do it, so had to make it at home tonight – said a few prayers for Doris. Phoned Mary to tell her we'd go shopping tomorrow night, she said June's sister had been to see June in the funeral parlour and she looked lovely, the undertakers had done a great job on her, so Mary is going to see her tomorrow morning before she goes to work.

Wednesday 10th August

A mad rush this morning to get things ready for Nan's and Terri's trip to Southend with my friend Mary Mac and her husband. Ciarán and Fiona had decided they weren't going for some reason best known to themselves. When I got into work, Doris said to me she had seen Harry and told him about yesterday's incident. He told her Mr. Jacobs (the man who had told her off) had gone on holiday and they would sort it out when he came back, in the meantime we could do our own work during our lunch hours. Being optimistic, I had brought Ciarán's trousers to do, so was quite pleased with the news. Had asked Mary last night to get some chicken portions from Marks for dinner, and told her I would collect her on my way home from work. Instead of getting some already cooked, she bought fresh ones and stuffed and cooked them with some lambs' hearts. She also cooked cabbage, so I just had to cook potatoes. After our lovely dinner, we went shopping, after which left Mary home and went in to see two of June's sisters, they were busy getting things ready for tomorrow. Rose's husband had a look at my still-leaking petrol tube, said I need a smaller clip on it. Stayed chatting for three-quarters-of-an-hour. Came home thinking they would all be back from Southend, but they didn't come back till after ten o'clock. They'd had a lovely day and all had the look of the sun. Before going, Terri had bought a swim suit in Marks, her skin looked really the better for her day out. She said Fiona and Ciarán really missed a great day.

Thursday 11th August

Took a suit with me to work this morning to wear at June's funeral, also my harness. With the heat, I've got so used to going without my panty girdle as I couldn't possibly work with it on – at the moment I'm letting everything hang out. Doris and myself did some production work today, we are both getting fed up doing them. Doris is very upset about it, she said to come to work as a sample machinist – which of course I did too – and to end up doing production work is very annoying, but with Lizzie being on holiday there are no samples cut. I don't mind too much as long as I'm getting paid the same wages, it's all work, but I must say production work is very boring. Asked Harry if I worked my lunch hour could I go half an hour early, he said yes, so I left at 2.30. Got up to June's house at 2.50. There were quite a few people there, and the driveway of the house was covered with the most beautiful flowers. I never saw so many wreaths at a funeral, there was a few hundred pounds worth. It seemed a shame to spend so much on flowers, particularly as June used to say she didn't want flowers at her funeral. There was a very nice service at the crematorium. Wouldn't like to be cremated myself, not too keen on being buried either – still, won't have much choice when the time comes. After the funeral, we all went back to the house, had a very nice buffet. Terri rang me there to say they were all going to the pictures in Wood Green; they brought Leena and her mother. They weren't home till after eleven, Leena's husband was really annoyed.

Friday 12th August

Nan should have gone home this morning, but last night we persuaded her to stay till Sunday. More moans and groans from Doris today about production work. She said she is not coming back to work when she goes to Jamaica. Was very tired today due to the fact I had sat up last night talking to Nan till 1.30. Called into Mary on my way home.

She said one of June's nephews had phoned, said he wanted the name and address of June's solicitors as he wanted a copy of her will. Rose's husband said he would send him two copies; I'd love to be a fly on the wall when he gets them, I'm sure there's going to be trouble when they find out Rose has been left everything. Mary said Rose told her she can have anybody she likes to stay with her in the house, as it will take some time before everything is fixed up, but if I were Mary I wouldn't fancy staying in that big house on my own. Rose's husband is going to write a letter to the council to see will they give Mary a flat. After dinner, Bernie wanted to go to his work club. Didn't fancy going (hate pubs and clubs), but was nagged rotten till I agreed to go; we brought the kids of course. Fiona and myself played a game of darts. Then they all wanted to play the slot machines, went with them to see they didn't put too much money in them. Got playing myself, won £15.00. Nan won £3.60, Terri £2.40 and Fiona £1.60, really was our lucky night.

Saturday 13th August

When Terri brought me my cup of tea this morning, she said she'd read my stars and they said I was going to have car trouble, hope they are wrong. Went out shopping before Nan got up. Changed a foot pump I'd bought last Saturday in Halfords, got one with a gauge instead. Bought some things in Marks, came to £9.94, paid in 50p pieces from my winnings last night. A woman behind me asked had the gas man been, told her no, that I had struck it lucky on a slot machine. Went to Walthamstow with Nan, then later on called for Mary, and we all went to Wood Green to buy a grandad's shirt for Ciarán. He chose a white one, hope he washes his neck before wearing it. Met Bernie Fitzpatrick, who told me Niall is over on holiday and would call to see us. Mary stayed to dinner, she also stayed the night. Bernie went to the Dogs hoping to make his fortune. Leena came in to see Nan as she is leaving in the morning. She gave her two table mats and a key ring. While Leena was here her brother called in, it was his birthday and it's their custom to visit each other on that day. He is a very nice person, he told us his best friend is an Irishman from Galway. He had a cup of tea and stayed about half an hour. Bernie came from the Dogs, poorer and wiser. Ciarán had a bath, but somehow or other his neck escaped the water. Phoned Euston station twice tonight to know what the situation was at Holyhead, was told the boat which had broken down was fixed and everything was back to normal.

Sunday 14ᵗʰ August

Everybody up early this morning for Nan going away. Bernie and Ciarán went to eight o'clock Mass as usual, Ciarán to serve and Bernie to do the bingo for me. Myself and the girls went off to Euston with Nan. The station was in complete chaos, hundreds trying to get on the train, which was already packed. Saw one seat in a carriage which had a reserved ticket on it, dragged Nan in and made her sit down in it. A bloke next to her said, can't you see this seat is reserved? I said yes, probably by a porter who'll give it to anybody for a good tip. Things got so bad the police had to be called. There was a carriage reserved for a group of disabled people, but they were late, and by the time they got there all their seats were taken. In the end the police got it sorted out, and one of them passing said to me, bring back the football crowd. The train was 20 minutes late pulling out. I was glad to see it go, I was afraid somebody would come along and claim the seat Nan was in. Had hoped to be in time for 9.30 Mass, but we didn't get home till ten o'clock.

Took Bernie to the off-licence. After getting a few flashes from other motorists, realised my headlights were on – it had happened again, they wouldn't turn off. Went to a spare parts shop in White Hart Lane. Luckily for me they had the second-hand part which was needed to fix my lights; new it would have cost £14.00, but the bloke there fixed it and the whole lot only cost me £8.00. The stars were a day late in their predictions about my car.

Monday 15th August

Lizzie back from her hols, as she calls it. Also, the new trainee pattern-cutter (Penny) was in, she seems very nice, comes from Bristol. She's got digs in Mount Pleasant Road. Doris very upset today, said she has evil spirits in her house, they come every time her husband goes to work. He works on the buses and is on the 4 am shift, so she's not getting much sleep. Told her I'd bring her in some holy water tomorrow, wrote it on my hand so I wouldn't forget. When I came home from work, Fiona was all excitement – Niall had called to see us. Was sorry I missed him, but he had to rush away as he was leaving for home at 5.30. They gave him a cup of tea and heard all about his life in Ireland, which made them very envious. They said he hadn't changed a bit, except of course he's a lot taller. He thought they hadn't changed much, except they had got taller too. Terri told him to be sure and tell his mother that our mother was writing a diary for her. They all said he should have called sooner so that they could have seen more of him. Mary called over to go to six o'clock Mass with us in St. Edmonds. Terri went home to sleep over with Mary last night, but didn't go home with her tonight. Fiona couldn't make up her mind whether to go into Leena's in the morning or not; she [Fiona] is very disagreeable, so in case she wouldn't go, Terri said she'd go.

Tuesday 16ᵗʰ August

Fiona went into Leena's after all this morning, but, unlike Terri, she doesn't give me a cup of tea before going, with the result I didn't waken until 8.10. Felt really ill. When I got out of bed, had a dreadful headache, runny eyes and nose; my legs even felt weak. Thought of ringing Harry and telling him I wasn't well enough to go to work, but decided against it. Took two tablets, hoping I'd feel better as the day went on, arrived in just five minutes late. Gave Doris the Lourdes water. She asked me, what would she say when sprinkling it? Told her to say, 'Sacred Heart of Jesus, protect us, in the name of the Father and of the Son and of the Holy Spirit, Amen' – I'm really entering into the spirit of things, still, I hope it will set her mind at rest. Really think it's all in her mind, she is a very superstitious person. Don't know how I got through the day. Didn't get any better, thought I'd never get home to bed. Mary came over early, had a cup of tea with her. Got a dinner ready for Bernie – Ciarán and Fiona didn't want anything, they had already eaten, and Terri wasn't home from Geary's. So when Bernie came in, went off to bed with some hot whiskey. Terri went home with Mary. I slept for a while. Woke with the phone ringing – it was Nan, phoning from Ireland. In spite of all the chaos at Euston, she said she had a very nice journey home. All the rest of her news was sad – a neighbour of ours at home (50 years old) had died of cancer, another had one of his eyes removed, he had a growth at the back of it. Spent the night crying my eyes out, what with the news and feeling so ill.

Wednesday 17ᵗʰ August

Didn't feel much better this morning, found two Lemsips, took one before going to work, felt a lot better after a while, they really do work.

Did alterations most of the day, made a pair of trousers for Ciarán in my lunch hour. The forelady in the factory gave me another Lemsip when she heard I had a cold, it seems they keep a stock of them. They have a stock of medical supplies for all emergencies. Doris said I was very foolish coming to work when I wasn't well, but I don't like staying out. Doris is still talking about the spirits in her house. She shook the holy water all round her bedroom and got a great night's sleep; thank God for holy water. Rushed home from work, thought Mary would be over early, but she didn't come till five o'clock. Terri is working afternoons in Geary's all this week. Had to wash up a load of dirty dishes before getting the dinner ready. Fiona was up the road in the Turkish house; gave her a piece of my mind when she came in, [she] said it wasn't her week for washing up. Told her if she went up to that Turkish house again, I'd kill her – she spends all her spare time there. Terri, Mary and myself went shopping after dinner – much easier to get round Tesco on Wednesday nights. Took my shopping home and put it away before leaving Mary home with her shopping. Felt sad going into June's house, kept thinking of the last time I saw her sitting in her armchair, little did I know then I was seeing her for the last time. Her house looks lovely. I wish I had £65,000.00 to buy it, it's right at the back of Alexandra Palace.

Thursday 18ᵗʰ August

Terri gave me a cup of tea before going into Leena's. When I got out of bed, felt really awful. Had some Cornflakes and toast for breakfast, couldn't taste either of them, seem to have lost my taste buds. Had an argument with myself about going to work. Had a Lemsip with its magic formula and went off to work. Couldn't stop coughing when I got in, Doris said I seemed to be worse than ever; still, managed to struggle through the day, between listening to Doris about her spirits. Her daughter rang her this morning at seven o'clock to tell her she thinks she has spirits in her house too. She asked me would it be alright if she gave her some of the holy water, and could I get her some more. She said the Mormon religion she belongs to doesn't believe in holy water; was tempted to ask her how come she did, but hadn't the energy to bother. Was very pleased when I got home from work – Mary had been there from midday, it was her day off, and the house was all nice and tidy and the dinner almost ready, she had also done all the washing. Fiona was in work. Her manager had rung this morning to ask her to go in. Ciarán had met Reg, and he asked him to help him, and Terri was in Geary's, so all my family were well occupied today, thank God. We are still killed with the heat here. Bernie got into his Bermuda shorts the minute he came in from work. I kept praying nobody would call in because they'd die of shock if they saw him, he's certainly not a sight for sore eyes. Terri went home with Mary to keep her company.

Friday 19th August

Felt a bit worse this morning. Had breakfast again without tasting anything. Thought I really won't make it to work. Fiona and Terri went off to work. I sat wondering what to do, then remembered it was Friday and, as I needed the money, decided I better go to work. Managed to get in by nine o'clock. Lizzie didn't come in till after nine, was gone out by 9.30, up the West End to see a buyer from Dorothy Perkins. I made a skirt and jacket. At lunch hour made a night dress for myself; Doris fitted it on and wants the pattern of it. When Lizzie came back, she said the buyer liked our skirts but said they are too good for their market. At two o'clock Lizzie told me to go home, said I looked really ill. Got home just in time for my friend Mary Mac. Had cooked some bacon and cabbage yesterday for dinner, so only had to heat it up and cook some potatoes. After dinner, Mary Mac and myself went up to Tesco to get a leg of lamb for Sunday's dinner. My cousin, Anna O'Malley, her husband and son are coming on Sunday from Ireland to stay with us. Had asked Dan would he clear all the rubble out of the garden before they came, he said he'd be over Wednesday or Thursday but he never came, I'm really disgusted with him. Asked Bernie could he put some sort of shape on it, said he'd do it tomorrow (he started three weeks' holiday today). Mary Mac went out to the garden and sorted things out. Bernie wasn't too pleased because he was shamed into helping her and our Mary.

Saturday 20th August

Woke before six o'clock this morning, couldn't stop coughing. Got up to go to the loo, felt very weak. Bernie got up and made a cup of tea and brought me up some Benylin. Later on, when the children had gone to work, Mary gave me another cup of tea, told me to stay in bed, didn't really need telling. Was just going off to sleep at about nine o'clock when Bernie came up and said we have visitors. Mary Mac and her husband, Jack, had come over to take all the rubble out of the garden and down to the dump, she really is a friend indeed, Bernie said she's better than ten men. The three of them worked hard loading stuff into Jack's car and carting it down to the dump. Later on, got up, couldn't lie in bed with everybody else working – even took a load of stuff down to the dump myself. Felt really bunched. Phoned the surgery and asked could I have some antibiotics. Teresa (the nurse) said to call up at 11.30. Went to Marks to get some chicken portions for the dinner, Bernie came with me and went into the bookies. On the way home he went in to collect my prescription. There was a note with it from Dr. Watson, he wants to see me on Monday, please God. When we came home, was in a state of collapse, could hardly drag myself up to bed, was very tired but couldn't sleep because of my troublesome cough. Mary came at 4.30 and got dinner ready. Got up and had some. Bernie went off to the Dogs. Mary stayed the night.

Sunday 21ˢᵗ August

No better this morning, it was a terrible effort to get up and go to Mass. Had a dreadful pain up the left side of my face. When we got home, Mary was up and ready to go to 9.30 Mass. Fiona got breakfast ready while Bernie and myself checked the bingo tickets – got a full house, the first time in years. Mary said I wouldn't get much, as it was won last week and only paid £3.50; still, it's nice to win no matter how little. Had dinner early today because I wanted to have my afternoon nap early as I had to meet my cousin Anna, her husband and son at Euston station at 5.45. Arrived there at 5.30, but the train was delayed and didn't get in until 6.35, so Bernie and myself had quite a wait and not a place to sit down. Usually I love watching the comings and goings at Euston station, but all I was interested in was getting home. Was really relieved when my cousin arrived. Mary and the girls had tea ready when we got home. Anna had brought presents for everybody – whiskey for Bernie, brandy for me, Yardley make-up, soaps and perfume for the girls, Mary and myself, and a box of chocolates for Ciarán. After tea, we all went down to Bernie's work club, except Mary, who said she'd rather watch telly. Wasn't so lucky on the slot machines, lost a few bob, but everybody enjoyed themselves. The girls weren't too happy going home to Mary's to sleep, they're afraid they'd miss something.

Monday 22nd August

Felt no better this morning. Bernie went in to help Leena in the shop – Terri was to have gone in, but her having to stay in Mary's made it impossible for her to get over early enough. Hated going to work what with not being well and having such a late night, felt really bad. When I got into work, phoned the surgery to make an appointment to see Dr. Watson at 5.30. Had a couple of Lemsips during the day, which I find very good. Didn't do a lot of work, and at 2.45 Lizzie said I could go home. Nobody in when I got home, so had a bath and got the dinner ready just in time before everybody arrived in. Just had time to give everybody their dinner before going off to keep my appointment with Watson, who said he wanted to see me to nag me for being back on the cigarettes again. He said I was an eejet. Gave me antibiotics for sinus, which he said had gone down on my chest. Told him about the pains in my big toes – [he] said I had arthritis, gave me another prescription for tablets; told him about my hot flushes, he said, I don't see you very often (actually it's two years since I've seen him), but when I do you make up for lost time with all your complaints. We all went down to the club again tonight except Mary. When we came back, had to leave herself and the girls home, after which Anna and myself were up till after three o'clock talking about old times, a sure sign we are getting old.

Tuesday 23rd August

What with being up so late last night and not being well, couldn't go to work this morning. Struggled out of bed to cook breakfast, intending to get back into it as soon as everybody had gone out. My cousins, Bernie, Fiona and Ciarán were going to London to visit a museum.

Terri had to go to work, which upset her very much – so much so, that instead of going back to bed, I took her to Wood Green to see a dress which Fiona wanted copied for a Turkish wedding they are all going to on Saturday 3rd September. Had phoned Harry before going to tell him I was too ill to go to work; prayed I wouldn't meet him or anybody else out of the firm while I was out. Intended having lunch out with Terri, but by the time we got to Wood Green and had a look at the shops, had just time to get home, have a quick cup of coffee and take her to work at one o'clock. After that, got a few bits and pieces in Marks, came home and got into bed. Was just dozing off when Anna, Bernie and Fiona came in. They had got tired going round the museum, but the boys wanted to stay, so Kevin (Anna's husband) stayed with them. Had to get up and get dinner ready. Finished it just as Mary came in, then the rest of them. After dinner they all wanted to go to the club. Told them I was too tired to go, so Bernie and Kevin took the children over to the Northumberland Baths. They came home at ten o'clock. Had supper, then drove Mary and the girls home.

Wednesday 24th August

Didn't feel a lot better this morning, was wishing I had another day off work. Bernie gave me a cup of tea before he went into the shop. Still have dreadful pains in my face. When I got to work, Lizzie said they hadn't expected me in for the rest of the week – wish I'd known that, I wouldn't have come in at all. Made a few samples and Fiona's dress during my lunch hour. Was glad when it was time to go home. Everybody was out when I got home. Got dinner ready just before everybody came in. They'd been on a shopping spree. Anna had bought quite a few things in Argos, said things were an awful lot cheaper than in Ireland. Bernie phoned Sonny [Vera's brother] to know would he like to come down to the club – said he would, so when he came I drove all the men and the two boys down and had to come back for Anna and the girls. Couldn't believe my eyes when I saw another of my cousins coming into the club. It was Anna's sister, Betty, her husband and sister-in-law. They had been staying with Betty's husband's brother in Middlesex. They've been here for a week and are flying home tomorrow, for which Betty said she is very glad. She's had a miserable time. Her mother-in-law came with them, she is over 80 years old and is very troublesome. She said tonight was the first time she's been out since she came here. They had a couple of drinks with us, then they had to go.

Thursday 25ᵗʰ August

Had a Lemsip after my breakfast this morning, they certainly do help. How I envied everybody in bed. Went off to work feeling very sorry for myself. Didn't do anything exciting in work – as a matter of fact, felt I wasn't really needed. Made a T-shirt for Ciarán in my lunch hour. Was only home from work when everybody came in. It seems they hadn't gone far, just to Wood Green and up to Angel Coaches to book a trip to Margate tomorrow. Terri was a bit put out when she heard about it, as she can't go – she has to work tomorrow. Poor Terri, she hasn't had a rest since she got her holidays. Got dinner ready while Bernie and Kevin had a drink. After dinner, did some cutting out. Everyone decided they wouldn't go to the club tonight, for which I was very thankful – getting a bit tired making two trips there and back every night. We all sat round watching telly. Fiona didn't go home with Mary tonight because of going to Margate in the morning. So Anna and myself dropped Terri and Mary home. Showed Anna round June's house, she thought it was lovely. When we got back, made supper. Kevin insisted on washing up, for which I was grateful. Then everyone decided to go to bed early because they had to be up early in the morning, but as usual Anna and myself sat up till all hours talking about our mothers, who were sisters and such very different people.

Friday 26th August

Everybody up bright and early for their trip to Margate. Poor Terri couldn't go, she had to go to work in the afternoon – told her I'd take her out to dinner tonight. When I got to work, discovered all the factory hands weren't in – they had all been given the day off because there was no work for them, wish I worked in the factory. Didn't do a lot of work myself. On the way home, called in to Mary, told her I was going to Edmonton Green to get some ham for sandwiches to give them when they came from Margate, she said she'd come with me. Got back in time to collect Terri from Geary's. Drove Peggy (the lady she works with) home, drove Mary to the W3 bus stop. Terri and myself drove to Wood Green to find somewhere to eat. Didn't realise there were no restaurants there apart from McDonalds and Wimpy, both of which only sell junk food. Finished up in a fish and chip shop in Turnpike Lane, had a very nice meal there. Was home by eight o'clock, got sandwiches ready and put the kettle on for them coming from Margate. Was expecting them home by nine o'clock. At ten o'clock, Terri and myself went to the door to see if they were coming, found Peter working on his car – they are all going to Ireland in the morning, but the car wouldn't start, felt very sorry for them. Prayed they'd get it going, between praying nothing had happened to the others coming from Margate. They didn't arrive home till 10.30. They'd had a great day. Anna bought Terri a lovely musical box and myself a cut-glass honey jar.

Saturday 27ᵗʰ August

The house was very peaceful this morning with Terri, Fiona and Ciarán gone to work. Ciarán came back at nine o'clock for a cup of tea, then off again as quick as he had come. I cooked breakfast for Anna, Kevin, Colm and Bernie, after which Anna and myself went out to do some shopping. Kevin, Colm and Bernie went out for a walk. Mary came at four o'clock and got the dinner ready. Arrived home at five o'clock, and before I even had time to park my car, Ciarán ran out of the house to tell me Declan was in there. Asked him, Declan who? He said Declan Moffatt, my nephew whom I haven't seen in over three years. Was delighted to see him. He said he was working for a firm on West Road. He stayed until 11.30. Drove him home, the girls came with us. They seemed really delighted that their cousin came to see us. Asked Ciarán this evening to water the flowers in the front garden with the hose; my car got in the way, so he hosed that down too and also himself, he came in soaked. He's nearly as handy as his father.

Sunday 28ᵗʰ August

Everybody up at seven o'clock. Just had a cup of tea and toast, then off to eight o'clock Mass, which Father Roderick said – Father Hegarty is in Ireland. After Mass, we set off for Wembley market, which is held every Sunday in the car park of Wembley Stadium – Bernie and Kevin didn't come. Thought it would take an hour to get there, but we did it in less than 20 minutes. Didn't think a whole lot of it, but there were loads of material stalls there. Bought some material for Fiona for the wedding. Anna bought a canteen of cutlery supposed to be silver plate (51 pieces) for £15.00, have my doubts about it, it's marked A.P. whatever that means. Was home by 11.45, much to Bernie's surprise. Himself and Kevin hadn't even washed up the breakfast things. It seems Bernie had done the cooking, which I'm sure wasn't fit for human consumption. However, much to Bernie's annoyance, I insisted they wash up. Mary came at 12.30, helped me to get the dinner ready, after which I had my usual afternoon nap, which was rudely interrupted by the girls taking a snap of me sleeping. It seems they had also taken one of Bernie and Kevin asleep in the garden on deck chairs. Mary got the tea ready then went off to Mass. She came back, but left early, and then we all went down to the club. Bernie and Kevin played snooker for the night. Anna and myself had a go on the slot machines, I lost £3.00 but Anna won £5.00. Made a vow, I'm not putting money into those machines again.

Monday 29th August (Bank Holiday)

Was up at 8.45, cooked breakfast for everybody. Left Bernie and Kevin to wash up, while Anna, Colm, the girls and myself went off to Queensway market, which we discovered, when we got there, wasn't on, so we decided to try Petticoat Lane, which we discovered wasn't on either. Rather than go home so early, we drove up to the West End and got behind a coach which was taking people on a tour of London. Saw more of London in one hour than I've seen in the 18 years I've been here. Hadn't realised just how beautiful London really is. We went all over the bridges, saw Big Ben, Downing Street, Westminster Abbey, the Houses of Parliament, the Tower of London, Trafalgar Square and all the places of interest. Can't remember when I enjoyed myself so much. Finished up at St. James's Park. Put the car into a car park, and we all walked up The Mall to Buckingham Palace. Saw the Changing of the Guard, which Terri took a snap of. Also got a quick glimpse of

Prince Philip, who for a brief second came out onto a balcony. All this time was thinking – Bernie will be furious with us being out so long, and would be waiting on his dinner, but when we got home at about 1.45, himself and Kevin were out. Mary said when she came at 12.30 Bernie said they were going to back a horse and I'd be in any minute. Cooked dinner, which we didn't have till near four o'clock. After tea, Bernie, Kevin and Colm went to the club. I cut out a dress for Terri for the wedding.

Tuesday 30th August

Bernie (who is still on holiday) gave me a cup of tea at 7.30 this morning, then he went in to help Leena so that Terri could have a lie-on. Herself and Fiona haven't gone home with Mary for the past few nights, they are sleeping on the bed settee in the sitting room. Hadn't much to do in work – made one skirt, then Lizzie asked me would I take an early lunch or do production work. Didn't fancy having an early lunch, so did the production work instead. Asked her could I not have my holidays now [an Irish construction, to mean 'ask her if I could have my holidays now'!], but she said they needed me this week and next week. Could do with some time off with all the late nights I'm having. Made Terri's dress in my lunch hour, wasn't pleased with it. When I got home, Bernie said my cousin, Mick Emerson, had phoned, he and his wife Dorrie are coming over. He told them I'd ring tonight to know when exactly they are coming. After dinner, everybody went off to the club except myself. I cut out another dress for Terri and one for Fiona. Phoned Dorrie – was amazed when she said they were arriving tomorrow evening. Told her I'd meet them, but she said there was no need as they were taking their car. Phoned Mary to tell her that they would have to stay with her as I had no room, [Mary] said they should have given her more notice. Anna and the girls came home early from the club. Were very annoyed when they heard Mick and Dorrie were going to stay in Mary's, they even offered to stay there themselves and let Mick and Dorrie stay here.

Wednesday 31st August

Bernie went in again this morning to help Leena, I think he fancies himself as a shopkeeper. Brought me in a cup of tea and my morning newspaper (the Daily Mirror) – only buy it hoping I'll win the bingo one day. Before going to work, left strict instructions the house was to be cleaned up before Dorrie and Mick came. Was very busy today in work. Made a dress for Fiona in my lunch hour, she wanted it with a very baggy top. Knew it wasn't right when I made it, but it was as she had said she wanted it. Couldn't tell her it was too baggy. When I brought it home and fitted it on her, she had to agree there was too much fullness in the top. You can't tell her anything, she knows it all. Had to re-cut the whole thing. She'd been out shopping with Anna this morning and bought a pullover for school which was a bit too small. Had to ring Mary and ask her to come over while I took her back to change it, in case Mick and Dorrie arrived. While we were out, tried to get a crest for Ciarán's school blazer in Wades, but was told I'd have to have a letter from the head master. When I got home, cut the crest off his old blazer and Anna stitched it on while I was getting the dinner ready. Mick and Dorrie didn't arrive until 8.30. Bernie, Kevin and Colm had gone swimming, Ciarán was too tired to go. Later on, collected them all from the baths and went down to the club. Lost over £1.00 on the slot machines. Mick didn't seem too pleased going off to stay in Mary's place, would rather have stayed here.

September 1983

Thursday 1st September

Ciarán and Fiona weren't very happy this morning – their first day back to school after the holidays. Ciarán had made up his mind he is not going to like the upper school. Because she is now a sixth-former, Terri doesn't have to start back until Monday. She hasn't had much of a holiday, between going into Leena's and Geary's. Ciarán was halfway up the road when I had to call him back. I had made him new trousers, but he had on an old pair which were about six inches too short – between that and his new blazer which is about a size too big for him, he looked like the village eejet. He wasn't too pleased having to change them. Doris wasn't in work today – phoned to say she wasn't feeling well and had gone to the doctor last night. She said he told her it was all in her head; I could have told her that, she imagines all sorts of things wrong with herself. Cooked dinner for eleven of us today, after which Mary and myself went shopping.

215

When we came back, everybody wanted to go to the club except Mary, who stayed at home to watch telly. Bernie, Mick and Kevin played snooker, the two boys played pool, and Anna, Terri, Dorrie and myself played table tennis – or tried to; none of us any good at it, but we did have a good laugh. Had a go on the slot machines, but had no luck. I'm convinced now that when we all won something on it that night, it must have been out of order. Terri went home with Mick and Dorrie to Mary's so she could show Mick the way to get back here in the morning.

Friday 2nd September

Very tired this morning, all my late nights catching up on me. Got the usual cup of tea from Bernie before he went in to help in the shop. Thought I was hearing things when Ciarán asked where his toothbrush was, as he never cleans his teeth – think maybe one of his new teachers told him off about them yesterday. Hope they are a bit more strict than the lower school. Doris wasn't in work again today – was really annoyed with her as I was hoping to have next week off. Asked Lizzie about it, said she'd ask Harry. He said he'd rather I didn't take next week off, that he had me down for two weeks in October, which of course I had asked for in the first place, but as Mick is really over here on business, thought Dorrie might be lonely on her own. Terri hadn't to go to work today, so she went with Bernie, Mick and Colm to Braintree, Mick had business there. It seems they were to be back by 12.30, but when I got home at 3.30 they weren't back. Only Anna, Dorrie and Kevin were in. Kevin made me a cup of tea, which was very welcome. The others didn't arrive in until near five o'clock. They got lost on the way to Braintree, which is about 20 miles from here, but according to

Mick they drove about 200 miles. Himself and Bernie so tired, after dinner they fell asleep. Very stormy tonight, a very sudden change in the weather. Did a bit of hand-sewing on Fiona's dress. The men went down to the club, the women watched telly, which was very bad due to the storm. Ciarán went to bed early. Fiona went home to Mary's to show Mick the way here in the morning. Anna and myself reminisced till two in the morning.

Saturday 3rd September

Everybody up early this morning. Anna, Kevin and Colm going home to Ireland. Didn't envy them, it was still very stormy. They didn't like going, but Anna has to be in work on Monday and Colm has to go back to school. Felt so sorry they were going, really enjoyed their company, wished I lived near them. Bernie and myself left them to Euston Station but we cut it very fine, we didn't arrive there until 9.55, the train was going out at ten o'clock. As usual there were a lot of reserved cards on some of the seats, but one of the porters took three cards off when Kevin gave him a tip; I know the tip I'd have given him, the tip of me boot. There's a racket going on with the porters. When we got home, Bernie and myself had just finished tidying up when Dorrie and Mick arrived. Fiona had the day off work on account of the wedding. She wanted a backless bra, so herself, Dorrie and I went to get one. All the shops round Tottenham and Edmonton were sold out of them, so we left Fiona at the hairdressers and myself and Dorrie went to Wood Green. We finally got the bra in Dorothy Perkins. We came home foot-sore and weary to great excitement, the big three getting ready for the wedding. It seems Ciarán was going without even washing himself until Mick undressed him and nearly threw him into the bath. They all looked very nice going off. They weren't home until one o'clock, all very tired. Went to Mary's with Dorrie to collect hers and Mick's clothes, they are both staying with us now for the rest of their holiday.

Sunday 4th September

Crawled out of bed very tired this morning after all the running around I'd done yesterday plus the late hour going to bed, however we all went to eight o'clock Mass. When we got home, cooked breakfast – everybody helped with the washing up. Then Mick wanted to go up to London sightseeing. Had to wait for Mary, who didn't arrive until midday. As Mick is not very familiar with London, I was to lead the way, with Mary and Dorrie in my car. The two girls and Bernie in Mick's car (Ciarán didn't come with us). Well, talk about the blind leading the blind. I'm not too familiar with the centre of London myself, but felt quite pleased that I managed to lead them to Buckingham Palace without mishap. We all got out and had a look round, then a copper came along and told us to move our cars. With me still leading, set off to find Tower Bridge. Went over Blackfriars Bridge twice, Westminster Bridge four times, and round Trafalgar Square four times, with Mick following close behind. It was when I went round a roundabout three times that Mick finally lost his cool. Hooted to me to stop. Said after a few heated words that he'd lead the way; all into the cars again, this time with me following meekly behind on our search for Tower Bridge. Everything going grand until we came to a road with three turnings. I still don't know what happened, but Mick turned right and I turned left and that was the last we saw of them till we got home at 4.30. Don't think I'm ever going to be let forget today.

Monday 5th September

Hated going to work this morning, would have liked to have taken Dorrie round the shops, and was twice as annoyed when I was asked to do production samples. Felt, if that's all I have to do I wasn't really needed there today as they have a production sample machinist in the factory. Was really glad when it was time to go home, especially as my eyes were giving me trouble due to the fact I was using Dorrie's glasses. Mary had taken mine home with her last night by mistake. When I came home, found Dorrie there on her own. She had been busy cleaning the house, I was very pleased with the result. Bernie and Mick were out somewhere. With Dorrie's help, got the dinner ready before they all came in. Afterwards, we all went down to the club. The girls and Ciarán put a few pounds given to them by Bernie and Mick in the slot machines, but won nothing. Just as they left the machine, a bloke walked in, put 10p in it, and won £100.00, we all felt a bit sick. Asked Mick to put a bulb in the chandelier in the dining room, Bernie has tried putting it in several times but it keeps popping out, missing hitting us by inches. However, Mick had a look at it and said what I needed was a new chandelier. Had intended getting one when the house was finished, but said I'd get one in the morning if he'd put it up for me. He said he'd do it before they leave for home in the morning. They are leaving at about 10.30.

Tuesday 6th September

Got up a bit earlier this morning to buy the new light-fitting which Mick had said he'd put up for me, intended being at the shop before it opened. Phoned Harry to tell him I'd be in a bit late, but Mick insisted he'd go for it. Told Bernie to be sure and get me a nice one. Set off to work looking forward to getting home and seeing the new light-fitting up. Made a tartan blazer (a sample) which didn't turn out so well – it was too big, will have to be re-cut; Lizzie was working on the pattern when I left for home. Was surprised when Terri opened the door and told me Mick and Dorrie hadn't gone home, they were out somewhere with Bernie. When I asked her about the light, she said it's lovely but you are not going to like it. That was an understatement. I nearly had a stroke when I saw it. It was one single light hanging from the ceiling with a bulb in it like a balloon, but it only showed the equivalent of 40-watts. After being used to 3 x 100-watt bulbs, it was like going into a dungeon. The shade on it was lovely but more suitable in a hall. I said to Terri, I'm going out to buy a new chandelier. So the two of us went up to an electrical shop in Edmonton Green. Selected one I liked, then realised I hadn't enough money with me. Told the man in the shop I'd be back by 5.30. When I got home, Bernie, Dorrie and Mick were there. Mick asked me how I liked the light, told him I didn't – to take it down and put it in the hall. Told Bernie when Mick had done that to handcuff him to a chair in case he escaped before I got back with the new chandelier.

Wednesday 7th September

When I got up this morning, went into the dining room to have another look at my new chandelier, I'm really pleased with it, it looks lovely. It's got five lights, each with a 60-watt bulb. Mick also put a dimmer switch on it which is very handy. Mick and Dorrie definitely leaving this morning, I'm letting them go now I've got my light fixed. Mapped out a route for them to get to Holyhead, hope they don't get lost. As I left for work, they were putting their cases in their car. Made four samples in work and a school skirt for Terri in my lunch hour. When I got home, told Bernie I was going to change the standard lamp Mick had bought me for the dining room, he said he'd come with me. Hadn't a big selection in the shop they had bought it in as they were closing down and had sold most of their stock. Finished up getting a reading lamp in the shape of a ginger jar. It's not marvellous, but I prefer it to the standard lamp. The girls said it is lovely, so did Mary, who was there when we got home. She was very upset. Rose (June's sister), whom June left everything to, and her husband had come up from Sussex to see Mary. Told her they wanted her out of the house by the end of September, they said if the house was empty they wouldn't have to pay rates on it. They had told Mary after the funeral she could stay in the house until it was sold, which will take about a year or more. They had the phone and gas cut off. These are the people Mary thought were her friends.

Thursday 8th September

Terri went in to help Leena at 7.30 before going to school, then Bernie took over at eight o'clock. Very cold and dull this morning, the weather has changed very suddenly. Made a school blouse for Terri in my lunch hour and had a long chat with Lizzie, who is moving to a maisonette tomorrow, somewhere in Holloway, she said it's a bit nearer to work. Doris went out to the bank in Stamford Hill, and Penny, the new pattern-cutter, went out to lunch with some friends. Mary and Bernie went to the Citizens Advice Bureau to see what her position is with June's house. She was told, according to law, they had to give her a month's notice to get out; if she didn't get out by then, they'd have to take her to court to get an eviction order, and she would then have to get out within three months. So what she'll decide to do remains to be seen. It seems Rose has invited her sisters up at the weekend to take whatever they want out of the house, but according to law they must leave Mary with a bed and cooking facilities. I don't know where they are all going to sleep when they come. There is no doubt about it, the love of money really changes people. Mary was always singing Rose's praises, but now she doesn't seem to be the nice person Mary thought she was. Was so tired after dinner, fell asleep on the couch. Rang Dorrie and Mick to see did they arrive home alright, Dorrie told me they had been burgled while they were away.

Friday 9th September

Thank God it's Friday, don't think I could stand another day in work, I'm so tired. Lizzie was late getting in, she was getting things ready for moving – thought she would have taken the day off. Altered a dress and skirt for Mr. South's (my landlord) wife during my lunch hour. Lizzie re-cut the tartan blazer, I did some of it before I left work. Mary Mac was at home when I got there. Told her about Mary and June's sister, she couldn't believe it. Bernie was helping in the shop until 1.30, Leena had to go to the doctor, she is covered in a rash. She told Terri later the doctor gave her a prescription for cream, she said her husband will go mad having to pay £1.30 for cream, she really has a dreadful life with him. Bernie said she was crying in the shop this morning over the way he gave out to her. After dinner, Terri, Bernie, Mary Mac and myself left Mary home, they said June's house was lovely. Bernie said if he won the Pools he'd buy it; if I won the Pools

I'd like to buy a house somewhere better than Hornsey. Fiona went to bed before 8.30, she is tired after all her late nights. Jack called for Mary at 9.30. When we had supper and they had gone home, Bernie, Terri and Ciarán went to bed. I sat watching the last episode of 'The Godfather', then I watched a film called 'Freaks', which was really horrifying.

Saturday 10ᵗʰ September

Was given two cups of tea in bed this morning, one by Terri before she went off to work (the house was so peaceful with them all at work that I thought I'd have a lie-on), but just as I was going off to sleep, Bernie brought me another cup of tea. Just then, Leena knocked to ask him would he stay in the shop while she went somewhere or other. Got up to go to the toilet, had a look at Ciarán's room and thought, what a dump. While still in my nightie, started pulling the paper off the wall, thus making it worse. Decided I'm going to change it all around. Had a look at the bathroom, which still needs some more tiles putting up over the window. Will have a rest this weekend, then it's 'operation house' again as from Monday. Was all washed and dressed by the time Bernie came in from the shop, had another cup of tea with him. Then went to St. Joseph's Home, where they were holding a bazaar. Saw Sister Catherine, who asked me would I help out on one of the stalls, told her I wanted to have a look round first. Was very disappointed – it wasn't the big affair they usually have, just what they call a mini bazaar. Bought a few raffle tickets and bits of jewellery for the girls. Met Eileen Buckley who was serving at a stall for Ethiopia; told her I didn't feel very well, she said I didn't look well. Asked her to tell Sister Catherine I was sorry I couldn't help and went straight home to bed. Got up at five o'clock to cook dinner, didn't feel much better. Bernie went off to the Dogs. I watched telly with the girls.

Sunday 11ᵗʰ September

Summer has really gone, pouring rain this morning and very cold as well. We all went to eight o'clock Mass, which Father Hegarty said. He asked the people to take more bingo tickets, as the takings are going down and the money was needed to pay for the new church hall, which is nearly finished at last. Everybody is invited to have coffee there next Sunday after the 9.30, 10.30 and midday Masses. Said a few words to Father Hegarty about not having coffee after the eight o'clock Mass, and guess who's making it now – me. Peter and Sheila came home from Ireland today, bought me a beautiful present, a Royal Tara, bone-china candlestick holder. Sheila said you can't buy Belleek china, it's gone so expensive, so my little collection must be worth quite a bit. Mary came to dinner, she is still upset over being told to get out of June's house. Was really glad when dinner was over and I could go to bed, still very tired. Terri gave me my tea in bed. When I got up, cut out two suits for herself and Fiona (had bought a very nice jacket at the bazaar yesterday just to take a pattern off it) – one is a light grey flannel, the other a dark grey – Lizzie gave me the material. Helped Fiona with her homework, which was fashion and textiles.

Monday 12ᵗʰ September

Wish I had been born rich, I'm so tired working. Very cold this morning, had to wear my coat going to work. Bernie's last day of his three weeks' holiday. He went in to help Leena in the shop at eight o'clock, Terri had been in there from 7.30 before going to school. Mary stayed last night; left her in bed when I went out to work, she doesn't go in to work until about 10.30. Lizzie re-cut that tartan blazer again, it looks a bit better but couldn't finish it, waiting on shoulder pads. Made the little jacket for Terri in my lunch hour, it looks very nice, will put the lining in it tomorrow. When I got home from work, Bernie was in the shop again – Leena had gone to collect her little girl from school. Cooked dinner for Bernie, Ciarán and myself. Fiona didn't want any, she's on a diet again, and Terri didn't have any because she doesn't like lamb – can't please everybody. Mary didn't come over this evening, can't get in touch with her now since June's sister had the phone cut off. Our bathroom still needed more tiles to finish it, so went up after dinner to do them. All the tools had been shoved in the shed before the visitors came, had a bit of a job finding them. Had a few words with Adam and James about their punk records, told them they are not to be played in my house anymore. They both said their mothers don't mind them listening to them, told them I didn't care what their mothers allowed, I'm not having dirty records playing in my house.

Tuesday 13th September

Pouring rain again this morning, this must be our rainy season – how England ever runs short of water I'll never know, we certainly get enough rain. Having trouble with my windscreen wipers, they are not working. Fed up with this car, there's always something wrong with it. Terrible traffic on the roads since all the schools re-opened. Made a nice sample jacket in work today, loose-fitting with a sailor collar. Lizzie told Doris, Penny and myself to take some material before she sent it out to the cutting room. I took four pieces, one of them is grey with a white pinstripe. I cut a suit out of it for Fiona tonight, a straight skirt with a short, boxy jacket. Made the skirt of Terri's suit in my lunch hour. Mary came over after work, she brought some sheets and towels to wash. Put them in the washing machine and had a flood in the laundry room, discovered the seal round the door is broken. Thought if we could get it off we could turn it upside down, but it wouldn't budge; was afraid to force it off in case it did more harm than good. Looked up the Yellow Pages, picked out two phone numbers for Mary to ring tomorrow and get the one who'll come quickest to mend it. It poured rain so much tonight, Mary couldn't go home. I never saw such rain, you wouldn't even put milk bottles out. Late again getting to bed, stayed talking to Mary till one o'clock.

Wednesday 14th September

Envied Mary lying in bed while I went off to work. Left home at 8.30, didn't get in until 9.10, the traffic was chaotic. There was a tail-back from south Tottenham High Road right back to Park View Road. Thought there must have been an accident, but saw no signs of one – may have had something to do with the rain, pouring again this morning. Terri was up at 6.30 to go into Leena at seven o'clock. I'm getting a bit annoyed over it, because the minute she comes from school she's in there again. She'll even do without dinner to go in and help out, she's getting no rest at all. Mary went to see a lady in the council about a flat – she said she'll have no trouble getting a council flat, but it will take a couple of months or more and there is no question of her having to get out of June's house by the end of September, and she is going to write to June's sister and tell her so; I think Mary is a bit happier about the situation now. Doris had a chat with Harry today, she doesn't know whether to leave or not. He told her Mr. Jacobs, one of the directors, thinks she's too slow and he doesn't like the idea of her taking five weeks' holiday, she's off to Jamaica on Sunday. She is to let Harry know by Friday whether she's leaving or not, would have slipped out quietly had I been her. Went shopping with Mary and Fiona tonight – didn't buy very much, but it cost £29.72.

Thursday 15th September

Could do with that extra half hour sleep in the morning, which I don't get now that Terri goes into Leena's at seven o'clock instead of 7.30. Once she gives me that cup of tea I'm afraid to go asleep again in case I don't wake up in time to call Ciarán for school – he'd like that. Lizzie didn't come in till lunch hour today, she'd been in the showrooms up the West End all morning, but she left plenty of work for Doris and myself. At about 11.30 Mr. Jacobs (the man who told Doris off) came in and asked where Lizzie was, then turned to Doris and said, I hear you're off on holidays, I hope you have a nice time and I wish you the best of luck. He shook hands with her and all she could say was, I can't believe it. Afterwards, she said he only said all that because he was so pleased to know he was getting rid of her. She left work early today to go for an interview for a job up the West End – doubt if anybody will hold a job for her till she comes back off her holiday. After dinner, Bernie burnt the paint off the bathroom window. Burnt is the right word – was really annoyed when I saw it. Was annoyed also with Terri, it's her week for washing up and she was so bent on getting into the shop that she cleaned the cooker very badly. When I gave out to her, she said I didn't care about helping people. After I got through with her, she didn't go into the shop. Could do with some help myself, not very happy.

Friday 16th September

Really can't understand what's gone wrong with the traffic – what used to be a 10 or 15 minute journey this morning took 40 minutes. Never left the house so early, was trying to get into work early to make a skirt for Fiona before nine o'clock. Finished up being late for work, never saw so much traffic in all my life. Bernie said it was the same on The Angel, he thinks there must be a road closed somewhere that's causing all the traffic to come through Tottenham. If it continues like that, I'd be better off getting a bus to work, although even the bus lanes were packed this morning. Doris left today, feel sorry to see her go. She said when she comes back from Jamaica she is going to the agencies. Never heard of them myself (agencies for sample machinists), but apparently they do exist. You just work for two or three weeks at a time, but she said the wages are twice as much as you get in a permanent job. The job Doris went after yesterday was gone – the lady she saw said she had got somebody from the agency. Cooked dinner for Mary but she didn't come over, can't get in touch with her now that her phone has been cut off. So tired after dinner, went into the sitting room and fell asleep till seven o'clock. Bernie must have fallen asleep too while watching the telly, he did no work tonight. I cut out a school skirt for Terri, who was in helping Leena as usual.

Saturday 17th September

Everybody off to work this morning, even Bernie, who didn't think the firm would have any more Saturday work; the house was so peaceful. Was just settling down for a long, looking-forward-to rest, when I remembered the man was coming to fix the washing machine, and very reluctantly got up. Did some tidying up, then cut out a couple of patterns while waiting for the man, who came at ten o'clock. Took a look at the seal of the washing machine, pressed it in with his thumb, turned it on and tested it, said that's ok now. Then gave me a bill for £14.95 for that small service, he was gone by 10.10. Went to Walthamstow market, was very disappointed, there were very few stalls there due to the fact it was a Jewish holiday. Went to the shops in Stoke Newington, which were also closed, it wasn't my day. Went to Ridley market, where I got some lovely satin for nighties for the girls. Then I went to Edmonton Green, bought some coat material there. Spurs lost 2-0 to Everton today. Couldn't park my car outside Geary's where I get my bread, there were traffic wardens everywhere, they were giving out tickets like their lives depended on it. Mary came to tea and stayed the night. Bernie nearly went berserk tonight, he caught James jumping up and down on Ciarán's bed, what he didn't say wasn't worth saying.

Sunday 18th September

Where, oh where, has all the sunshine gone – pouring cats and dogs this morning and freezing cold. It's hard to believe we had such a lovely summer, it all seems so far away now. The new church hall is not finished yet so there was no coffee morning. Dick Johnson was really furious with Adam Kelly this morning, it seems he was beating Henry up in the vestry after Mass. He said he's not letting him serve Mass anymore if he doesn't behave. I said a few words to him too about beating Ciarán up last week – he's really very troublesome, Judy really has her hands full. Father Roderick said Mass. He's so fussy, he even started before the candles were lit. When we got home, Fiona cooked breakfast and then Mary went to 10.30 Mass. Leena's birthday is on Thursday week, Terri bought her a cut-glass fruit set. She went to wrap it today and discovered it has a flaw in it, she'll have to change it tomorrow. She's not well at all today, she seems to be getting a cold and has a sore throat; still, it didn't keep her from going into the shop. Fiona went to bed after breakfast, said she's exhausted. Had my usual afternoon nap. Fiona brought up my tea. Listened to the 'Top Twenty' while reading a book of Dublin sayings my cousin Anna had bought for me. It's called, 'Janey Mac' [a popular Dublin expression to avoid blasphemous swearing], it is very interesting. When I got up, cut out a dress for myself. Terri has me annoyed to go to a dance in the new church hall next Saturday, the bishop is going to open it. Would rather not go, still, it might be interesting. Bernie said he'll stay home with Fiona and Ciarán.

Monday 19th September

A really lovely morning, a bit of a change from yesterday. Thought my car wasn't going to start, it doesn't like the cold weather, probably won't go at all when the winter comes in. The traffic wasn't bad at all this morning, got to work at 8.50. Overlocked another school skirt for Terri before starting work at nine o'clock. Made a couple of sample skirts and a jacket. Made Terri's skirt in my lunch hour. After lunch, Ann (the cleaner) came in, asked us were we missing Doris. When I was going through the factory at three o'clock, I said to an Irish lady there, I bet that Doris is sitting under a coconut tree; she said, I hope a coconut falls on her head (joking of course). Mary phoned to say she had rung the Gas Board about my freezer, which is not working properly since one of their men fixed it a few weeks ago. They sent me a bill for £25.00, which I'm not paying till it's put right. Said they'll send a man on Thursday. Laura also phoned this evening, said she had a great time in America, said business is booming. They are opening a new factory, she has two other designers working with her now. Said she'll call over one evening when they are going to visit Ben's parents. Bernie and myself put some hardboard on the bathroom floor – what a job that was cutting round the toilet. Gave strict orders to Bernie and Ciarán not to miss their shot when going to the toilet.

Tuesday 20th September

A beautiful morning, a bit cold but lovely and sunny. No problem getting to work this morning; Bernie seems to have been right about the traffic last week, there must have been a road closed that brought all the traffic round Tottenham. Lizzie was in the West End this morning. Penny cut out a skirt for me to make – for a person who's been to college for three years studying design and pattern-cutting she has an awful lot to learn. The people teaching these kids at college would need somebody to teach themselves. I learned more in a few months at the Grafton Academy in Dublin, and then I only went there once a week – couldn't afford to go more often. Mary came over this evening, she's very upset. June's sister (the one who's been left the house) and her husband were in the house when she got home last night. The husband said, I hope you'll be out in a fortnight's time. Mary said, I can't go till the council give me a flat. He said, I thought you'd do the decent thing and get out. June's sister had told Mary she could stay till the house was sold, which might take a year or more. When Mary reminded her of this, she denied ever having said it. How can you reason with people like that, but Mary made it quite clear to them that she is not getting out till she gets a place to live. I think what's upsetting her more than anything is the fact she thought so highly of these people.

Wednesday 21st September

Nearly had a stroke when I looked into the girls' bedroom this morning – had I seen it before they went to school, they wouldn't have gone, was really furious. Paper bags of rubbish everywhere, clothes thrown all over the place. Fiona had changed the sheets on her bed and had thrown the ones she had taken off on the floor. Even the window-sill was full of books and boxes. Gathered up everything and put them on their beds. On my way to work, kept going over what I would say to them when they came home from school, even contemplated not giving them any food for a week. Lucky for them, by the time I got home from work I had cooled down quite a bit. Nevertheless, when they did come home I sent them flying in all directions with all I said to them; I never saw a room cleared so quickly in all my life. I told them, in future I'm inspecting their room every morning from now on. We have the rain back again, it never stopped all day, came down in buckets. Went shopping with Mary and Fiona today. Bought some lino tiles for the bathroom floor. Left Mary home, she then reminded me that the man was coming tomorrow to fix my freezer. As tomorrow is her day off, she said she'd come home and stay the night and wait for him to call.

Thursday 22nd September

A beautiful morning after all the rain. Before leaving for work, told Mary what to say to the gas man about the thermostat they had put on and which didn't work. Terrible tail-back of traffic when I got to south Tottenham High Road; luckily for me it was going in the opposite direction or I'd never have got to work. On my way home from work I discovered the reason for the hold-up – every few yards along the High Road they had built islands, which now means single file. I wonder whose stupid idea that was, it had to be a man, a woman would have more foresight. I suppose in another few weeks they'll be knocking them down when they find out their mistake, at the expense of the rate payers. Couldn't believe it when Mary told me the gas man hadn't been. Rang up and gave out yards. It turned out they gave the bloke who was to have called the wrong address – instead of 21, they had put down 27; they said I could make another appointment for next week. When I had finished telling them I was going to sue the Gas Board for two days' loss of pay (one day last week and today), they had a bloke up within ten minutes. He said the freezer hadn't needed a new thermostat at all, just a service, which he did, and told me not to pay the £25.00 I'd been billed for it. Went to get some radiator paint in Wickes, but they hadn't any.

Friday 23rd September

Summer has come back again, thank God – it's been a really beautiful day, up in the seventies all day. Had a couple of flashes of lightning and a very heavy shower of rain tonight at about 8.30. Got to work bright and early this morning. The traffic was very good, little or no delays. Made some samples of summer skirts, we are now doing next year's summer range. Finished off a dress for Mary in my lunch hour; was making it for myself, but didn't care for the colour, it looks very well on her. Thought she wasn't coming at all this evening, didn't arrive until nearly six o'clock. She said at the last minute Father Hegarty told her there would be 12 people (including the bishop) tomorrow to dinner, so she had to go out and buy more meat. We both went down to Queensway tonight to look for that radiator paint, but they hadn't got it there either. We had a look at the furniture while we were there. This assistant came over and asked us were we interested in anything, I said no, everything is much too expensive for me. He said yes, I look very rich got up like this (I had on an old dress and cardigan which had seen better days), he said it's only the very rich people who go round like that. Still can't make up my mind whether he was paying me a compliment or not. Peter (next door) got the front of his house double-glazed today, it looks very nice. Sheila said they'll get the back of the house done later on.

Saturday 24th September

Very warm and sultry this morning but not complaining, love the warm weather. Got up at 8.30, tidied round and did some ironing before going off to Edmonton Green to do some shopping. Got the radiator paint in Tesco – very expensive, a very small tin for £3.25. Took Mary's dress over to her, she was very busy, there were 15 people coming to dinner not 12, told her I'd go over later and give her a hand. Went off and had my hair set in Tiffany's. Selina went berserk with the lacquer, came out with my hair feeling like a board. Tried to comb it out when I got home but couldn't get the comb through it. Got dinner ready and rushed over to the chapel house before seven o'clock. Dinner was to have been at seven o'clock, but at 7.45 the bishop still hadn't arrived and Father Hegarty was saying Mass. Dick Johnson came into the kitchen, he spoke to the other people and they all agreed to go ahead without the bishop, which was just as well because he didn't arrive until 8.30, said all he needed was a cup of coffee as he had already eaten. Went into the church hall after we had washed up, the dance was in full swing. Saw all the old familiar faces. Nobody could believe how Fiona has grown, even Johnjoe and Mary said they wouldn't know her if they met her out.

Sunday 25th September

Oh God, did I pay for my dancing session last night, could hardly walk this morning with the pains in my legs. That's what I got for acting the fool, showing the girls how to do Irish dancing and old time waltzes. Still, we all had a great time and the hall is really lovely, which I suppose it should be, it cost £100,000.00 to build. It has got everything – a lovely kitchen, toilets, community room upstairs and another room upstairs which is to be called the Father McCarthy room, loads of store rooms, all with fitted carpets and central heating, and of course the dance hall downstairs. The girls and myself served coffee and tea there this morning after eight o'clock Mass. Thought I'd never get dinner over with so that I could get to bed to rest my weary legs, my dancing days are really over. The next time I go to a dance, I'll sit very sedately in a corner and watch the younger crowd dancing. Fiona is not well tonight, she has a bad cold, don't think she'll be able to go to school tomorrow. No better myself – when I got out of bed, still had dreadful pains in my legs. Had a Radox bath and took a couple of tablets, can't say they did much good. Was busy doing some cutting out when Leena called – she thought Bernie was on a week's holiday and would help in the shop, was disappointed to hear he had finished all his holidays.

Monday 26th September

Another beautiful morning, thank God, hope it lasts a bit longer. Fiona couldn't go to school today, she has a bad cold and a sore throat, which is not surprising since she goes out in the rain with no coat or umbrella. She keeps saying rain never did anyone any harm, now she knows different. Lizzie wasn't in work today, she went to Paris at the weekend at the firm's expense. Penny and myself worked hard. I made three sample skirts and a dress for Fiona in my lunch hour. Mary phoned the Gas Board this morning for me, to tell them my freezer still isn't working, said they would send somebody tomorrow. When I came from work, phoned to know what time the man would call, morning or afternoon – was told, not too politely, they couldn't tell me. Gave them a piece of my mind, said I thought with all the inconvenience I'd been put to I should be getting preferential treatment, they said I was. Asked to talk to Mr. Simpson or Mr. Francis, both managers there, but was told they were at a meeting. Was so furious, got into my car and went down to the gas depot on Garmen Road. Saw a supervisor there that I've come to know through all the aggro I've had from the Gas Board in the past few years. Said a few words to him about the incompetence of his fitters. The outcome of which was, a man is calling before 10.30 in the morning to fix the freezer; Bernie is taking the day off.

Tuesday 27th September

Very dull this morning but very warm, had to open the kitchen door, but even with that there was no breeze. Left Bernie a list of jobs to do while waiting for the gas man. Lizzie wasn't in work today, she phoned in to say she wasn't well. Later on, Penny phoned her and she said she sounded as if she had a bad cold. In spite of her cold, Fiona went to school this morning because she didn't want to miss her German lesson, which is one of her favourite subjects. When I got home from work, was really annoyed – not only had Bernie not done any of the jobs I'd mapped out for him, but it seems there were three men working on the freezer. In the end, they came to the conclusion that what was needed was a new unit, which one of them said I would get free if I hadn't got the freezer more than five years. I thought I only had it about two years, but when Mary came this evening she said she thought it was about five years old or more, I hope she's wrong. The annoying part about it is I'm going to be without it for at least two weeks or more. Phoned Mr. Simpson, who said he'll do his best to get it done as soon as possible, the hold-up will be the manufacturer supplying the unit. Bernie stripped some of the wallpaper off Ciarán's bedroom tonight while I cleaned off a door. We have started on the house again; whether it will be done before Christmas remains to be seen. Left Mary home, it's all go here.

Wednesday 28th September

Dull again this morning but still very warm, too warm to wear a coat. Was surprised to see Lizzie in work when I got there, she hasn't got rid of her cold but she said she feels a lot better than she did yesterday. Found Paris very tiring and nothing really exciting happening in the fashion world. Clothes are pretty costly there, the average price for a skirt is around £50.00, which the French women don't mind paying. Lizzie said French women are definitely prettier than English women. Harry has an ad in a few newspapers for a sample machinist, but so far he hasn't had one reply. Was hoping he'd get one soon so that I could have a couple of weeks off in October. Will have to do a Novena he gets somebody. Mary came to go shopping. Terri didn't come with us – Leena asked her to stay and have a meal with them. Fiona didn't come, she said she had too much homework to do, but when we came back she was in keeping Helen (next door) company; [I] said a few words to her. Left Mary home. Was expecting June's sister and husband to be there, but they must be leaving it till next week to come up from Sussex, when they expect Mary to be out of the house, but the council workers have been on strike and she hasn't been able to get in touch with the woman there who told her she'd get her a flat. Spurs played Drogheda tonight and beat them 8-0.

Thursday 29th September

Leena came in at eight o'clock this morning with a Black Forest cake, today's her birthday. Terri gave her a very nice cut-glass fruit set, I gave her a vanity bag and hand cream – she was so excited. Hadn't much time to talk to her, was rushing to get ready for work. Dull and misty all day, but still very warm. Made some very cheap cotton sample skirts. The firm is trying to do a cheaper line in skirts in an effort to get orders from Tesco and Woolworths. Think it's a pity that a company that makes such skirts should bother to make trash, but I suppose it all brings in the money. Started on a pair of trousers for Ciarán during my lunch hour, but one of the directors (the one who told Doris off) came in and I didn't get much done. When I came home from work had a phone call from Mary Mac to say she's coming to dinner tomorrow. My electric sander broke. Asked Leena's husband if he could fix it; he couldn't, but he reminded me that it's still under guarantee, so I can have it repaired free of charge. Could have done with it tonight. Bernie finished taking the paper off Ciarán's room. Could have killed him when I saw he had taken the ceiling paper off as well. Leena sent her husband out to get two cauliflowers and he brought her back a beautiful diamond ring, she said it's the first thing he's ever given her since they got married. Sending Bernie for the shopping the weekend.

Friday 30th September

The weather has changed again, quite cold this morning and drizzling rain. Had to put my car lights on going to work; was halfway up the stairs to the design room when I remembered I'd left them on, had to go all the way down and turn them off. Very busy today making all those cheap samples. Had to get Lilly (the Irish lady who works in the factory) up to help, she's a hard nut. Harry's father said to her, "How do you like working in this five star place?" she said, "I'd rather be in a four star". She doesn't like making samples, said she doesn't like the responsibility. Finished off Ciarán's trousers in my lunch hour. Mary Mac was waiting for me when I got home, told her all the latest news while getting the dinner ready. After which, herself, Mary and me went upstairs to take everything out of Ciarán's wardrobe – had decided it was too big for his room. Had a look round during the week for a new one, but any I saw are all made of chipboard, which I hate. Answered an ad I saw in the paper last night; the lady who answered the phone said I could have a look at it tonight, she lives in Enfield. Mary Mac, Fiona and myself went there. It's a very nice wardrobe, all solid timber, dark oak, too nice really for Ciarán, he's so careless with his paint. The lady wants £50.00 for it, the problem is getting it home. Told her I'll let her know tomorrow if I was taking it or not.

October 1983

Saturday 1st October

A dreadful day in more ways than one, never stopped raining once and foggy with it. Spent the morning looking for the key to the bureau in Ciarán's room, where I keep most of my private papers, birth certificates, policies and such like. Didn't find it – I put it away safe, too safe. Gave up looking and went off to the Black & Decker shop about my sander. Spoke to a very nice man there, who told me it would take a week to repair. When I told him I wanted it in a hurry he had it fixed there and then, no charge of course because it's still under guarantee. Went off to Stoke Newington to get some canvas and trimmings for coats I'm going to make for the girls, was very sorry to hear the shop is closing down, it's been there for years. When I came home, Bernie told me the lady who's selling the wardrobe phoned – she said she'd found a man who'd deliver it for £4.50. Still can't make up my mind whether to have it or not, it's so much smaller than the one he has. Ciarán came in very upset this evening. Adam Kelly told him that I was taking all the punk records and tapes over to Father Hegarty – I was supposed to have told this to Mary O'Brien. Since I haven't seen Mary for years, I don't know when I'm supposed to have told her. Couldn't convince Ciarán I hadn't said it, so went over to Adam who was having a bath. Told Judy what he'd said; she seemed to think Ciarán was telling lies, but Adam said John O'Brien told him. He was so cheeky to me, I told Judy if Ciarán spoke to her the way Adam spoke to me, I'd kill him. Went to see Mary O'Brien and John, who said he didn't say that to Adam. It seems Adam just says these sort of things to upset Ciarán, he's a real stirrer.

Sunday 2nd October

Not a bad morning, quite a change from yesterday, warm and dry. Father Roderick said Mass. Father Hegarty is not well at all, he was in bed all day yesterday with a very bad cold, Mary said he couldn't eat a thing. Didn't think we were to serve tea and coffee again this Sunday, but Mrs. Dunn got everything ready, so the girls and myself went round to help. Only four people came in, one woman was over here on holiday from Ireland. Had told Ciarán I wasn't giving Adam Kelly a lift home from Mass, but while I was helping in the hall both of them walked home. Judy had said to me last night – in future Adam and Ciarán will not be together; I said I thought that was the best thing, but here today Ciarán told him his father said they could be together, but Ciarán wasn't allowed to go into their house and Adam wasn't to go into our house. But Ciarán wasn't too happy when I told him I wasn't letting him be with Adam. I've had enough trouble with him telling lies about me. Ciarán said he was leaving home today and asked me for the £2.00 back which he gave me from his milk round, but later he thought better of it and stayed; didn't know what to do with himself all day. Spurs played their first Sunday match against Nottingham Forest, beat them 2-1.

Monday 3rd October

Very warm morning. The traffic was chaotic, something wrong on the High Road, even the buses had to go round the one-way system. Couldn't do a thing right in work. Harry cut out some skirts on Saturday for me to do in a hurry today, you'd think a bad carpenter had cut them, there was nothing right with them. Between that and me leaving my brains behind, it was a pretty awful day, was really glad to get home. Cooked dinner but there was nobody in to eat it, everybody was late home for some reason or another. When Ciarán came in, he was in the hungry horrors – finished up eating two dinners, which makes a change for him, he usually lives on Cornflakes. Fiona went round to see Dr. Watson, she thinks her hair is falling out. He gave her a prescription for shampoo – if it does her any good, I'll try it myself, going a bit thin on top. After dinner, Bernie cleared out Ciarán's room, so he'll have to sleep in my bed, I'll sleep on the bed settee. He told his father if he wakes him up snoring, he is going to sleep on the little couch in the dining room. I spent the evening until nine o'clock sanding down two bedroom doors, took them to the kitchen to do. Dyed one of them to see how it would turn out, or would I be breaking it gently to Bernie that I wanted them painted white – that's why I did it while he was upstairs. It's really ironic everybody liked it except myself.

Tuesday 4th October

Very warm today, the temperature 72 degrees. The traffic here has really gone haywire, couldn't believe it this morning, everywhere leading to Park View Road was choker block full [another Vera original, for 'chock-a-block']. Tried all the turnings, but one was worse than the other. In the end, had to turn back and go up on the High Road, which was also packed with cars. Went up Lordship Lane, down Bruce Grove, up The Avenue, down Mount Pleasant Road, down Laurence Road, up Avenue Road N15, then out onto St. Ann's Road and out onto south Tottenham High Road – took me exactly one hour to do a journey which should take 15 minutes at the most. Didn't have a very happy day in work either. Lizzie was at the showrooms up the West End. Everything I went to machine had something wrong with it. Penny is as good, or should I say as bad, at cutting as Harry is; fed up altering badly cut work. Made a skirt for myself in my lunch hour, no problems with that. When I looked at the width of it, thought to myself, it's time I went on a diet. Mary came over this evening, so far June's sister and her husband haven't come round. Sanded some more doors tonight out in the kitchen, never saw such a mess in all my life – I really do need my head tested, layers of dust everywhere. When I was finished, cleaned up – even washed the floor. A few minutes after, everywhere looked as if it needed cleaning all over again, don't think I'll ever get rid of the dust.

Wednesday 5th October

I don't know what's gone wrong with the weather – yesterday we were sweltering with the heat, this morning it was really cold and remained so all day. The traffic was a little bit better today, not a lot, but at least not as bad as yesterday. Things not too bad in work, Lizzie was there to see to things. Harry asked me could I postpone my holidays for a while, we are so busy. Lilly from the factory came up again to help out. Wasn't long in from work when Leena knocked at the door to know was Terri in, she was to have been home early from school and had promised to collect Tina from school and Leena was getting a bit anxious. Told her I was sure Terri would collect her on her way home, which was exactly what she did do. It seems she missed a bus and was delayed waiting on another and so went straight on to the school for Tina. About half an hour after, Tina banged down our door to know would we come quickly – they were being murdered. Terri and myself ran into the shop; only Leena's mother was there and she was in a state of collapse and couldn't talk, I told Terri to make her a cup of tea. After a while, Leena came in – she was in a terrible state – she had been out chasing three chaps who had robbed the till and beaten herself and the mother up. I phoned the police, who came at once, got an ambulance for the mother, Fiona went with her. Ciarán came from school very ill, had to take him to Dr. Watson. Then up to the hospital to get Fiona and the mother, then up to Stamford Hill for Ciarán's prescription, then got the shopping and left Mary home. God, what a night.

Thursday 6th October

Ciarán wasn't any better this morning, he wasn't able to eat anything; wouldn't have gone to work at all but for the fact Mary said she'd come over and look after him and we are so busy in work. Gave him strict instructions not to get out of bed and on no account to open the door to anybody. Left the keys in Leena's for Mary. The traffic was back to normal this morning. Lizzie wasn't in, she had gone to the fabric show at Olympia. Lilly was up again today to help out, spent a very pleasant day chatting about this and that. Phoned home at midday to enquire how Ciarán was, was amazed to hear him answering the phone. Mary hadn't arrived (was really annoyed with her), but Ciarán said he was alright and had just taken one of his tablets. Finished off a skirt I was doing. Phoned half an hour later intending to go home if Mary hadn't come by then, but it was she who answered the phone. Said a few words to her about not coming down earlier. She said the person who used to clean for June came just as she was coming out. She didn't say anything, but Mary thinks it means that June's sister and husband are coming up from Sussex. I went home with her again tonight intending to have a few words with them but they weren't there.

Friday 7th October

Ciarán still not well, Terri stayed out of school to look after him. Gave him one of his tablets before going to work, told Terri to give him another one at 11.45. Rang her at midday, luckily I did, she had forgotten to give it to him. She told me she had given him soup for his lunch, she had also done jelly and custard for him and loaned him her tape recorder, so he was quite happy. Worked very hard today, still a mad rush on for samples. No Lilly today, she had a rush of her own in the factory. Some of the samples I'm doing are for Arnotts of Dublin. At two o'clock Harry's father came in and asked me would I come in to work tomorrow as they badly needed samples. Much as I hate Saturday work, I didn't like to refuse, told him I'd come in at nine o'clock. He said Lilly was also coming in. Saw Lilly when I was going home, who told me she was coming in at eight o'clock and would leave at midday.

Don't know if I can manage the eight o'clock, will have to see how I feel in the morning. Mary came over this evening. Everybody was soaking wet coming in, it poured rain nearly all day. Bernie put Sandtex on Ciarán's ceiling tonight, not awfully keen on it but at least it saves me having to paper it. I dyed another door. Terri went into Leena's. Fiona went to a disco with a school friend and her parents. Felt sorry for Mary going home to that house, it's really miserable for her with no heating or light upstairs.

Saturday 8th October

Ciarán's birthday, he's still not very well, could not do his milk round. Mary and Terri gave him a fiver each, Bernie gave him £10.00, my cousin Nan also gave him £10.00. He wants me to buy him a pair of shoes, but he'll have to wait until next Saturday when he's well enough to go out. Hated going to work this morning, had planned to do so many things in the house as Bernie wasn't working today. Lilly and myself worked very hard, I made four samples, we left at midday. Called into Mary on the way home, she was very upset. June's sister and her husband had come up from Sussex – gave her a letter from their solicitor which said she had to vacate the house by Monday or the bailiffs would be sent to evict her. Didn't know what to do. Then I thought of a lady I used to know who worked for the council, went to see her. She is such a nice person and so helpful. She phoned a person from the housing community. When I explained Mary's situation to the lady on the phone, she said Mary was to sit tight. Said she must go to the council first thing Monday morning and they would take action against June's sister and her husband. They had also told Mary they are going to change the locks on the door, it's all very worrying.

Sunday 9th October

Don't know what was wrong with Father Roderick this morning – he said Mass in record time, didn't even give a sermon. Poor old Tom was there, he's just come out of hospital, God help him. He didn't look well enough to be out, especially as it was pouring rain, but otherwise he was his usual cheerful self. Mary was down very early, she hadn't even had a cup of tea – she said June's sister and husband were in the kitchen and she wouldn't go in while they were there. Decided to take all the white skirting boards off Ciarán's room, and asked Dan to cut the doors off his old wardrobe into lengths 6.5 inches wide – that will mean no more painting on skirtings. Dan took the doors up to the shop in his van. Later on, Ciarán and myself went up to the shop, it's a while since I've been there. He has quite a lot of second-hand stuff, he said he's doing better with that than the DIY. Bought a few bits and pieces from him, including an inlaid cribbage board for 50p which Bernie thought was lovely, I'm going to French polish it. Dan came over tonight to turn on the central heating – everybody is complaining of the cold here. Told him I was buying a second-hand wardrobe for Ciarán's room, he thought £50.00 was very dear for it. Told me he had made two small cupboards in his small bedroom each side of the window, said it wouldn't cost much more than I was paying for the wardrobe and it would make the room look better finished. So have asked him to do two cupboards for Ciarán's room, hope I won't have to wait till next year for them.

Monday 10th October

The house was lovely and warm this morning thanks to the central heating, but wasn't prepared for the cold outside, bitterly cold and pouring rain. Ciarán went back to school this morning, wasn't too happy about him going as he's now got a bad cough. He was gone when I discovered he hadn't worn a coat, just his blazer – gave out to him when he came home, he needs looking after like a baby. No problem getting to work this morning, not a lot of traffic on the roads, thank God. Still rushing samples. Penny (the trainee pattern-cutter) finished off some of them for me as she hadn't a lot of her own work to do. On my way home from work, called in to see Mary to find out how she got on this morning with the council. She was told they are putting her on the housing list as an emergency case, she is to go back to see them in two weeks' time. They said she cannot be put out of June's house. When Mary was going out this morning, June's sister's husband asked would she mind if they put her bed down in the sitting room; she said she didn't mind, so it doesn't sound as if they are going to turn her out today as they said – they must have had a change of heart, thank God. Dan came over tonight to measure up for Ciarán's wardrobes, one for hanging clothes in and the other with shelves. He will have them done the weekend. I'm not going to hold my breath, I know Dan too well for that.

Tuesday 11th October

Very cold this morning going to work but at least it wasn't raining. Still very busy in work. Started making a coat yesterday in my lunch hour for Fiona, she told me she wouldn't wear it because it's red; this evening she wanted to know when I'd have it finished, so she must have changed her mind about it. Didn't do much to it today. Lizzie was interviewing a designer. Harry asked me today did I know of another sample machinist who wanted a job, told him I knew of one person.

I had met a friend of hers on Saturday who said she wasn't very happy in her job so maybe she would come and work for him. I went to see her tonight. Told her about the job and how nice Harry and the rest of them were to work for. Even phoned Harry, who was still at the factory, and arranged with him to see her tomorrow morning. Came home and did some more work on my doors while Bernie painted Ciarán's bedroom window. At ten o'clock, had a phone call from Barbara to say she'd been thinking it over and was a bit wary of changing jobs. She's a very good sample machinist but has always worked at dresses and thinks she might be bored doing skirts all the time. However, she said she'll give me a ring the weekend – wish now I hadn't said anything to Harry. Bernie said Mary didn't look at all well tonight; I was too busy to notice, I expect it's all the worry over the house, I hope she gets a flat soon.

Wednesday 12th October

Harry was very disappointed this morning when I told him Barbara wasn't coming. His father asked me did I tell her that I was happy working here, said I did and also told her how nice you all were to work for. They are really desperate for another sample machinist. They've had loads of replies to their ad for a designer but not even one for a sample machinist, we seem to be a dying breed and, unless they get one, I'll get no holidays at all. Think I'll have to do one of my Novenas. When Mary came over, she said she had told June's sister since she was getting rid of everything in the house, could I have the hall heater (which I had given to June) back; she said yes, they had put it aside for me. She also told Mary she was sorry for all the trouble – that it was the solicitor who wanted her out. Mary told her she hoped to be out within the next couple of weeks. She said don't worry, there's no rush now. I don't know what brought about this change of heart, but I'm very glad for Mary's sake. She also told Mary I could have a Westminster chime clock belonging to June. Took it home tonight, not only will it keep us awake chiming but the whole street as well. It's a lovely clock and I'm very pleased with it. No work done tonight. Went shopping and then to Wickes to buy a pasting table. Didn't buy one – they were £7.00 there, saw them somewhere for £5.00, wish I could remember where.

Thursday 13th October

Very wet this morning, and my windscreen wiper is not working right since Ciarán washed my car a few months ago; when I get time, will have to swap with the one on the passenger's side. Worked hard today, made six skirts, Penny finished them off for me, which was great. Still more replies from designers but none for sample machinists. Still working on the coat for Fiona in my lunch hour. Pouring cats and dogs when I came out of work. Called to Dan's shop to get some moulding, he was just closing – didn't know he closes early on Thursdays. Mary's day off. Left the keys in Leena's for her, so she did a bit of tidying up for me. Said she couldn't stand the clock chiming, Ciarán said it would get on his nerves too. Heard every hour it chimed myself during the night, so it's not very popular here except Terri, who thinks it's lovely, but then it didn't keep her awake all night. Think I'll have to stop the chimes or I'll be very unpopular with the neighbours. This is Indian Festival week, so Leena took Terri out to some celebrations. I put a few strips of wallpaper up in Ciarán's room, bought it in Wickes for £1.25 a roll. It looked a lovely, thick embossed paper but when it was pasted it was just like newspaper, so thin it kept tearing. The air was blue while I was hanging it, but once it was up it looked quite good. Bernie not in the best tonight, never is when there's work to be done. You'd want a feather to keep him in good humour.

Friday 14th October

Lovely, sunny morning but quite cold. Nothing exciting in work, made a couple of skirts and altered a couple. Told Lizzie I'd ask Barbara again about coming to work for the firm. Harry wasn't in, but he phoned and Lizzie told him what I'd said. He said he'd phone me at nine o'clock tonight to know what she'd said. Called to Barbara's house on my way home from work; knew she wouldn't be home from work, but wanted to know her phone number so that I could ring her later on. Her mother said she didn't know whether she'd take the job or not – had it been for dresses she would have jumped at it, but skirts she thought would be too boring. However, said I'd ring her later this evening. After dinner, went up to Ciarán's room to put the skirtings on. Bernie was to help but threw one of his tantrums, went down stairs and watched telly for the night. This house would be finished long ago only for him and his tantrums, he makes me sick. Couldn't manage to do the skirtings myself, as the blocks of wood which they get screwed onto were missing – will ask Dan to do them. Phoned Barbara at eight o'clock, she was very definite that she wouldn't take the job. She's doing built-in wardrobes in her bedroom, said she couldn't go into a new job with so much on her mind. Harry phoned at exactly nine o'clock. Hated having to tell him I'd no luck with Barbara. Mary came over and stayed the night.

Saturday 15ᵗʰ October

Was up at eight o'clock this morning, after Terri had given me a cup of tea before she went off to work. Bernie doesn't go to work on Saturdays now. Wasn't talking to him over last night's performance, gave him the silent treatment. As I wasn't going out until this afternoon, decided I'd put the self-adhesive lino tiles on the bathroom floor. Made my first mistake when I started laying them from the wall out, found as I got to the top they weren't running straight. Had to quickly take them all up and start again from the centre of the room. What a mess that was, adhesive all over my hands. Had to spread the tiles sticky side up on the wash hand basin, the bath, and anywhere I could find a space. What with my feet sticking to the floor and my hands sticking to everything I touched, I was in a right state. Was missing one tile, looked everywhere for it. Since I hadn't moved out of the bathroom, knew it had to be there. It was, discovered it was stuck to my bottom. Had left it on the toilet seat and then sat on it, it just wasn't my day. Had intended taking Ciarán out when he'd finished his milk round to buy him a couple of jumpers and shoes, but he came in at 4.30 like a drowned rat. It had started to rain at one o'clock, I never saw anything like it, there were gale-force winds with it, so that put paid to our shopping spree. Only went out to collect Terri from work. Fiona was soaked to the skin when she came home. Terri went to another Indian festival with Leena.

Sunday 16ᵗʰ October

A lovely bright morning after all the rain yesterday but very cold – shivered in the church at Mass. Never saw so many people at the eight o'clock Mass, but all we took in at the bingo was £1.40, and 50p of that was mine and 30p from Bernie – it's not worthwhile standing in the cold for. Finished the floor in the bathroom this morning. It took me exactly one hour to put two tiles round the toilet pan, what with having to cut a pattern for it first. However, now that it's finished I'm very pleased with it. As it had rained so much yesterday, thought I better get a new windscreen wiper for my car, so after Bernie and myself had been to the off-licence, went to a car accessories shop in Bruce Grove. Was amazed at the price of them, £3.19, but they hadn't got the size. Tried another couple of shops without success. Went to James Clay's in White Hart Lane. Bernie went in to get it, had the old windscreen wiper with him, came out with just the rubber part. The bloke in the shop told him all he had to do was slip the old rubber out and fix the new one on. Knowing how handy Bernie is, I went into the shop and asked the bloke had he not got the whole fitting, as my husband wouldn't have a clue how to do it. He said, I'll do it for you, which he did at no extra charge, only cost me £1.50. Dan came tonight and fixed the two wardrobes in Ciarán's room – very pleased with them, they certainly improve the room. He's going to make a hi-fi unit to match for Ciarán's record player and also put a light over his bed.

Monday 17th October

Very cold morning, but at least it wasn't raining, not a lot of traffic on the roads. Think a lot of people are away on their winter holidays, wish I was one of them. Lizzie wasn't in today, she's gone to Paris to look at some fabrics, she'll be home tonight so should be in work tomorrow. She left plenty of work for Penny and myself to do. Just about to finish a skirt I had started on Friday when Harry came in and asked me to do four samples in a hurry, had them done by lunchtime. After lunch, finished off the one I started on Friday, then started on another one, it was all go today. Mary didn't come over this evening. This morning she said she'd go home after work as there might be some letters for her, she's expecting one from the council. Not talking to the girls, I'm sick of all their bickering and fighting – they've only to look at each other and they are off. Wouldn't let Terri go in to Leena's for the way she behaved this evening. She spends too much of her time in there altogether, she's there from seven till eight o'clock in the morning then from 5.30 until nine o'clock, sometimes later at night. Didn't know what I was letting myself in for when I told Leena we would help. Later on, Leena came in to know what was wrong. She thinks Terri and Fiona are angels, told her a few home truths about them. Terri spent the rest of the night crying her eyes out, Fiona defiant to the last, couldn't care less.

Tuesday 18ᵗʰ October

Very breezy this morning but lovely and sunny. Traffic great, got to work in ten minutes, was there by 8.50. Bert and Harry were in the design room looking at samples; the ones that Harry wanted in such a hurry yesterday were still there. When Lizzie was in, she said her trip to Paris was very enjoyable but tiring. A while after, Harry's father and another director came in and asked me why I put badly matching zips in three sealing samples. Told them I had told Harry we had no matching zips, and those were the ones he had told me to use. His father was furious and gave out yards to him. Felt sorry for him, but would have been twice as sorry for myself had I put them in without asking. The outcome is, I have to make three more sealing samples, not feeling sorry for Harry anymore, I could kill him. Lilly came up from the factory this morning to help out, had a good laugh with her. Called to Dan on my way home from work to get some more moulding, think I'm his best customer, never anybody in the shop when I go there. After dinner, did some more papering in Ciarán's room – can't finish it until Dan does the light for over his bed; knowing him, I hope I don't have to wait too long. Turned on the central heating a week ago, but for some reason it's not working. Dan said there might be air in it, it's certainly not hot air because the rooms are freezing. Mary didn't come over this evening. Phoned the chapel house but she had gone home, don't know how she goes back to that empty house.

Wednesday 19th October

A lovely, sunny morning – wish the weather could be always like this, ideal for working in. A new designer was talking to Harry when I got in to work, she had come for a day's trial. She seems very nice and quite good at her job I thought. I made a skirt which she designed and cut the pattern for – nothing really exciting, but at least she knows how to cut a pattern, which is more than can be said for a lot of designers; whether she'll be the one to get the job remains to be seen. Made two of the samples for BHS, this time with matching zips. Later in the day Harry said to me, we are giving you the first week in November off, I said is that a promise, he grinned and said no. Lizzie told me she's having that week off as they thought it would be best if we took our holidays the one time. Hadn't the heart to say I was expecting two weeks off, however, have to be thankful for small mercies. Mary came over this evening – asked her why she didn't come yesterday, she said she was so tired she went straight home to bed. Left her home after shopping. That house looks so miserable now that all the furniture is out of it. Mary is sleeping in the dining room – all it's got in it is her bed, a table, one chair and a small fireside chair, not very comfortable-looking. Dan left over the flex tonight for the light in Ciarán's room. Last night, Bernie channelled out the wall for it; tomorrow night, he'll sink the flex, plaster over it and leave it ready for Dan to connect.

Thursday 20th October

Fell asleep after Terri had given me my early morning cuppa, Fiona was washing her hair and hadn't thought of calling me. Terri as usual was in helping Leena before going off to school. Shouted to Ciarán to get up quick or he'd be late for school, he got out of bed in record time. Came down to breakfast, which he was bolting down when he suddenly realised he hadn't to be in school until ten o'clock, and would be finished at 2.30 because of some army thing going on in the school. He was also doing the Bronze Medal exam for swimming, he had to bring his pyjamas with him for it. In spite of getting up late, managed to get into work before nine o'clock. Lizzie said Anna, the designer who came yesterday, is starting work here in two weeks' time when we both come back after our holidays. Lizzie is not too keen on her as a person, but she said if her work is suitable that's all that matters, so it will be interesting to see what happens between them. This morning Ciarán bet me a pound he'd be home before me, but he wasn't, don't think I'll get that pound. He was very pleased with himself – he passed the swimming exam, but was a bit hurt when the teacher told him he had to pay 50p for the badge. Was busy dyeing the moulding round the bedroom door when I had a phone call from Miss Campbell, she used to be the girls' head mistress, she wants me to make her a dress. She said she has just moved back into her flat, it went afire four months ago, caused by a chip pan.

Friday 21ˢᵗ October

The traffic was very slow this morning, thought I'd never get to work. Made four samples today, and in my lunch hour shortened the curtains for Ciarán's bedroom – they are too long now that the radiator is there. After two o'clock, Penny got a phone call; she went out of the room, and when she came back she looked really strange. After a while she said, I've been given a week's notice, I thought she was joking until she started to cry. I couldn't believe it, I felt really sorry for her, she couldn't stop crying. They told her she needn't work the week if she didn't like but she said she would. Don't feel a bit happy working here now if they can dismiss people so casually. When I got home from work, Mary and Mary Mac were here. It was Mary's day off and she'd been to the council about a flat. Told her she'd have one within the next two months; if that's their idea of an emergency case, I hope I'm never homeless. Did some more dyeing tonight. Bernie put two doors back on, think they look ghastly. Bernie seems to think they'll look fine when they are varnished; hope the days of miracles are not passed, that's the only thing that will improve these doors. I think all my labours have been in vain, all I've done is make the house worse than it was. Mary Mac had done the same with her doors but has now decided to paint them white. Mary stayed the night.

Saturday 22ⁿᵈ October

All off to work this morning except Bernie and myself. After breakfast, dyed the last of the doors for upstairs. Bernie varnished two of them – it does improve them, but they still look very dark, I expect when the wallpaper goes up it will look alright. Ciarán came in for his usual cup of tea and a jacket, it wasn't as warm as he thought it was. Told him I'd take him to Wood Green when he had finished his milk round to buy him some clothes and shoes of my choice – that didn't please him. Terri came in to lunch, and as usual went into Leena's and bought some junk food in a carton; the smell alone would put you off eating, but she seems to like it. Had told Mary this morning I'd call for her at 3.15 to do a bit of shopping. Phoned her later to tell her I was waiting for Ciarán. He didn't come home until 3.45, James was with him, and by then Mary had come over so we all set off for Wood Green. Went to every shoe shop there, but Ciarán couldn't see the shoes he wanted. Finished up going into the shop where Fiona works. Mary bought a pair of shoes from her, she got £4.00 discount off them. In the end we got nothing for Ciarán; he wasn't too bothered, I think he'd rather have no new clothes than wear what I like. Got home just in time to collect Terri from Geary's with her usual bag of cakes. Dan was to come over tonight, but true to form he didn't come. Didn't do any work tonight, fell asleep watching telly.

Sunday 23rd October

Freezing cold this morning and very foggy as well, wouldn't have been surprised if the car didn't start, it doesn't behave well in cold weather, but thank God it did, so we were all in time for Mass, which Father Hegarty said and Ciarán and Adam Kelly served. Adam doesn't wait for a lift home now. Didn't do too bad with the bingo, took in £3.60, which is a great improvement on last week. There's a disco for the youngsters next Friday night, but the tickets aren't selling very well because Father Hegarty wants the parents to come and buy the tickets for their children – he thinks by doing that he won't have any trouble there, but the youngsters resent that very much and don't want to go at all, so he may find himself with only the disc jockey. Had a surprise visit from Ben, Laura and Katie tonight, they had spent the day with Ben's parents and were on their way home. They all looked very well, especially Katie, who has got very tall since I saw her last. Told me about the new factory they are opening soon in East Ham. They stayed for about an hour – told them I'd call to see them when I get my week off. They had only gone when Dan called, he brought over the cabinet which he made for Ciarán's record player. Said he'll come tomorrow night to do the light and plug, I'll be very surprised if he does, with Dan I just live in hope.

Monday 24th October

The traffic was great this morning, had a clear run all the way to work, it should be like that for the rest of the week because the schools are closed for half-term. Was first in the design room, Lizzie came in a few minutes after. Penny was so late thought she wasn't coming in at all, but she was very cheerful and seemed quite confident she'd get a job soon, hope she's not disappointed. Lizzie was very pleased with herself today, she bought a new sports car over the weekend, she said it's really super. Made a skirt for Fiona in my lunch hour. When I got home from work there was nobody in and I had no keys. Knew Terri was in work, and swearing vengeance against Fiona and Ciarán for not waiting in for me, when I thought of going into Leena's – and sure enough she had the keys. She told me Fiona's boss had phoned and asked her to go into work as two of the girls who were to have gone in were ill. Fiona was only glad to oblige, as she needs the money badly for a trip to Florence her art teacher is planning for early next year, it's for seven days and it costs £140.00 plus spending money. Phoned Mary, but she said she wouldn't be over this evening as she was too busy making chutney with all the tomatoes Father Hegarty had grown and hadn't eaten. She's run out of recipes for tomatoes and I think this is her way of getting rid of them once and for all. Dan didn't come over after all, Ciarán was very annoyed, he said his room is never going to get finished.

Tuesday 25th October

A lovely, sunny morning but the traffic wasn't as good as yesterday – quite a long tail-back at Park View Road, had to go up the back ways and come out at the top of Chestnut Road. Lizzie wasn't in at all today, she was in the West End showrooms seeing some reps about cloth. Penny cut out five BHS samples for me to do – you'd think a bad carpenter had done them, they were all the same style but in sizes 10 to 18. Harry came in to see how we were getting on. He was only fit to be in bed, he had such a dreadful cold, eyes and nose running all the time, really felt sorry for him. Made another skirt for Fiona in my lunch hour, she was really pleased when she saw it. Mary came this evening, she had a letter this morning from the council to say a man would call to see her on Friday morning between nine and twelve – hopefully it will be a step nearer to her getting a flat. Couldn't do much work tonight on the house, waiting on Ciarán's room to be finished. Dan was to come over to do the light for over his bed and the skirting boards (can't put the carpet down till that's done), but he sent James over to say he couldn't come, as he had a visitor. Was really annoyed, really can't depend on him at all. Can't even tidy the bedroom, Ciarán's bed is up against the wall in the girls' room and the rest of his things are in the other bedroom.

Wednesday 26th October

Brilliant sunshine this morning, the weather is really great. The traffic wasn't bad either; was in work by 8.40, so started making a sleeveless jacket for Fiona to go with one of the skirts I made her – worked on it until 8.55. Lizzie came in at nine o'clock, said she spent a very pleasant day yesterday in the West End. At about midday, Jim (the cutter) came into the design room and said I was wanted on the phone. It was Terri – she said, I hung out the washing for you; I said, I hope you haven't phoned up just to tell me that; she said, no, I wanted to tell you I think I got a Saturday job in Woolworths in Wood Green – she's to go back on Friday, and the lady she saw today will let her know for sure. Finished off the jacket for Fiona in my lunch hour, it looked really nice on her. Gave me orders to make the one to go with the other skirt tomorrow, she's never satisfied. Went shopping with herself and Mary tonight. Left Mary home, then stayed a while chatting to her. Freezing cold in that house, don't know how she stands it. When I got home, Dan was there. He had put the skirting on Ciarán's room, it looks very nice. He said our house is very badly wired and I should tell my landlord; I'm sure that will please Mr. South, he only had it re-wired four years ago, but Dan said it's very dangerous. Things get worse in this house. If only I could win the Pools, I'd run out of it and never come back again, it's really a curse to be poor. Bernie has been asked again to take early retirement.

Thursday 27th October

Another pile up of traffic on Park View Road this morning, never know what to expect, however was in work bright and early. A mad rush all day to get samples done which were wanted in a hurry. Lilly came up from the factory to help out, she livens things up a bit. Made the other jacket for Fiona in my lunch hour. Lizzie bought in some fresh-cream cakes today, had them in the afternoon just before I left. On the way out, one of the directors asked me not to put my car in the car park for a while as they were having some pipework done, which entailed digging up the ground. He forgot to mention they had already started on it – had an awful job getting my car out, was in danger of driving into the holes. Ciarán was in when I got home, he hadn't been out all day. James had been helping his father in the shop so he had nobody to go out with, he said he was bored to death. He used to say if he had a record player he wouldn't be bored; now he has one, but I suppose there's a limit to how much punk you can listen to. Mary came over and we went down to Wickes after dinner to buy some varnish – got Ronseal, £8.99 for 2½ litres, and £3.00 for a 2" paint brush – Bernie nearly had a fit when he heard the price. Dan came over without any tools (left them in the shop), so he couldn't fix the central heating or do the plug. However, he did manage to do the light and promised he'd come over tomorrow night and finish the job.

Friday 28th October

The traffic's gone haywire again – took me 40 minutes to get to work, which proves me wrong about the school children being the cause of the hold-ups – the schools are still on their half-term and the traffic is worse than ever. Penny's last day at work. She went for an interview for another job yesterday evening, and when she was coming home at six o'clock she was mugged by four youths on Spurling Road. They took her bag with £16.00 and all her sketches, she was more upset over them than the money. Without them she doesn't stand much chance of getting a job, and it would take her weeks to do them all again. However, she cheered up later on – Lizzie gave her a very nice sewing basket, the two lads in the cutting room gave her a box of Terry's All Gold, and I gave her a bar of Roger & Gallet soap. Mary saw the man from the council this morning. He just asked her where she'd like a flat and whether she'd like one with a separate bedroom or a bed-sitter and kitchen. Asked a few more questions, and then told her to ring the council on Tuesday. Terri and Fiona went to a disco in the new church hall tonight. Father Hegarty said if there was any trouble at it he would never have another one. Called for the girls when it was over. They said it was great, and Father Hegarty said he was very pleased everybody behaved so well. Dan came over and did the plug in Ciarán's room. Said he'll come over on Sunday and fix the central heating – could do with it now, it was really cold today.

Saturday 29th October

Ciarán didn't do his milk round today – Reg is on a week's holiday and the man in his place doesn't have help. Finally got his room finished this morning, it looks really nice, hope he'll keep it so. It's amazing how much bigger the room looks with the two smaller wardrobes rather than one big one. Was able to sort out the other bedrooms now that all Ciarán's stuff is out of them. Even got the landing cleared, so now we can walk on it without risking our lives falling over something or other. Bernie was going to the bookies, so asked him to get me some white spirit and two lengths of five-eighths quadrant. He came back with the white spirit and 2 x 6 foot lengths of expanding curtain rod.

When I gave out to him over it, he said Ann Banks never heard of quadrant (neither had he), so she gave him what she thought it was. Sent Ciarán back with the curtain rod, but she said she doesn't change anything cut off a roll (gone off her); Bernie and I are not talking. Took Ciarán to Seven Sisters Road (the Holloway end) to buy him a pair of shoes which he had seen there and liked. He was very put out when I told him I didn't like them, nor was I buying them. They were pointed, with big brass buckles on the sides, they were £18.99 and looked like something off a pantomime. Bought him a Fred Perry jumper instead. On the way back to the car, dropped into a bazaar. Bought a couple of necklaces; one I find really fascinating – it's made from a horseshoe nail, very heavy, probably meant to be worn by a horse.

Sunday 30ᵗʰ October

Couldn't believe my eyes when I looked out the window this morning, thick frost everywhere, including my car, and I had to scrape it all off myself because Bernie is still not speaking. Fiona didn't come to eight o'clock Mass with us, herself and Terri were at an 18ᵗʰ birthday party last night. They weren't home until after midnight, so Fiona had a lie-on and went to midday Mass. Terri was up early as usual. Father Roderick said Mass, which Adam Kelly and Ciarán served. Adam doesn't talk to me now, but he gives me bulls' looks. I said to Mary today – if looks could kill, I'd be dead on the spot. After breakfast, Bernie took up his positon by the fire while I put up a shelf in the kitchen, it's six foot long and took me nearly two hours to do, could have done it quicker had I got some help. In the midst of it all, Bernie had the cheek to send out to know was I driving him to the off-licence. Was tempted to tell him where I'd like to drive him, but thought better of it and just said no, which really didn't improve our relationship. It's at times like this that I wish we weren't related at all. Was quite pleased with the shelf when I finished it, put all my plants on it. After my usual afternoon nap, cut out two pinafore dresses for Terri, won't be able to make them till I go back to work in a week's time. Dan was supposed to come over today to fix the central heating, but true to form he didn't come. Told James when he came tonight to tell his father we are all freezing over here – hope he gets the message.

Monday 31st October

Day one of my week's holiday. Was looking forward to having a lie-on, but had to get up at 7.40 to call Ciarán otherwise I'd have had him keeping me company for the day, he hates going to school. Got his breakfast ready and had my own. Called Mary at nine o'clock, had another cup of tea with her, then she went off to work. I set to work too. Varnished three bedroom doors back and front and the mouldings in one-and-a-half hours flat. Had another go at putting quadrant on the skirting at the bend of the stairs, what a job that was. Steamed it, soaked it in water to try and get it into the right shape – just when I thought I was winning, it snapped. Gave it up as a bad job – that had taken well over an hour to do. Got some finer moulding, which was more pliable, doesn't look as well as the quadrant but it will have to do. Dyed the rails of the stairs and up along the sides, was so busy didn't even stop for lunch, had to stop of course to get the dinner ready. Was quite pleased with my day's work. Intended doing some more after dinner, but Mary came to say June's sister and her husband were in the house when she got home from work. They weren't very friendly, and asked her to tell me to take my hall heater as they couldn't be responsible for it if it were stolen. It was only when I sat down I realised how tired I was. Mary left at 9.30. She said it was warmer on the street than in our house. Was in bed just after ten o'clock. Bernie still not talking.

November 1983

NOT TALKING

Tuesday 1ˢᵗ November

Up at 7.15 to call Ciarán, the girls hadn't to be in school until ten o'clock. Terri went into Leena's before seven o'clock, Fiona stayed in bed until 8.15. I went off to nine o'clock Mass in St. Edmonds, the church was packed, had to stand. Went to Edmonton Green after Mass, did some shopping there. Bought myself a fresh-cream apple turnover to have with a cup of tea when I got home, but with one thing and another didn't get home till after midday, so had it for lunch. Was going to strip the paint off the dining room door; spent nearly two hours looking for two scrapers, but couldn't find them – in the end, had to go out and buy two. By then it was nearly three o'clock, so I thought I better start getting dinner ready, and in between took the door off the dining room and stood it up against the wall in the hall. I have come to the conclusion that I have the strangest family. They came in one by one and not one of them said a word about the door being off the dining room, talk about taking everything in your stride – I suppose I should be thankful none of them fell over the door in the hall. Mary came this evening – herself, Fiona and Bernie (still not talking) went to eight o'clock Mass. I took the door out to the kitchen and stripped the paint off. Said some prayers for Bernie for putting emulsion on for a primer, had to plane it off. Dan came to fix the central heating, but he couldn't find the fault. Said he'd come over tomorrow morning and drain the system, hope he knows what he's doing.

Wednesday 2nd November

Terri gave me my usual cup of tea before seven o'clock – drank it and fell fast asleep, didn't waken until 7.45, Fiona and Ciarán were still in bed. Wasn't worried about Fiona, she hadn't to be in school until ten o'clock, nearly dragged Ciarán out of bed. Had him out in record time, vowing he'd be in bed tonight by nine o'clock. Told me later he was early for school, he must have caught an express train. Dan came over at nine o'clock to have another go at the central heating. He drained the system and bled all the radiators, took him the best part of three hours. In the end he got them all working except the one in mine and Ciarán's bedroom, said he'd come back again some time and try and get them working. The gas man came and put the new thermostat on my cooker; still haven't heard a word about my freezer, luckily for the Gas Board the weather is cold or I'd be giving them a piece of my mind. Was just getting into bed last night at 11.30 when the doorbell rang, everybody was in bed, was a bit scared going down to answer it. Was amazed to see Mary – she said when she got home there was a note from June's sister wanting to know where the clock had gone (the one she had told Mary I could have). She said she had to come down and tell me; wish she'd left it till morning. Don't know what June's sister is playing at, but took the clock back tonight. She wasn't there of course – herself and her husband are staying somewhere else. Neither of them spoke to Mary at all, she doesn't know what to make of them.

Thursday 3rd November

Up at seven o'clock this morning, didn't feel very bright, but felt better after I'd had breakfast. After the children had gone to school, set to work. Starting sanding the skirting in the hall; after spending about an hour at that and not very pleased with the result (the timber is too old), decided I'd have a bash at putting new skirting boards on it. Dan had brought over skirting boards and moulding to do the dining room. The hardest part was getting the old stuff off, but it was worth all the hard work, I'd never have got the old timber to look so well. I must admit, a couple of times I did ask myself was I right in my mind. This time last year I had not a marvellous house but it was comfortable and fairly presentable, no-one could call it that now. A stranger seeing it could be forgiven for thinking we are either moving in or moving out. However, after doing the skirting I decided I'd have a go at replacing the moulding round the door. Dug an old mitre block out of the shed, did round the sitting room door. Rang Dan to tell him I'd used up all the timber for the dining room, told him to bring me some more tonight. Wish I thought of doing this in the beginning, it would have saved an awful lot of hard work and would have got things done much quicker. Mary had a day off, she came at about 1.30. She cleaned my bedroom, it looks a bit more normal now. Dan brought the timber tonight, set me back £30.00.

Friday 4th November

Last day of my hols and still haven't had a lie-on in the morning. Started work as soon as Mary went out. Took a piece of skirting off a bit of a wall in the hall, and nearly half the wall came with it. It's the same with anything you do here – I go to replace what looks like a fairly simple thing and it turns out to be a major operation. Thought I'd put some moulding round the door under the stairs – the part the door swings on was very ugly-looking with the cut-outs for old hinges on it. Did a lovely cover-up job on that with moulding, had to cut some off the stair frame to fit it in. That job took me exactly four hours, but I'm really pleased with the result. If only I had somebody to clean up and get the dinner ready I could keep going forever. Replaced the moulding round the other two doors, the hall is really beginning to take shape. Wish I had another week off work. Dan came over tonight to put a new frame round the patio doors in the dining room, he also put down some new skirting boards. Watched him very carefully to see if I could learn anything from him. Must admit he's an awful lot faster at doing things than I am, apart from that I think anything he can do I can do… I'm joking of course. Mary went home to see was there any post for her. She said the clock is still there, so they haven't taken it back to Sussex with them.

Saturday 5th November

Finally had my long-earned rest this morning. Terri gave me a cup of tea at eight o'clock before she went off to her new job in Woolworths, didn't get up until after ten o'clock. Had breakfast and gave Ciarán's door another coat of varnish – it really looks lovely, will be very pleased if all the doors look as well. Bernie hasn't spoken a word to me since last week, nor has he done anything to help in the house. He spent all today watching telly. Whatever has gone wrong, there is no sound coming from it, just a picture, but that didn't seem to worry him – maybe he can lip read. It's well he's not a mind reader or he'd have a shock if he could read what I was thinking about him. Called to the chapel house for Mary. We went to Edmonton Green, got some lovely coat material for the girls. On the way home called to Geary's for my bread. Chatted for a while with the ladies there, they were saying how much they missed Terri today. When I came out, my car wouldn't start; thought it had run out of petrol, got a can from a garage opposite but it still wouldn't go. With the help of a lad from the fish and chip shop, pushed it to the garage and filled it with petrol, still wouldn't start. Asked a bloke there would he give me a jump, which he kindly did. A mad rush after that to get dinner ready on time. Fiona was the first one home, she was going to a Guy Fawkes' party. Terri came home foot-sore, she'd worn a new pair of shoes and was on her feet all day. She also went to a party tonight with Leena.

Sunday 6th November

That rotten car let us down this morning. Terri, Ciarán and myself got into it at 7.50 to go to Mass; Bernie still not talking, so he left the house at 7.30 to walk over, he must have had second sight. Fiona had stayed the night with her friend. Put the key in the ignition, but it was as dead as a door nail. Ciarán ran all the way to the church but still wasn't in time to serve Mass. Luckily, Father Hegarty was saying Mass – he never starts before the time, unlike Father Roderick. Quite enjoyed the walk over and back. After breakfast Dan called over to take me to a new

DIY wholesalers which has opened up at the bottom of our road – it is only open to traders. Terri came with us. Was amazed at the price of things there, half the price the shops charge, and they sell all sorts of household things. Bought a smashing pasting brush for 99p, basin, bucket, cleaning brushes, fairy lights, Christmas decorations and a load of other things – would have bought more only Dan was in a hurry. Terri bought me a Quartz kitchen clock, am very pleased with it. Hope to go there again, it's like Aladdin's cave, it's got everything. Took the battery out of my car and put it on charge, hopefully there's nothing more wrong. Didn't do any work on the house today, the shopping trip took up too much of my time. Cut out a coat for Terri tonight out of one of the pieces of material I bought up The Green yesterday. There was only 2 yards 6 inches in it and cost £3.00, so was very pleased to get a full-length coat out of it.

Monday 7th November

Hated getting up for work this morning. Left my battery on charge all night, got ready in record time in case it let me down but thank God it didn't – wasn't looking forward to going to work by public transport. Everybody asked me how I enjoyed my holiday, some said I had lovely weather for it; told them I hadn't noticed, I was too busy working hard. Harry said there was a sample machinist coming in today. I thought – great, I can have another week off soon, but she didn't turn up, neither did the designer who had come for a day's trial a fortnight ago. Harry's father phoned her and she said she didn't feel she could cope. Called to Mary on my way home from work, she said Ben phoned this morning just after I'd left for work, he said he'd ring when I came from work as it was very urgent. So phoned when I got home. Laura answered and said they were really desperate for a sample machinist and did I know anybody who would come and work for them. Told her I didn't, that we were having the same problem in our firm. Also told her if she didn't get one during the week, I'd come on Saturday and help them out. Fixed the rest of the skirting in the hall. Bernie sat for the night watching telly. I'm really cheesed off, and more so when he told me he has put in for early retirement and will finish work at Christmas; I'll be really doing a moonlight flit.

Tuesday 8th November

Every bone in my body was aching when I woke this morning – really thought I wouldn't be able to go to work, but by a supreme effort had my breakfast and got myself ready. Was just starting to rain when I got into my car, and then noticed the windscreen wipers wouldn't work. Drove straight down to Murphy. He had the wipers fixed in a second, all it needed was a new fuse. Lizzie wasn't feeling too good either, she's not having a very pleasant time with her husband – she said she nearly didn't come to work she was so upset. However, she had a couple of buyers in today and I think they took her mind off her troubles for a while. Met Mary in Bruce Grove after work. After dinner, did some plastering in the hall while Bernie was stretched out in the armchair watching telly. Fiona got supper ready at 9.30 and Bernie went wild because she didn't give him his quick enough. He finished up saying he was getting a separation tomorrow for the way he's treated here. I think he's very well treated here, he doesn't lift a finger to do anything for himself; he thinks now his daughters are grown up they should wait on him, and if not them, I should.

Wednesday 9th November

Didn't feel too bad getting up this morning, thank God, in spite of the fact I didn't get to sleep till all hours last night. After midnight (we were all in bed), Sheila rang the doorbell to tell us we had water pouring from the overflow in the loft. Bernie rang Dan to know what to do, he told him to go up into the loft and push the ballcock in the tank down to the bottom and flush the toilet, which he did, but when I got back into bed I couldn't sleep for hours after. My machine in work also broke yesterday; was supposed to be fixed when I left work, but when I got in this morning it was still broken, had to use Doris's machine. Lizzie is a bit annoyed – the firm wants her to design cheaper skirts and tops, which limits her to very basic designs, but they are anxious to capture the Woolworths and Tesco market. Mary, the girls and myself went shopping tonight. Bought some school shirts for Ciarán, at one time he wouldn't be seen dead in a white shirt, but now, for some reason best known to himself, for the past week he doesn't want to wear grey ones. Also bought some BioTex to soak them in because he will not wash his neck. I'm really pleased when Wednesdays come round and he has to go swimming in school, it's the only day he looks clean. When we came home after leaving Mary home, couldn't get a parking space, had to leave my car at the bottom of the road. Spurs were playing Arsenal, they lost 2-1. Bernie never mentioned anything about his quickie separation tonight, as a matter of fact he offered to walk down the road with me to bring my car up.

Thursday 10th November

Lizzie wasn't in work today – Jim (the cutter) said she wasn't well and was going to the doctor. There was a skirt on my machine which Harry had cut out yesterday; when I started to make it, discovered it was all off grain. Showed it to Jim, who said he'd cut another one, which he did, but that one wasn't nipped right – no fault of Jim's, the pattern was wrong. Re-nipped it myself and finally got the skirt made up. Started on another one which Harry had cut – that wasn't right either, Jim had to re-cut the front skirt. Was feeling a bit fed up, I was getting nowhere fast – by lunch hour hadn't even made two skirts. One of the older directors came in at 1.30 and asked me had I enough to keep me going, I could have hit him with the ironing board. Was really glad when it was time to go home. Not much joy at home either. Bernie took up his usual position in the armchair in front of the telly while I was busy working. Told Mary any minute I was going to explode, after two weeks of this just couldn't take any more, so gave Bernie a bit of my mind. Told him in no uncertain terms what I thought of him. When he got over the shock, came out to the kitchen and asked me what I wanted done. Told him to sand a door upstairs which I had varnished the other day. He hates sanding, afraid it might affect his chest, but he made a good job of the door.

Friday 11th November

Lizzie was in this morning, thank God. She went to the doctor yesterday – told her she's suffering from nervous exhaustion (me too). Had a much happier day than yesterday, everything went much smoother. Lizzie had a clear-out of material, gave it into the cutting room. She said any material they don't use for production they cut out in their most popular style and sell to the market stalls, so it does pay to buy things in the markets after all. Jim (the cutter) is having a surprise party for his girlfriend tonight, she is 21 years old, Lizzie is going to it. She was altering a dress and coat to wear at it. She bought them second-hand in a charity shop, they are 1940s style. I'm amazed at what young people wear these days. My friend Mary Mac came to dinner tonight, and for once didn't let her do any work. We sat chatting while I altered a coat for Mr. South's (my landlord) wife. It's a Laura Ashley model in corded velvet made like a bell tent. He said it was very cheap, just £100.00, made in Dublin. Ciarán went to a pop concert in his school tonight, James went with him. Told him not to sit down or he'd do himself an injury – he had his jeans covered in safety pins with writing all over them as well. Was a bit worried when he wasn't home by eleven o'clock, but he came in soon after and said the concert was kosher, whatever that means. Bernie sanded another door tonight.

Saturday 12th November

Was up at 7.15 this morning – Laura phoned last night to know would I go over to do some samples for her. Drove the girls and Helen to work on the way, arrived there at 9.10. Ben and Sam were out moving things into their new factory. Katie was there, she's really lovely and very amusing, she never stopped talking all the time I was there. She was driving an imaginary car – Laura and myself were supposed to be in it, we were going to her house for the weekend. Made eight tops, a skirt and a pair of trousers while I was there. Told Mary I'd meet her outside Marks in Wood Green, but with the traffic didn't get there until 4.20. Had a mad rush round Marks to get some chicken portions for the dinner, also bought a nice cardigan for myself. Suddenly remembered I hadn't collected the bread from Geary's. A mad rush back to the car to try and make it to Edmonton by 5.30. Managed to avoid the Spurs crowd, although they were coming in the opposite direction. There were police at all the traffic lights supposed to be directing the traffic but causing nothing but confusion. Didn't get home till 5.45, so no bread. No work done tonight, Bernie is recovering from his sudden burst of energy. I fell asleep while watching telly, had a rude awakening when Fiona gave me a puck and said I was snoring too loud.

Sunday 13th November

Very cold this morning. All up bright and early except Fiona and Mary who both went to midday Mass, lazy pair. After breakfast, went upstairs to varnish two doors. Did one, and Bernie said he'd do the other one, so left him to it – it might be an offer that won't be repeated. I put a handle on Ciarán's door, it looks really nice. Bernie finishes work on Christmas Eve, he has decided to take early retirement. We are thinking of buying this house with the money he'll get – it won't be quite enough but we may be able to raise the rest, please God. Bernie will be in his alley [Irish: delighted with himself, or 'in his element'], sitting on his bum all day doing nothing – that's his life's ambition, hope I can stand it. I suppose whether I can stand it or not I'll have to put up with it. Hope he takes up gardening, but knowing him the only thing he'll take up is the newspaper to study the horses. Don't want to but I may have to work full-time to make ends meet, or I may strike it lucky and win the Pools, chance would be a fine thing. Had a nearly cold bath tonight, not from choice but because we had little or no hot water. Phoned Dan to tell him. He came over and said somebody must have changed the water temperature, but since nobody here knows how to change it, it must have been done by Mr. Nobody.

277

Monday 14th November

Didn't hear Terri bring me in my tea this morning and nearly slept it out. If I didn't get up, Ciarán would stay in bed all day – don't know how he gets to school on time. The new designer came this morning, she seems very nice, she's called Cathy. She'll only come in Monday and Tuesday, she has another job the rest of the week. Lizzie had a phone call this morning, took it in the main office. When she came back she said, that was a sample machinist but I think she's too good for us. She said, if you give me Laura's phone number I'll tell her to go over to her. Gave her the number, and at one o'clock I had a phone call from Laura to ask me did I know the person who had come to her for a job. Couldn't tell her much as I had to take the call in the main office and there were three directors there. Told her I'd ring when I got home, which I did. Told her what had happened and how I couldn't understand why Lizzie didn't get the sample machinist for our firm, and about her saying she thought she was too good for us – I'm still wondering what way to take that. Laura thinks Lizzie wants to get her a machinist in case I might go back and work for her. Asked Lizzie today did the directors know a lady had applied for the job as a sample machinist, she said no; the mind boggles.

Tuesday 15th November

Very cold this morning and the traffic was dreadful. The new designer is very nice; I asked her was she married, she said no, but she lives with a man and are very happy together. Lizzie and herself are getting on great, they seem to like each other. Called into Dan's on my way home from work, parked my car a bit down from his shop. Bought a few bits and pieces from him. When I came out there was a sticker on my car saying, 'the number of this vehicle has been noted and if it is parked here again the police will be called to remove it', horrible people. Poured rain on the way home. After dinner, did the hem on Mr. South's wife's coat while Mary, Bernie and Terri took the wallpaper off the dining room. Bernie also took the old tiles off the ceiling, which I was very glad to see go, never liked them. A terrible job getting the paper off. Must say Polycell paste is very good. What a mess to clean up afterwards, and yours truly had to do it with some help from Mary. Had a bit of a shock tonight when I discovered the radiator in the bathroom was leaking. Phoned Dan. He came over with his spanner and found another leak. Tightened up some nuts and said it should be alright but to keep an eye on it. I'm keeping an eye on so many things here, I haven't enough eyes.

Wednesday 16th November

Bernie woke me at 5.30 this morning to know where his keys were, had I taken them by mistake. Could have murdered him, didn't sleep after that. Got up at 7.30. Got all the bags of old paper and put them in my car to take to the dump. Before going off to school, Ciarán asked me to sign a note which he had written himself (in his worst handwriting) asking to be excused from swimming as he had a chest infection. Wasn't too pleased when I told him I didn't put my signature to lies – apart from which I like him to go swimming, it's the only time he looks clean. Dropped the bags off at the dump and on to work. Most of the people in the factory are knocked off for two days as there's no work for them – also the two lads in the cutting room, who have plenty of work but the cloth hadn't arrived for it;

wish I worked in the factory. Called to Mr. South's office on my way home from work, but he wasn't in. Just Mary and myself went shopping tonight, Terri went into Leena's and Fiona had homework to do. Left Bernie stripping the rest of the paper off the dining room. Bought some ceiling paper in Tesco, it was only £1.49 a roll, not looking forward to putting it up. After leaving Mary home, cleaned up the mess in the dining room. It just needs the ceiling sanded and I can start on the papering.

Thursday 17th November

Really exhausted this morning when I woke – would love to have stayed in bed, wish I didn't have to work. A mad rush on today, Bert wanted four samples for tomorrow morning, all in cream linen. Lilly from the factory came up after lunch to help out. She was her usual cheerful self – told me herself and her husband always go to Pontins for Christmas. Would love to spend Christmas in a hotel, but with my lot would cost a bomb. Fiona went to St. George's Theatre today with the school to see 'Twelfth Night'. She wasn't home till after six o'clock, said it was very good. Fiona brought the telly out to the kitchen to watch 'Top of the Pops', so we all sat out there, I was doing a bit of hand-sewing. Thought, any minute now Bernie will explode because he was the only one working. Later on he came out to watch 'Miss World', he fancies himself as a judge of beauty. You'd think somebody had given him a bang of a flour bag – he was covered in white, even Minnie (the cat) was covered in white. The room was in a dreadful state, everywhere covered in white. Cleaned it up as best we could, but will take some time to get rid of it completely.

Friday 18ᵗʰ November

Lilly came up to the design room again this morning to help out, which was just as well because everything I started to do had something wrong with it. They were samples the new designer, Cathy, had cut. The first one I started on had too much work on it for the production workers, so Lizzie said to leave it and she'd get Cathy to alter it on Monday. Started on the next one, which was a navy, pleated skirt on a basque; it was cut on the wrong grain and was shaded, so had to leave that for Cathy to alter. The next one needed some alterations too, which Lizzie did – that was the only one I completed for the day. Mr. South came for his wife's coat. Bernie asked him could we leave a deposit for the house when he got his money at Christmas. He was decent enough to tell us there was no need to pay a deposit until the last month of the transaction, said to put it in the bank until then and we'd get some interest on it, he really is a very good landlord. Wanted to paper the dining room ceiling tonight but had no plank. Asked Leena if she had one. Showed me one which she said I could borrow, but it was too long to go across the room. Bernie asked her husband if he'd mind if he cut it, but he didn't seem pleased. With Peter's help, managed to get one (but that's another story) which was just the right size. So, with Bernie holding me on the plank, I papered the ceiling.

Saturday 19ᵗʰ November

Thought I'd feel crippled this morning after my night of running up and down the ladder and onto the plank, but strange to say I didn't feel too bad – very tired, but no aches or pains. Put the last strip of paper on Ciarán's room, had left it till the moulding round the door was finished.

Then sanded down the bathroom door again, much to Bernie's annoyance. He thinks I'm being ridiculous. Can't get it through to him that the reason I stripped the doors in the first place was because they were so rough through not being sanded down between painting. If it was up to him I'd be back to square one with doors and mouldings I can't clean. At three o'clock called for Mary to go shopping. She said Father Hegarty wanted to talk to me, it was about Ciarán and his Confirmation. He was to make it next year, but he [Ciarán] told me so often that he was only making it to please me that I told him he wasn't making it, as I didn't think that was the right attitude – this is the result of children being allowed to make up their own minds about Confirmation. The parents have no say in the matter now. In spite of what the clergy think about it, I think it's wrong. However, Father Hegarty said he'll have a talk with him, that perhaps he's too young at 14 years old and he could wait another year or two; probably won't want to make it at all then, even to please me.

Sunday 20th November

A funny thing happened after Mass this morning. Had just finished selling the bingo tickets, [and] Bernie and myself were chatting to Dick Johnson, when this tall, Indian man went into the church. He went over to the statue of the Sacred Heart and lit a cigarette from one of the candles. Betty Murphy went in and told him smoking wasn't allowed in church. He came out very quickly and came over to me and said good morning and kissed my hand. Then he started ranting and raving about how upset he was; I told him to sit down and take things easy. Then he put his hand on the case the bingo tickets were in and said, "Give me that money till I get out of here". I told him not to do that,

that there was only £2.00 in it and it's not worth committing sin over. He said, "Give it to me, I'm not going to walk that High Road again". Dick Johnson told him, no, you can't have the money, it's not ours, it belongs to the church. After a while of arguing, he went off swearing like a trooper; thought afterwards we were lucky he didn't turn violent. After breakfast, went down to Stax with Dan, spent £44.00 there. It was what they called 'Open Day' when everything was nearly half price; they were also giving all their customers a glass of wine. When I got to the check-out, the cash register broke down. After spending about 20 minutes trying to fix it, they got another, which wouldn't work either. Didn't get out of there until 12.45, not my day.

Monday 21st November

Bitterly cold this morning, had to scrape the frost off my car before going to work. Didn't feel very well in work, had an upset stomach. Lizzie told me to take a rest, but felt a bit better as the morning wore on. Lizzie was doing some pattern grading, she got a staple stuck in her hand, helped her to pull it out. She went to the toilet to wash her hand, came out about ten minutes later, she looked ghastly. She said she nearly passed out, it must have been the shock but she didn't look well for the rest of the day. Called to Dan's shop after work to pay him a few pounds I owed him. Told me to check my bill from Stax, he had been over-charged £60.00 yesterday. Checked my bill when I got home but it was ok. Thought I was seeing things when I saw Bernie standing at the front door. Said he didn't feel well in work – went to the nurse, who told him to go to his own doctor, which he did, and was told he had an ear infection, so he's having a week off. Said he did a bit of sanding, but I saw no signs of it. Between us we put the door back on the dining room; sounds simple but it wasn't, took half the night to do. Glad it's back on, certainly makes the room warmer. Mary didn't come over this evening, she must have gone home straight from work, she'll freeze in that house. Terri went up to bed and came back down to tea later. Everywhere is covered in frost.

Tuesday 22ⁿᵈ November

Frost everywhere again this morning, had to scrape it off my car. Bernie was still in bed when I went off to work. Harry was in the design room when I got there. Lizzie asked him about us having Thursday and Friday off – he said we could, it would give us time to buy him a Christmas present, told him I thought the employer always bought the employee a present. Stayed in work until 3.20 to finish a sample Harry wants first thing in the morning. When I got home, was really furious; Bernie hadn't done one thing in the house. He must have sat on his bottom all day, he's really going to drive me mad when he retires. He's the laziest person I ever met. Nobody but himself could sit all day in a house that's in such a state. As soon as dinner was over, got to work on the dining room, did some plastering first. Terri did a bit of sanding for me. Mary came over, and herself and Terri cleared everything out of the dining room and I got to work with the sander. Worked with it for about one-and-a-half hours. Was quite pleased with what I had done. Still had the skirting to do when the rotten sander packed up, I suppose like myself, it's over-worked.

Wednesday 23ʳᵈ November

The weather gets worse, thick frost everywhere again this morning. Hate the cold, wish I could hibernate all winter. It's a shame I'm not rich, I'd be off to Spain until the summer. Really envy Eileen Buckley, she's off to visit her son and his family who live in Australia, she'll be staying for three or four months. Had frozen fingers by the time I'd scraped the frost off my car. Harry was in the design room when I got to work. Lizzie was to have finished the sample which Lilly and myself had rushed yesterday but she hadn't got the buttons for it, they were to have come first thing this morning but they hadn't come. So, when Lizzie came in we both got busy putting on what there was in stock. We had nearly finished when the buttons arrived. We had to take off the buttons we had first sewn on and put the new ones on, was glad to see the end of them. When I got home, could have killed Bernie, he had taken the paint off a door and left the moulding round the glass, which means when it comes to burning that off it might leave burn marks on the door. He has a happy knack of doing everything wrong. Mary came over tonight, said she is getting fed up waiting for the council to house her. She said when she got out of bed this morning her hands were so cold. They really should heat that house, she's afraid the pipes will burst. She's ringing the council tomorrow.

Thursday 24th November

The first day of my two days' holiday. As usual, had to get up at 7.20 to call Ciarán but went back to bed, where I stayed until ten o'clock, only to come downstairs to face a load of dirty dishes in the sink, was really annoyed. Bernie had been up an hour before me. After I'd banged a few things around, he said he'd do the washing up, but by then I had it done. Mary's day off, she came at eleven o'clock. I was stripping the paint off the kitchen door, Bernie was as usual sitting on his bottom – said a few words about him to Mary, made sure he heard me. After a while, he came out and asked what could he do – was tempted to tell him, but sent him to Black & Decker instead to have my sander repaired. Told Mary to ring the council to enquire about a flat. She was delighted to hear they had two to offer her, one on Northumberland Park which had just been done up except for the kitchen, and the other one on Lansdowne Road, it's in the process of being done up and wouldn't be ready for another few weeks. She said if Mary went down to Bromley Road she would give her the keys to look at the one on Northumberland Park. Mary flew down and got the keys and the two of us went to have a look at the flat. It's really lovely, a big sitting room, bedroom, a nice fitted kitchen, loads of cupboards, hot-press, central heating, and even a small store room – told Mary I could fill that for her.

Friday 25th November

Was very tired this morning, but got up early to try and put some sort of shape on this house. Bernie started to give the dining room ceiling another coat of emulsion, he's like the queen making a cake, everybody has to dance attendance on him. Mary and myself cleared out all the furniture for him. When we'd finished, Mary went off to work and I sanded the kitchen door. After a while, had a look in to see how Bernie was getting on, told him he'd missed a bit on the ceiling, he nearly had a fit. Thought I'd better keep my mouth shut, so got lunch ready. Bernie said the ceiling would look better when it dried out. At 3.45, stopped work to get dinner ready; just as I did, Johnjoe came in with Bernie's wages, stayed for nearly an hour, so dinner was later than usual. Fiona came from school soaked to the skin, it hasn't stopped raining for the past two days. Terri and Ciarán were just as wet when they came in. After dinner, stained all the woodwork in the dining room, including the £400.00 fire, which had got terrible abuse when Bernie was scraping the ceiling before I had time to prepare it. Bernie hadn't bothered to cover it up – that's him, he does one thing and spoils another. After supper, was so tired I couldn't keep my eyes open, was in bed by eleven o'clock.

Saturday 26th November

Bernie was wrong about the ceiling being alright when it dried out, it was worse – all patchy; nothing for it but to give it another coat. So Mary and myself gave a repeat performance moving out the furniture, would love to have said I told you so, but I thought I better hold my tongue or he mightn't do it at all. Mary went off to work. I went upstairs to varnish the bedroom doors while Bernie got on with the ceiling. Had just started when the doorbell rang, it was the man from the Pru for the house insurance. I'm sure he got a shock when he saw the state of the house, it's like a disaster area, he must have wondered what we are insuring. Bernie told him we are going to buy the house. Worked until two o'clock. Tidied round a bit, then called for Mary to go shopping. Saw Father Hegarty, who told me he was going to have a talk with Ciarán after Mass tomorrow morning. Took Mary to a second-hand shop in Hornsey to see would they have anything suitable for her new flat. They had some beautiful things, but unfortunately most of them were already sold. We did manage to get a very nice Slumberland bed (brand new) with a lovely headboard. The man told us the woman who had it didn't like it, she thought the mattress too hard. Fortunately, Mary likes a hard mattress, she got it for £60.00.

Sunday 27th November

No excitement this morning after Mass. Dick Johnson told us the man who had tried to take the money last week was a drug addict, God help him. Still raining, hasn't stopped for four days, but it has got a lot warmer. Saw Martha McGregor. Asked her if she'd teach Ciarán maths (which he is hopeless at) – she gave me her phone number. Father Hegarty came out to tell me he was going to give Ciarán a cup of tea and have a man-to-man talk with him about his reason for not making his Confirmation. After breakfast, we all, except Ciarán, went over to see Mary's new flat. Had a good look at it this time, it's really very nice but the kitchen does need a lot doing to it. Measured the windows for curtains. The bedroom and sitting room windows are 9 foot wide. In the sitting room there is a radiator which runs the whole width of the window, so will have to have the heavy curtains come just to the top of it, but in the bedroom the radiator is on the opposite wall, so can have the curtains down to the floor. Took some stuff over to put in Mary's store room, told her I'd fill it for her. It's really a very compact flat, ideal for a married couple with no family. If I had my children off my hands, wouldn't mind having a flat like it. Don't think Bernie would like it, he'd miss having a garden to laze in.

Monday 28th November

Oh God, why do I have to go to work, would much rather stay at home, would never be bored, I'd find so much to do there. Wish it was myself who was taking early retirement and not Bernie, he'll just waste the rest of his life sitting in an armchair watching telly, he'll just vegetate. Keep telling him he won't feel as healthy as when he was working, but he just laughs. My car is giving me a lot of trouble, keeps cutting out all the time, could really do with a new one, really had no joy with this one. Johnjoe said Murphy has three nice Cortinas, he's to find out how much he wants for them. Didn't feel too bad when I got to work. The day passed very quickly. Lizzie, like myself, had spent her two days off working in her new flat, painting and making new curtains. Harry asked me did I buy him his Christmas present while I was off, told him he shouldn't expect anything, it's not his Christmas. Called to Mary on the way home to collect some meat I had asked her to get. Said she'd been down to the council, and the lady there told her she could keep the keys for the flat and start paying rent from Monday next – also told her to apply for a rent rebate. She went to the Electric Board to have the electric turned on, but they won't be able to do it until next Monday, so she won't be able to do anything in it until then. She's really delighted with it, said she owes St. Anthony £10.00 for getting it for her.

Tuesday 29th November

The traffic went mad again this morning – left home at 8.30, didn't get to work until 9.20. Having trouble with my car cutting out all the time, I have visions of somebody running into my back. Poor Ann Delaney (she's the cleaner where I work) had a phone call this morning in work, she ran before anybody could ask her what was wrong. Her son, who is 23 years old, went to Ireland in January to attend a wedding of a friend (he was just a year married himself); when the plane touched down at the airport he had a stroke. He was rushed to Jervis Street hospital in Dublin. He came out of the stroke paralysed. He spent months in a rehabilitation hospital in Dun Laoghaire, he only came back to London in September. I phoned Ann when I came home from work. She told me her son went to hospital this morning for a brain test, and while having it done he got very upset and seemed about to have another stroke, that was why they phoned Ann. She said she managed to calm him down. God help her, she was very upset, he's her only son, he was a policeman. She has a daughter who is also married and lives in Ireland. Varnished all the woodwork in the dining room tonight while Bernie gave the bedroom door a light sanding, ready for another coat of varnish. Can't make up my mind whether I'm going to like the dining room or not, but I'm stuck with it now.

Wednesday 30th November

Could hardly drag my weary bones out of bed this morning, but thank God the traffic wasn't as bad as yesterday, got to work by nine o'clock. Spent the whole morning on my own. Lizzie had gone to the West End showrooms and didn't arrive in until near one o'clock. She had asked me to make two skirts for her hairdresser, started one of them in my lunch hour but one of the directors came in, so that put paid to that, didn't like doing it while he was there. Ann came in after lunch. God help her, she looked worn out. Asked her about the skirts they were making in the factory out of all the remnants. She said she bought a few of them – £2.00 for the unlined ones and £4.00 for the lined ones. She intended buying some more on Monday, but there wasn't one skirt hanging up in the factory, Harry and Bert had taken them out over the weekend. Would like to have got some for the girls. Had a really hectic night. After dinner, took Mary and Terri off to collect all Mary's things out of June's house. Never saw so much stuff for one person, don't know how the car held it all. On the way back, dropped Terri off at Woolworths, she was working from 6.30 till 8.30. They had a late night opening for disabled people, and some of the staff gave their services for free, including Terri. Took all the stuff back to Mary's new flat, Ciarán gave a hand to carry them up the stairs. After that went shopping. Left the shopping home, then over to the chapel house and back to Wood Green to collect Terri. She was very tired but they all had a lovely time.

December 1983

A SURPRISE AT CHRISTMAS

Thursday 1st December

Thick frost everywhere this morning and Fiona washes her hair before going to school, goes off with it not quite dry, she really looks for trouble. Really have to have a home-tune done on my car again. It jumped all the way to work this morning, which is highly dangerous in traffic. Have to drive it on choke all the time, you'd think it had whooping cough. Very cold in the design room, kept my coat on till Lizzie came in and lit the heater. Had to rush a skirt for Harry who was in the West End. When it was finished, Lizzie phoned for a taxi to take it up to him. After that, did a couple of things Cathy had designed. In my lunch hour, did some work on Lizzie's friend's skirt. Jim (the cutter) got me some chips for lunch, wish I hadn't eaten them, felt really full after them. It was Mary's day off, she spent it in the flat cleaning it up. She said it looks a lot better now, but she thinks she'll buy a new sink unit – the one in the kitchen is all defaced. Her bed arrived while she was there, she said it's lovely. Had to go to Fiona's school tonight about her O-level exams which she is sitting next year. Was lucky to get a place in the car park, but when I came out couldn't turn the car round, so had to back out. Was doing alright until this car came driving straight towards me. Got out to have a word with the driver, who also got out. I said, I'm trying to back out; she said (very indignant), I'm trying to park, I'm one of the teachers and this is the teachers' car park. I said, if the teachers were as punctual as the parents they'd have no trouble finding a space – she was an hour late. When I got back into the car, Fiona was hiding, she said that was her biology teacher.

Friday 2nd December

Dear God, the weather and the traffic get worse – late again for work this morning. Two lots of road works on the one-way system causing complete chaos, wish I had a helicopter. Lizzie thought something was wrong with me I was so late getting in. Ann brought me in the sweets she had promised me for the bazaar. Couldn't believe it when I saw them – there was about 5lbs of sweets and loads of chocolate bars. Asked Harry had he any skirts to sell, he said not at the moment but he would be bringing some samples from the West End showrooms next week. My friend Mary Mac came to dinner this evening, and her husband, Jack, brought me some plants for the bazaar. After dinner, Mary Mac and myself went to a lady in Moira Grove to collect some things, then on to the new church hall to get my stall ready for tomorrow, but when we got there the Brownies were in the hall. Had to wait until seven o'clock for them to finish. When I had my stuff all set out, Father Hegarty said to keep the best pieces back until half an hour after the bazaar opened. Said he had seen dealers buy things for 50p and sell them half an hour later for a fiver. So, took all my best pieces and put them in a box and put them under the table behind where I was going to stand. Left the hall about nine o'clock. Got home, had supper. Mary Mac and Jack left just after eleven o'clock.

Saturday 3rd December

After Terri had given me a cup of tea and gone off to work, got up and washed my hair. Mary got breakfast ready, after which I went upstairs and gave the two bedroom doors another coat of varnish, gave the bathroom its final coat too. Bernie got lunch ready, cheese sandwiches and tea. Then I put some things into the boot of my car for the bazaar. Brought out Jack's plants to put in the car, when before I knew where I was, I was sprawled the full width of the path. Got such a shock, I couldn't move. A young girl came along and asked me could I get up, told her I would in a minute. Asked her to ring my doorbell, which she did. Bernie came out, and between them they got me up off the ground. Had two badly cut knees and sore fingers. However, after a while, recovered well enough to go over to the bazaar. Was delighted to see I had a few more things on my stall, including a lovely hair dryer on a stand; told Kay Hunt it was too good for the white elephant stall, I said we should raffle it – she agreed, so put it under the table behind me. A very nice young girl named Mary was helping at my stall. When the bazaar opened there was the usual surge of people. Crowds round my stall when a woman told me a man had taken a food mixer without paying for it. She pointed him out to me and I ran after him and told him I wanted the food mixer which he hadn't paid for. He had it in a huge hold-all, took it off him. Later discovered the hair dryer and the good pieces I had hidden had also been stolen, rotten lot.

Sunday 4th December

Could hardly see in front of me driving to Mass this morning; Bernie had scraped the frost off the windscreen, but it freezed up just as quickly again. Father Roderick said the Mass in record time, gave no sermon. Terri and Fiona bought a very nice 3D picture of the Pope from Mrs. Dunn for Mary's new flat, they'll give it to her at Christmas. Our telly broke down yesterday. The bloke we bought it from brought another one that proved to be worse than the first, Bernie and Terri were very upset. Later discovered it's all due to the fact our outdoor aerial is bent over, the chimney stack needs repairing again. Have strict orders to phone South tomorrow and have him fix it or Bernie might leave home – that I should be so lucky. Was very stiff today after my fall yesterday, my knees are really sore. Did some carpentry work on the kitchen door. Have to do a Novena that one of the girls marries a carpenter, getting too old for this sort of work. Was really annoyed with Ciarán today – himself and James went up to Petticoat Lane to some punk shop there, didn't come home till after four o'clock for his dinner, so cut the plug off his record player. He won't be playing it for a while, which pleased everybody – except of course Ciarán, who said he'll buy a plug and put it on himself, will give him such a hiding if he does.

Monday 5th December

Wasn't too cold this morning, at least no frost to scrape off the car. Was late leaving for work, didn't get in until 9.05. Cathy and Lizzie came in a while after. I was delighted to read in the paper Alex Higgins won the Snooker Championships. Nobody in the factory except Lilly and another lady. The material which is holding up production still hasn't arrived. Nothing really exciting in work today. Called to Dan's shop on the way home but the shop was closed, he must have a big job on. Mary had a day off because the men were supposed to come and fix a broken window in her flat, but they didn't come. The man came and turned on the electricity. Am really annoyed with Mary, she went off tonight but never even said goodnight to me. When she was gone, Bernie told me she was sleeping in the flat tonight, which was more than she told me. Was busy working when the phone rang, it was my cousin Nan from Dublin to tell me a neighbour of ours (at home) had died, but I already knew, his sister had rung yesterday to tell me. Nan is looking forward to coming over for Christmas. Told her the house is in a worse state than when she was here in the summer, but she said she doesn't mind. Hope she won't be too shocked when she sees it.

Tuesday 6th December

Was up earlier than usual this morning, had to take my old banger to Murphy. Said he'd have it ready by 3.30. Got a bus to work, went upstairs – had forgotten how shaky buses are. Really see a lot on the top of a bus. Saw houses on Lansdowne Road that I'd never seen before – didn't even know there was a Lansdowne Lodge, looks like a big hotel. Arrived at work dead on nine o'clock. Was in before Lizzie. The design room was nice and warm – that is, until Harry came in to cut out some samples and turned the gas heater off. It's really a museum piece. It hangs out of the ceiling with chains out of it for on and off, but it does give off great heat. The room got so cold, had to put on another cardigan and scarf. Harry got the message and turned the heater on again. Then he started to complain of the heat because he was standing directly under the heater. They've got a 36-foot cutting table and he has to stand there – the mentality of men. In the end he decided to go out and buy a fan heater for me, so everybody was happy. Lizzie designed a skirt with a bag of the same material hanging from the waistband. I made it up, and both Lizzie and myself think it lovely, but Harry doesn't like it. He said, if they get an order for it, he'll take both of us out to a very good lunch. Called to Murphy on my way home, he had my car ready.

Wednesday 7th December

A really beautiful morning, cold but really sunny. Delighted with my car. Going like a bomb, hope it doesn't explode. The kids can't call it the tractor anymore, it just has a respectable hum. It seems to have got a new lease of life, thank God. Bert was in the design room when I got in. He was sorting out samples to take to the West End. Lizzie was so late I was beginning to wonder if she were coming in at all. Later on, Harry came in to do some cutting out. He has a new girlfriend, said he was cooking dinner in his flat for her tonight. Asked him what he was serving. He said, avocados, grilled steak and for sweet, pancakes. Asked him how does he make the batter for pancakes, he said, don't you buy that in the shops? Told him I'd buy him a cookery book for his birthday. Finished making a new serving gear for Ciarán in my lunch hour. How he wasn't strangled on the altar in the other one, I'll never know. It was up to his knees, and he had to take a deep breath in every time he put it on, but I didn't realise all that until last Sunday when Father Roderick sent himself and Adam Kelly down each side of the church to offer the sign-of-peace to the people. What with his surplice up under his armpits and his cassock up to his knees, with his blue trousers underneath that and his plantations of feet (he takes size 8 in shoes), he looked like something straight out of a Charles Dickens novel.

Thursday 8th December

Wrapped Lizzie's birthday present before going off to work. When I got in, she was already in before me. Said, "Hello Lizzie, Happy Birthday!" She gave me a funny look and said, it's not my birthday till next Thursday – that wiped the smile off my face. However, gave her the present and told her not to open it till next week. Thanked me and said she'd leave it in work. Lilly came up to help out, she was her usual cheerful self, had a right old chin-wag. At about 12.30 had a phone call from Fiona's school to say Fiona wasn't well and would it be alright to send her home. Asked to speak to Fiona, who said she had a bad headache and was very tired. Said she'd be alright coming home on her own, there was no need for me to call for her or to come home early. She's been up late these past few nights studying for a six hour art exam she is having tomorrow. The teacher told her if she's not well enough to do it tomorrow she can do it on Monday, but she was much better tonight, thank God, and went to bed early.

Friday 9th December

Terri brought in my usual cup of tea at seven o'clock this morning. Got up after I drank it, was afraid if I lay down again I'd fall asleep, I felt so tired. Made Terri stay out of school to go to the doctor – her hands are very bad, covered in a rash. She's had it on and off for the last 18 months. She's had all sorts of ointments which cure it for a few days and then it's back again, but it's never been as bad as it is now. Told her to tell Watson to give her a letter to a skin specialist. She said if she got an early appointment she'd go on to school, which she did. Dr. Watson gave her a letter to St. John's Skin Hospital off Leicester Square, she has to ring for an appointment. Harry was in the West End showrooms all day. Lizzie phoned him to know if we were still having Monday and Tuesday off. Spoke to him myself, he said he was going to see a buyer this evening and if she wanted some samples in a hurry we would have to come in both days. Said he wouldn't know until later this evening, and if I didn't get a phone call from him tonight it would mean I could have the two days off. Told Lizzie the same. Did a bit of praying on the way home he wouldn't ring. Thank God he didn't, looking forward to the two days off. Had to take Fiona to a concert in her school tonight and called back for her at eleven o'clock, she said it was really fantastic.

Saturday 10th December

Went to Marks early this morning, it was really packed. Then went up to Edmonton Green to look for wallpaper, couldn't see anything I liked. Went down to another DIY place which has opened on the North Circular Road (in opposition to Wickes). It's a marvellous place, much better than Wickes. Had quite a nice selection of wallpaper, but the girls are set on having the dining room done in white – that will last as many days as nights what with Bernie and myself smoking. In the end, didn't get any paper at all – decided to wait until I had somebody with me, don't trust my own judgement. That's the trouble in our house, there are too many chiefs all wanting their own way. Came home and did some sanding down while Bernie sat watching telly. Had a few words with him. Told him if I didn't get help, I'll leave it as it is for Christmas. Said he'd do some sanding when the racing was over. Mary phoned to say she'd be ready to go out at three o'clock. Went over and collected her. We went to Hornsey to see could we get anything for her flat in the shop where we got the bed, but there wasn't anything suitable. The bloke who owns the shop said he has another one in Kentish Town, so we went there, but there was nothing there either. Nearly died with the cold.

Sunday 11th December

Very frosty this morning. Father Hegarty said Mass, and afterwards took Ciarán into the chapel house for another chat. We were having breakfast by the time he got home. Said Father Hegarty gave him a cup of tea and he has now decided to make his Confirmation, thank God. Ciarán looked really nice this morning in his new serving gear, but when he got home he said, "Guess what you've done? You have my cassock buttoning to the girls' side and Adam kept jeering me over it". Assured him it was no problem fixing that. He went off to Queensway market and came back with a shocking pink, sleeveless T-shirt with black barbed wire painted all over it. He has now decided to give up his milk round after Christmas and go to art classes on Saturday mornings. He would like to design record jackets and T-shirts, punk of course. Don't know where he's going to finish up, hope it's just a phase he's going through. Did some varnishing in the dining room and hall. Had my usual afternoon nap. Fiona brought up my tea, Terri had gone into Leena's. Listened to the 'Top Twenty' in bed and read a book I had got from the library on varnishing, found it very interesting. Learned a few things from it – was surprised to read when a varnish brush is to be used the next day it should be left in varnish and not in turps as I'd been doing. When I got out of bed, cut out some cushion covers for the three-piece in the sitting room just to brighten it up for Christmas; really need a new three-piece suite.

Monday 12 December

Hadn't to go to work today, thank God, but had to get up early to get Ciarán up. Went back to bed afterwards until ten o'clock. Had my breakfast, then started work on the fire in the dining room. Never liked the colour of it, it's pine, decided to sand it down and darken it. Not as simple as I thought. When I put the wood dye on it, it just kept running off. Did another bit of sanding on it and tried again. Took a little better the second time, but still not great. Had another go at it, still a bit patchy but everybody said it was better than it was before. After dinner, put some varnish on it with disastrous results. The varnish caused the dye to run. Will have to start all over again on it tomorrow, hope I have better luck. Mary came with me tonight to the new DIY place, still didn't get the wallpaper. What I liked she didn't and vice versa, so decided I'll go down again tomorrow night and take The Boss (Fiona) with me. Didn't realise it was so frosty or I wouldn't have gone out at all, the roads were like a skating rink. They have a lovely garden centre in the DIY place, would like to have had more time to look round it, but the one thing I don't have is enough time.

Tuesday 13th December

Woke this morning thinking about that rotten fire surround when all of a sudden I had one of my brainwaves. Thought if I could buy some veneer, I could do the fire surround with that. Looked up the Yellow Pages, was surprised to see most of the veneer manufacturers are round Tottenham and Edmonton. Wondered would one of them sell me a small quantity. Phoned one in Edmonton, (Cuckoo Lane), asked the man who answered could I have a small amount of veneer, he said, yes, certainly. Jumped in the car and got there pronto – not only did I get the veneer, but he cut it all to the sizes I needed. On the way home, called into the library to get a book on veneering. Bought some Evo-stick too. Had lunch, then set to work and realised how hard it is – it's a job for the experts. Made a complete hames of the first piece, so took extra care with the rest of it, in between getting dinner ready. It was really tedious work. By the time everybody came home, had only got half of it done. Had another go at it after dinner, didn't quite finish it. Bernie did a bit of sanding down. He's going to his retirement lunch in the Chanticleer tomorrow, it's his treat from the firm. Wanted me to go with him, but couldn't take another day off work, so said he'll bring Johnjoe instead.

Wednesday 14th December

Hated going to work this morning, wish I could stay home and finish my fire surround, but after having two days off didn't like to be too cheeky. Lilly was up again today, had a laugh with her, she's a very cheerful person. Went to Cuckoo Lane on my way home to get some more veneer to replace the bit I had spoiled. While I was waiting for it had a look round. There were some beautiful inlaid doors and table tops, would love to have some things made there. Called into Halls and got some fancy moulding to put on the fire surround. When I got home there was a beautiful bouquet of flowers on the table. Apparently, I was expected to go to the lunch in the Chanticleer with Bernie, and the flowers had been bought for me. Bernie had a great time wining and dining. He never stopped talking about the steak he had, was too full to eat any dinner this evening. Got to work on my fire surround after dinner, was quite pleased with the result. Went shopping with Mary. Took some things over to her flat afterwards, including a Christmas cake Terri made in school. It looks really lovely, she iced it all on her own. If it tastes as nice as it looks, she'll have a standing order to make our cake every year. Was too busy to make one myself this year.

Thursday 15th December

Lizzie's birthday today. Took in the flowers which Bernie had got – left, it would be an insult to the flowers to display them in our house, it's such a shambles. [The idea here seems to be that the flowers are so lovely that their beauty would be insulted by the ugliness of the house. It's an interesting idea and one Vera uses again later]. Nobody except myself knew it was her birthday, but I caused a bit of a stir bringing in this huge bouquet of flowers. They all wanted to know who they were for, told them they were for Lizzie. On my way to the design room, Jim (the cutter) asked me about the flowers. He was really upset he hadn't been told it was Lizzie's birthday. Lilly was in the design room, told her how I had come by the flowers. When Lizzie came in she was amazed that everybody had wished her a happy birthday. She said (turning to me), you were the only one who knew. I said, well, I had to tell them why I was giving you the flowers. When she saw them her eyes nearly popped out of her head. She was so thrilled with them, she hugged and kissed me, said nobody had ever given her such a beautiful bouquet in her life. Had intended to tell her about Bernie getting the flowers for me, but she was so pleased with them hadn't the heart to spoil it for her by telling her the truth. Lilly said she never saw her looking so happy. Quite a few of the staff bought her presents in the lunch hour, Jim bought her a bottle of champagne. She was so pleased with everything, she said she didn't want this day to end.

Friday 16th December

Thank God it's Friday, couldn't have gone to work another day I'm so tired. A lovely morning, cold but very bright and sunny, ideal weather for walking or jogging – not that I'd be doing either, haven't the energy. Still, I thought to myself (as I was going to work), hard work doesn't kill you, or I'd be dead long ago. I really do need a rest. Everything back to normal in work today. Lizzie was also very tired, she'd been out to dinner last night with her husband and had a few drinks, which she is not used to, and she didn't feel too bright this morning. She said, when she brought home the flowers and the champagne last night and told her husband about the other presents she had got for her birthday, he never said one word – with a husband like that she hasn't a lot of joy in her life. He doesn't usually give her a present for her birthday because it falls so near Christmas, so she was really amazed when he gave her a camera last night, but I think she had to pay for the dinner they had. Mary Mac gave the girls some heated rollers a while ago; last night Fiona got me to put a plug on them. She tried them out on Terri – not only that, but she made her face up to go with the hairstyle, she really looked like Coco the Clown. Poor Terri had to work in Woolworths until nine o'clock tonight. All the shops in Wood Green were open late, so Fiona, Ciarán and myself went over to do some shopping. It was really great, so different from Saturdays when you can't move for the crowds. Poor Terri was really exhausted when we collected her.

Saturday 17th December

Went to look for wallpaper again this morning. Went to Edmonton Green, couldn't see anything I liked there. Finished up going to a shop on Church Road, got nice paper there, £5.95 a roll, got five rolls. The bloke told me I needed a special ready-made paste for it, that cost £6.80. The whole lot came to £36.55, hope it will be worth it. At least it's white, so that must please the girls. Did the rest of my shopping. When I got out of the car, took everything out of the boot. Rang the doorbell. Bernie opened the door and ran back in, left me standing with all the shopping. Shouted for him to come out and help me. He was furious – he said when I rang the bell, a horse he'd backed fell; can't think how my ringing the bell caused the horse to fall, but he seemed to think it did and was really annoyed with me; told him I never knew I had magic powers, he didn't think that funny. Had some lunch. Did some varnishing in the hall. Mary rang to say she was going to confession in St. Edmonds, told her I wasn't ready to go yet. Went up when I finished the varnishing, but Mary wasn't there, met her later when I went to Geary's for my bread. Bernie was in better humour when we came back. Was too tired to start papering. Fell asleep watching telly.

Sunday 18th December

Was very tired this morning due to the fact I didn't sleep very well because of falling asleep watching telly last night. Poured rain on the way to Mass, which Father Roderick said. He was very annoyed with a young child who kept talking out loud all the time, the parents sat there quite unconcerned. Had our usual little chat with Dick Johnson after

Mass. After breakfast, Terri and myself paid our usual weekly visit to the dump, we are as well-known as begging asses down there. Came home and started on the wallpapering. Added some water to the adhesive as it said on the carton, and measured the wall with the plumb-line. After applying the adhesive to the paper, had to wait five minutes before putting it on the wall, was really pleased with the result. The paper was very easy to handle and the adhesive is great. Had to break off to get dinner ready, but felt I had done a good morning's work. Had to have my afternoon nap, and listened to the 'Top Twenty' after my tea, then got up and did another bit of wallpapering. Didn't get much done, it's really very slow work with this waiting five minutes each time. Tried pasting two pieces at a time but it didn't work out – by the time I'd cut round awkward places the second piece was dry. Finished off the first carton of adhesive, so decided not to open the other one till tomorrow, so gave the fire surround another sanding down and a final coat of varnish.

Monday 19th December

Woke this morning with a sore throat, Ciarán wasn't too well either, he had a sore throat also – thought, this is all I need before Christmas. However, went off to work. Was expecting Lilly to be up today but she wasn't – could have done with her to cheer me up a bit, didn't have a very happy day. Was glad when it was time to go home. The weather didn't help, it poured down again today. A really miserable evening. After dinner, got started again on the wallpapering. Was really only fit for bed – only it's so near Christmas, would have left it. Didn't get an awful lot done. This waiting five minutes for the adhesive to set is really very time consuming, only Mary is here wouldn't get so much done at all. She does all the other jobs which I should be doing if I weren't wallpapering. Bernie is also helping, but his heart isn't in it – he'd much rather be sitting down watching telly, but the aerial has fallen down again, he is frantically looking for somebody to fix it. Realised tonight I may have to get some more wallpaper. Fiona thinks the paper is lovely, thinks I should do the whole house in it, but Terri and Mary are not too keen on it. I can't make up my mind whether I like it or not. When I asked Bernie and Ciarán, they just said it's alright.

Tuesday 20th December

Felt really bad when I woke this morning. Went into the bathroom to get ready for work, but hadn't even the energy to wash myself, so got back into bed, must have fallen asleep at once. The next thing I knew I was hearing Terri's voice asking where I was. She had gone into Leena's as usual at seven o'clock and I usually answer the door when she comes back at eight o'clock, but this morning when she rang the bell there was no answer. In the end, Ciarán had to get out of bed to let her in. I never heard the bell. Terri couldn't understand how my car was outside the door and there was no sign of me, she said I gave her an awful fright. She brought me up another cup of tea and an egg. When I'd finished it [I] got up, had a wash and rang Lizzie to tell her I wouldn't be in, then started doing some wallpapering. Only had a few pieces up when the doorbell rang, it was Pattie from up the road. She stayed talking for two hours. She has everything done for Christmas. She nearly died when she saw the state of our house, she said it would drive her mad. Told her if I had the time I'd probably go mad too. When she had gone, had to run up in the car to get another roll of paper and more adhesive.

Wednesday 21st December

Last day in work before the Christmas. [This is not a mistake, but a common Irish construction]. Didn't expect to have to do much work, but was kept quite busy. Lilly had told me they always finish work at lunch hour and then have a party, but this year everybody was disappointed there was no party, but we were told to go into the office to collect our wages. Lilly and myself went in together, as we both leave early, Harry and Mr. Jacobs were there. We were each given a glass of champagne, could have had crisps or nuts, which we both declined. When we were leaving, Harry gave us a kiss, wished us a happy Christmas and gave us a pound box of Terry's All Gold, just shook hands with Mr. Jacobs. He told us how bad things had been during the year, hence the reason they couldn't afford to give a party (nearly got out the fiddle). Called into Mary on the way home to give her some sheets I had washed. After dinner, finished off the wallpapering. Fiona said I'll easily get the stairs and hall papered before Christmas, they really think I'm a horse. It will probably take another twelve months before the rest of the house is done; still, at least one room downstairs is finished. Put the old carpet back on tonight so it doesn't look too bad, and have made some new covers for the chairs so when it gets a good cleaning, it will look a bit better.

Thursday 22nd December

Had promised myself a lie-on this morning, but the doorbell ringing at eight o'clock woke me. It was Reg, wanting to know would Ciarán give him a hand, he said he might get some tips – he was out of bed like a shot. Had intended doing some shopping this morning, but

Fiona and myself started doing some cleaning and tidying. I'm really pleased with the dining room now that it's cleaned up. Put some of my precious Belleek on the shelves of the fireplace; praying they won't get broken. Sure it will look nice when the new carpet goes down, which I hope will be before next Christmas. Terri went into Leena's and stayed there for hours, Fiona was giving out yards about her not helping. When she came back, we both went up to Dan's shop with a wardrobe door, which I asked him to cut to make a table out of for the sitting room. He brought it over tonight, and I put it on the legs of the old television stand – will have to get a bit of fancy moulding for the edges, then I'll have a nice table for the sitting room. Fiona said I'm very clever, which coming from her is praise indeed. The girls gave Ciarán £9.50 to buy a pair of earphones for his record player so that he won't drive everybody mad.

Friday 23ʳᵈ December

Woke this morning again to the sound of the doorbell ringing. Took me a while to realise it was Friday and it was Reg ringing for his milk bill. When I opened the door, Ciarán handed me 60 pence, which is my change out of a fiver for my weekly milk. Then he had the cheek to tell me my milk was outside the door. Talk about your friendly milkman, Ciarán is really spoiling the image. Don't know how Reg stands him. The girls said they saw him on the milk round a few times sitting in the milk float while Reg was doing the deliveries. They had a trainee milkman with them today, he crashed the milk float, he's going to take Reg's place when he goes on holiday in January. Ciarán said he doesn't think he'll help him unless he gives him danger money. Bernie didn't go to work this morning (his last day) – the management had told him he needn't go in, but they would still pay him for it. He went off to see the solicitor this morning about buying our house. Delighted to hear that they had found the deeds to our house, which they thought had been blown up during the War. They turned up in some bank, where they had been given as surety for a loan years ago. Went out shopping with Terri. Fiona said she would clean upstairs while we were out. Mary Mac and Jack came this afternoon to congratulate Bernie on his retirement. After dinner, we went to Wood Green station to meet Nan coming from Heathrow. The plane had to make an emergency landing and she was late getting in.

Saturday 24th December

Christmas Eve. After breakfast, stuffed the turkey and put it in the oven – always cook my Christmas dinner the day before. Put my piece of gammon into cold water to soak in case it would be too salty. Then went to Wood Green with Nan to do some last-minute shopping, it was a really miserable day, raining all the time. Went into Woolworths to see Terri, but she had gone to lunch. Met Fiona in Marks in her lunch hour, wish I hadn't, she asked me to get her a present for Leena and one for Terri, as if I hadn't enough to do. She also gave me strict orders to get a Christmas tree. Wasn't going to bother about one, the house is in such a state – felt it would be an insult to the tree – however, promised to get one. Had a look at some artificial ones in D.H. Evans, which were £26-£30.00; decided there and then to get a real one. By four o'clock, had got everything I needed except the tree, when I suddenly remembered I hadn't got my bread from Geary's. Made a mad rush to the car park. Managed to reach Edmonton by 4.30, collected the bread. When we got home,

Mary was there but she wanted to go out again, so back into the car again and up to Marks. Got what she wanted there, I still had to get a tree. Everywhere I went to was sold out, finally got one in Park Lane. Fiona was delighted with it. After dinner, she fixed it all up and put up a few chains in the sitting room.

Sunday 25th December

Christmas Day, my favourite holiday. All off to eight o'clock Mass this morning. There were a lot more people there than usual, all family groups, everybody seemed so happy. Father Hegarty said Mass, which Ciarán and Adam served. Fiona said afterwards, they were like two drunken men, Ciarán was all lopsided, standing on one leg, and Adam's head was nearly touching his knees when he sat down. After breakfast, did some last-minute gift wrapping. Dan, Colette and children called at 12.30. Then the Turkish family from up the road arrived with presents for the children, followed by Leena and Tina. Bernie poured drinks for everyone, he fancies himself as a bartender. All the neighbours left at three o'clock. Mary had been missing for ages, she was getting the dinner ready – I don't know what I'd do without her. Had our Christmas dinner, the turkey was really beautiful. Spent the evening playing cards and watching telly. Had some of Terri's lovely Christmas cake for supper. Stayed up talking to Nan and Mary till one o'clock.

Monday 26th December

Was having a lie-on this morning when the doorbell rang at about ten o'clock. Ciarán opened the door, then heard a voice saying, "I'm the new milk lady delivering your milk". Wasn't really awake, but I jumped out of bed when I heard that voice which I hadn't heard for four years. It was my good friend, Ann Fitzpatrick, who had gone back to Ireland. Herself, Jim and the four boys are here on a fortnight's holiday. It was so lovely to see her, how I've missed her. We had so much to say to each other, we could have gone on for hours. Jim had taken the boys to the Spurs and Arsenal match at White Hart Lane (Spurs were beaten 4-2) and they were all meeting in Bernie Fitzpatrick's house for lunch, so Ann had to leave at 11.30. Hope to see them all one night before they go back to Ireland, please God. Ann really looked wonderful and hadn't changed one bit, wish she could say the same about me, but I wasn't even washed when she called and knew I looked a bit worse than usual. Had intended asking Peter and Sheila in for a drink, but with the excitement of seeing Ann, I completely forgot.

Tuesday 27th December

Got up at 9.30 this morning, heard Mary in the kitchen getting ready for work. Had a cup of tea, then with Fiona's help got breakfast ready. Told Ciarán I was taking back to the shop the leather jacket which he had paid £36.99 for yesterday. Don't mind him having a leather jacket, but this was one the punks and skinheads wear – he looks bad enough without letting him out in that. He ranted and raved, cried and pleaded with me to let him keep it but I would not be moved. He said the people where he had bought it wouldn't refund the money and, as they only sold punk and skinhead gear, there was nothing else he could get. I told him if they didn't refund the money I'd get the police – that finished him altogether. He said he didn't want me making a show of him. He asked Bernie to go back with him, he nearly exploded but in the end said he'd go.

The two of them had gone up the road when Terri had to call them back – they had forgotten to take the jacket with them, they are great messengers. Later on, Terri, Nan and myself went to Wood Green just for a bit of air, most of the shops were closed. We met Ciarán and James there. Asked Ciarán had he got the money back for the jacket, he said they'll give it back on Thursday, the manager wasn't there today.

Wednesday 28th December

Got up at 9.30 this morning. Mary was in the kitchen having breakfast, had a cup of tea with her then got breakfast ready for all the lazy people who were having a lie-on. In spite of the fact that it was a beautiful morning, nobody seemed keen on going out except Mary and myself. It was her day off, so we went over to her flat and measured everywhere for carpet, then we went down to Queensway to see could we get any bargains. She chose a very nice, deep, rose-coloured carpet for her bedroom, and a mint colour for the sitting room and hall. She likes it very much, but I can't make up my mind whether I do or not. Will have to wait till I see it down – think I prefer a patterned carpet myself. We then went up to Edmonton Green to look for curtain material, but it was very dead up there, most of the shops were closed, including Tesco and all the stalls. Went from there to Jones Brothers, which was also closed, finished up in Wood Green but got nothing there either. Met Peter and Sheila in Marks, told them how disappointed I was they hadn't come in Christmas morning, said they saw I had a crowd of visitors. Said they'd be in New Year's Day. Didn't get home until six o'clock.

Thursday 29th December

Terri, Nan and myself went to Carnaby Street this morning to see would I get a refund on that leather jacket Ciarán bought, but they said they don't refund money, so I hope that will be a lesson to him – it's his loss because I won't let him wear it, he's bad enough, but that would really put the tin hat on him. I never saw such sights as I saw in Carnaby Street today – punks, skinheads and mods, you'd be afraid to look at them. If I hear of him going there again, I'll kill him. We went into Liberty's sale, but their sale is certainly not for the working-class. Then we went to D.H. Evans and John Lewis – the same thing, their prices are sky high. Was foot-sore walking. Had coffee and cakes in John Lewis, was afraid to have a meal there in case we'd have to take out a mortgage to pay for it. Didn't get home until nearly six o'clock, Mary had dinner nearly ready.

Friday 30th December

Bernie was up and out early this morning. He has got marvellous use of his legs since his retirement. When he came back he was in great form. Asked me to drive him to the off-licence. Bought a bottle of brandy and sherry, and some beers for himself. Told me he would pay my road tax, which is due next month. Asked him had he won the Pools. He said no, he won a few pounds on a double last week. Fiona had told him that there were still some seats left for the school trip to Holland next year, which Terri is going on. Bernie said he'd give her the money to go, £120.00. Wonder how much he did win on that double? Ciarán's hair has got quite long. I told him I'd cut it for him this evening. Said he didn't want it cut (still upset over the jacket). He said, he has decided to let it grow long so that he can become a hippie. Hope he's not serious. He's impossible, I really can't win.

Saturday 31st December

Terri was not working today, so the two of us went off to Walthamstow market this morning to get some curtain material for Mary, we went early and left Nan in bed. Hadn't bought her a Christmas present, so bought her a very nice pair of cameo earrings, they cost £26.50. There weren't many stalls out, so didn't get the curtain material, but got some lovely contour wallpaper for the kitchen, it was only £4.95 a roll, it's £8.00 in the shops. Came home and had some breakfast with Nan, then Terri went into the shop to help them with the stock taking. Nan and myself went off to Ridley market, but like Walthamstow most of the stalls were closed, but did manage to get some curtain material for Mary's kitchen, which will go very nicely with the wallpaper.

The last day of 1983, I'll be really glad to see the last of this year, please God next year will be a bit better. Hate the thought of going back to work next week. Wish I was rich and didn't have to go out to work. I'd have a big house with one room set out for sewing, with a flat-machine, an over-locker, a buttonholer, an industrial iron and a large cutting table. I'd spend all my spare time making clothes for the girls, Mary and myself. That is my pipe dream, and with the marks I get on the bingo and the Pools, think it will remain a dream.

Afterword

Sadly, a lot of people in the diary have now passed away. We remember them all fondly. They were good people and our childhood was made all the better for knowing them.

Of the friends and neighbours that are still alive, we remain in contact with most of them.

Terri lives in Surrey with her husband, children, two dogs and a cat. She works as a medical secretary. She is currently training to run her first half marathon.

Fiona lives in London with her husband, children and one dog. She runs a business with her husband and enjoys travelling.

Ciarán lives in London with his partner. He has been working as an IT consultant for a large media company for the last twenty years. He still listens to punk music and loves playing the guitar.